THE GARDEN YEAR

THE GARDEN YEAR

PRACTICAL GARDENING
MONTH BY MONTH

Richard Bird

Bramley Books

This edition published in 1999 for Bramley Books by

Ward Lock

Cassell & Co Ltd

Wellington House

125 Strand

London

WC2R 0BB

www.cassell.co.uk

A member of the Orion Publishing Group

First published in the UK 1998 by Ward Lock

British Library Cataloguing-in-Publication Data
A catalogue record for this book is available from the British Library

ISBN 1-84100-184-8

Designed and typeset by Ben Cracknell Studios

Printed and bound in Spain by Graficas Reunidas, Madrid

Frontispiece: A wall-trained peach tree, variety 'Peregrine'.

Jacket photographs (left to right): Jerry Harpur (designer: Susan
Whittington, London); Andrew Lawson (Rosa 'Pink Bells', courtesy of
Janet Dagnall and Mary Young); Ward Lock; Jerry Harpur.

CONTENTS

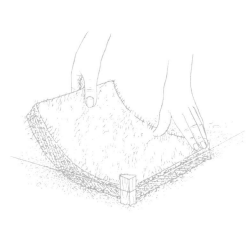

INTRODUCTION

Gardening is not an exact science. Many factors influence what a gardener does – soil and climate are the most obvious examples of this – and while a gardener in one area will swear by one technique, another, somewhere else, will swear by a different process. The maddening thing is that they are both probably right.

However, one thing is certain: *when* you do things is important. A gardener has to think and plan ahead all the time. At its most basic, this means that if, for instance, you want to harvest parsnips in autumn, you must remember to sow them in spring. This book helps you to do things at the right time, by reminding you, month by month, of the tasks you should be doing to keep your garden looking its best and being productive throughout the year. Not only does it tell you 'when' to carry out this work, however; it also explains 'how' you should do it.

One of the joys of gardening is that if you get it wrong one year you can always try again the next. If you forget to sow parsnips in time to eat them this year, there is always next year. However, timing, although important, is never that critical, and in most gardens there is a leeway of a week or so either way. Timing is also, of course, going to vary according to local weather conditions. Early spring will come to some areas long before it will in others, but it will come.

Unfortunately, in spite of what you sometimes read, there is no such thing as an instant garden. A proper garden needs to have time and energy spent on it. There are a few short cuts, but in the main you are in the hands of the weather, the conditions in your garden, time and your own experience. The best gardeners are undoubtedly those with knowledge and experience, but this does not bar anyone from starting. Even an inexperienced newcomer will have successes (and derive a lot of pleasure) right from the start, and it is worth bearing in mind that all gardeners go on learning right up to the day they finally hang up their boots.

This acquisition of skills and knowledge is one of the most enjoyable aspects of gardening, although you are not often aware that you are learning. Increasingly, you will get pleasure not only from what you grow but also from talking to other gardeners and showing people around your own plot, and one of the greatest satisfactions is having enough produce and flowers to give away to friends and neighbours.

There is no doubt that the vegetables and fruit you grow yourself taste better than shop-bought produce. You would be forgiven for thinking so no matter how they tasted, but vegetables from your own garden are always fresh, which is an important factor in flavour. There is also the fact that garden varieties are often bred with taste ranking high in the selection criteria, whereas commercial growers are more likely to regard factors such as pest or disease resistance, storage life, ability to travel without bruising and appearance more highly than taste. We do not generally buy carrots from one greengrocer rather than another on the basis of the flavour of the carrots, largely because it is impossible to distinguish among the varieties that are offered for sale. When we select seeds from which to grow carrots, however, we can choose among dozens of different named varieties. And even if there are a few blemishes when we come to dig them up, we can always trim them out.

The same principle applies to flowers. No house need be short of a posy or vase of flowers or foliage at any time of the year if they come from the garden. As with vegetables, the choice available if you grow your own far outstrips what is offered by the florist. Another advantage is that you do not have to buy a whole bunch if you only want a single flower.

To help your year in the garden, this book is organized on a month-by-month basis, beginning with January. At the beginning of each chapter is a checklist that summarizes all the tasks to be done in that month. The checklists are organized according to the various areas of the garden. The bulk of the text for each month is taken up by looking at these areas in more detail. First, there is an elaboration of the tasks to be carried out and then one or more topics are dealt with in more detail, with numerous cross-references to help you plan your gardening year. When looked at as a whole these topics add up to a complete manual of gardening.

Potting on cuttings of ivy (*Hedera*) and pansies (*Viola*).

JANUARY

At this time of the year the weather is likely to prevent us from doing very much in the garden, and many of us will take the opportunity to sit and browse through catalogues, planning the year ahead. Seed merchants seem to send out their lists earlier each year and now they often arrive in the autumn, and it is best, if you can, to get your orders off as soon as possible. Nevertheless, it is still pleasant to sit and dream about the year and to add a few last-minute requests. Looking through gardening books for ideas and information is also a satisfying way of spending hours that are too cold and wet for active gardening.

Even if we do little in the garden itself, now is the time to think about wildlife, especially birds. We can take short-term action by putting out food, of course, but it is far better to form a long-term plan. Choosing particular plants for the garden will not only provide food for all manner of wildlife but also shelter, and a pond will increase the number of available habitats and the diversity of the animals that visit your garden or make it their home.

The weather may be at its worst, but there will still be occasional clear, bright days that tempt us outdoors. Make the most of them and do as much work outside as you can. This is a good time, for example, to tackle borders that can be reached from the safety of a solid path.

CHECKLIST

General

- Shred all prunings and old herbaceous material (p. 23)
- Keep water pipes drained or lagged (p. 150)
- Continue clearing up when conditions allow (p. 173)
- Continue digging when soil conditions allow (p. 25)
- Plan next year's ornamental display (p. 124) and vegetable crops (p. 26)
- Order seeds and plants (p. 185)
- Thoroughly clean and oil any tools used in winter (p. 22)
- Clean and sterilize pots and trays (p. 158)
- Avoid walking on wet or sticky soil (p. 25)

Annuals and Tender Perennials

- Sow early half-hardy annuals (p. 20)
- Sow pelargoniums and begonias (p. 20)
- Check that overwintering annuals have not suffered wind-rock or frost upheaval (p. 50)
- Deadhead winter-flowering containers (p. 134)
- If not done, order next year's seeds (p. 120)
- Bring chrysanthemum stools into growth for cutting material (p. 134)

Bulbs

- Lift and divide early-flowering snowdrops (p. 21)
- Bring dahlia tubers into growth under glass for cutting material (p. 53)

Fruit

- Prune blackcurrants and other fruit bushes (p. 154)
- Heel in bare-rooted trees and shrubs when they arrive (p. 162)

- Plant new fruit trees and bushes when the weather and soil conditions allow (p. 162)
- Carry out formative pruning on new trees and bushes (p. 101)
- Winter prune fruit trees and bushes (p. 10)
- Keep netting over trees and bushes to prevent buds being stripped by birds (p. 53)
- Knock snow from netting to prevent it breaking (p. 187)
- Check stored fruit (p. 168)

Greenhouse

- Protect plants from frost if necessary (p. 171)
- Regularly check heating arrangements (p. 171)
- Water plants only when in growth (p. 38)
- Ventilate except in cold weather (p. 77)
- Bring dahlias into growth for cutting material (p. 53)
- Sow early vegetables for planting under protection (p. 55)

Lawns

- Lightly mow if conditions are right (p. 38)
- Remove fallen leaves and debris (p. 23)
- Prepare ground for laying lawns in spring (p. 141)
- Turf new lawns on previously prepared ground (p. 182)
- Service mowers and other lawn machinery and tools (p. 22)

Perennials

- Continue maintaining beds when conditions allow (p. 173)
- Continue preparing new beds for planting when conditions allow (p. 25)
- Shred and compost discarded material (p. 23)
- Continue sowing seeds (p. 39)

- Spread a general fertilizer around plants (p. 39)
- Mulch borders with well-rotted organic material (p. 172)
- Pot up or heel in bare-rooted plants that arrive from nurseries (p. 162)

Rock Gardens

- Prepare new beds (p. 63)
- Continue sowing seeds (p. 41)
- Carefully water plants under glass as they come into growth (p. 63)
- Order seeds from catalogues (p. 101)
- Order plants from nurseries (p. 101)
- Protect plants that dislike winter wet with panes of glass (p. 189)
- Protect delicate early flowers with glass (p. 144)

Trees and Shrubs

- Plant trees and shrubs if conditions allow (p. 162)
- Heel in bare-rooted trees and shrubs if weather prevents planting (p. 162)
- Prune wisteria (p. 129)
- Prune trees (p. 27)
- Protect flowering trees against bud loss caused by birds (p. 53)
- Protect marginally hardy shrubs and climbers with hessian in cold spells (p. 186)
- Remove snow before it breaks or disfigures trees and shrubs (p. 187)
- Check stakes and ties (p. 41)

Vegetables

- Sow early vegetables under glass for planting under protection (p. 55)
- Check stored vegetables (p. 165)
- Plant broad beans (p. 16)

FRUIT

TRAINING TREES

For many gardeners, one of the most daunting tasks is pruning trees. On the whole the problems are not too great with established trees, because you soon get into the rhythm of what to do after you have done it a few times. The main difficulty lies in getting the initial training right.

There are several ways of training fruit trees, which can either be grown as free-standing trees and bushes or supported and grown as fans, cordons and espaliers. The latter methods, especially cordons, have the advantage that they do not take up too much space, and although cropping is not as heavy as on trees, trained trees and shrubs allow you to have more varieties in the same space. Another advantage of the trained forms is that they can be used against walls, which provide a certain amount of warmth and protection. Trained forms nearly always look decorative, and they certainly enhance the appearance of a wall or fence. If the trees are trained against wire, they can be used to make good internal divisions between different areas of the garden.

The overall size of the trees depends on the rootstock used (p. 36), but it also depends on regular pruning, especially with the trained forms, which can quickly lose their shape if the gardener becomes inattentive.

TREES AND BUSHES

These can be divided into several different types, depending mainly on their size.

Standard
Standard trees are the old-fashioned, full-sized trees that once made up orchards. They are vigorous and will grow to heights of 5–6m (16–20ft).

Half-standard
These are similar in shape to standard trees, but they are not as big, achieving heights of 4–5m (12–16ft).

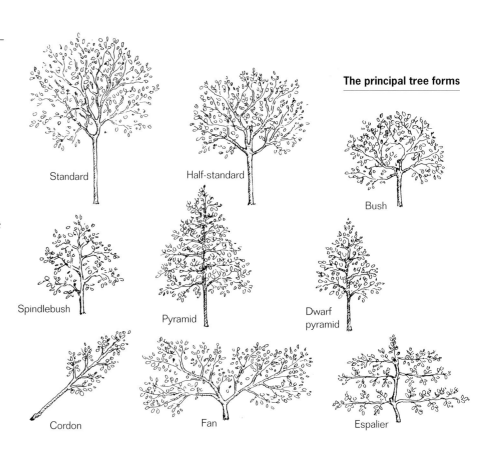

The principal tree forms

Standard

Half-standard

Bush

Spindlebush

Pyramid

Dwarf pyramid

Cordon

Fan

Espalier

Bush
A bush is smaller than either a standard or a half-standard, although the overall shape is similar. The branches more or less radiate from the top of the trunk. Bushes grow to heights of 1.5–4m (5–12ft), and they are suitable for small gardens. The smaller bushes are low enough to pick the fruit without the help of a ladder or steps.

Spindlebush
This is a carefully trained form of bush that has relatively few branches. Those branches that are left rise from a central leader, and they are trained so that – apart from the leader – they are all nearly horizontal to allow maximum light to penetrate and to promote the formation of the maximum number of fruiting buds.

Festoon
This tree is similar to the spindlebush except that the branches are tied in so that the tips are bent down, with the branches arched. This promotes the formation of fruit buds and produces a heavy cropping plant. The leader may or may not be left on.

TRAINED FORMS

Trained forms are not identified by size but by the final shape the tree takes. When you are planting against a wall

A pear tree that was originally trained along wires as an espalier. It is now well enough established not to need the wires, although it still needs regular pruning. Such a tree is decorative as well as productive.

or a fence remember that all trained forms should be at least 25cm (10in) away from its base.

Pyramid

A pyramid is a cross between a bush and a trained form. It is a free-standing plant, but its size is kept in check by regular summer pruning. The overall shape is pyramidal, and the overall height is up to 3m (10ft).

Dwarf Pyramid

This is the same type of tree as an ordinary pyramid except that it is on dwarfer stock and so is much smaller, growing only to about 2m (7ft).

Cordon

Cordon trees are trained against wires, which are usually free-standing but can be held against a wall or fence. The cordon is a single stem, angled at about 45 degrees to the ground, and allowed to grow to 1.5–2m (5–7ft) long. Cordons have the advantage that they take up little space, and it is, therefore, possible to grow several different varieties of apples or pears in a relatively small space.

Pruning a dwarf pyramid

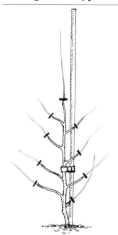  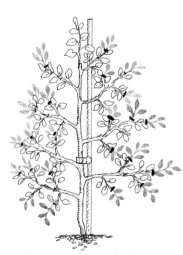 

Winter pruning: in the first year cut back the main shoot to 50–75cm (20–30in) from the ground, prune side shoots to 15cm (6in) from the leader and remove all low side shoots.

Winter pruning: in the second year prune the previous year's growth on the main shoot to about 25cm (10in).

Summer pruning: in the first year cut back new shoots growing from the main stem to five or six leaves, but other side shoots can be cut back to three leaves.

Summer pruning: in the second year cut back side shoots growing from the main branches to three leaves, and shoots from side stems to one leaf beyond the next leaf cluster. Repeat each subsequent year.

Fan-trained

Fan-trained fruit is normally grown against a wall or fence, although it can be trained on open wires. The branches radiate out in the form of a fan from the top of a short trunk. The trunk should be about 25cm (10in) long, and the overall height of the fan can be 2.4m (8ft) or more. Initially, the branches should be trained against canes tied to the wires, but these can be dispensed with once the branches have been formed.

Espalier

Espaliers look equally decorative whether they are grown against a wall or on free-standing wirework. The principle is to train a central stem from which selected laterals are tied in along horizontal wires. The side branches are allowed to grow two at time, and their number is increased each season until the required number of tiers is reached. Initially, grow each lateral against a cane held at an angle of 45 degrees to the ground. At the end of summer, gently lower the canes so that they are horizontal to the ground.

Stepover

This decorative method is not frequently seen, but it makes a beautiful edging, particularly for paths through a vegetable garden. Because of the limited size, stepover plants are not very heavy cropping. In essence, the method is the same as for an espalier except that only the bottom set of laterals is used and the overall height is not much more than 30cm (12in).

Pruning a cordon

Winter pruning: in the first year cut back side shoots longer than about 10cm (4in) to three or four buds.

Summer pruning: in the first year cut back all new growth to three leaves and trim side shoots to a single leaf.

Winter pruning: once the cordon is established remove overcrowded spurs.

Summer pruning: on an established cordon cut back the current year's side shoots to three leaves and new growth on woody shoots to a single leaf.

Pole

This is a relatively new form in which apples are grown on a single vertical stem or 'pole'. The plants can grow to 3.5m (12ft) or more, but they are best kept shorter than this or it is difficult to harvest the fruit. They are very useful for growing in small gardens and can even be grown in containers if you are prepared to water them every day.

Pruning an espalier

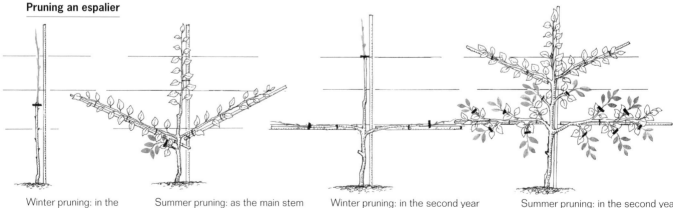

Winter pruning: in the first year cut back the main stem above three buds just above the level of the first wire support.

Summer pruning: as the main stem grows in the first year, tie it to a vertical cane. Tie two side shoots to canes held at 45 degrees. Cut back any shoots below the two selected side shoots.

Winter pruning: in the second year form the second tier by cutting the main stem above two buds. At the same time cut back the first pair by about one-third and cut any other side shoots right back to the stem.

Summer pruning: in the second year tie in new side shoots to canes and cut back to three leaves any side shoots between the first and second layer of shoots. Trim back side shoots on horizontal shoots.

TOOLS

One of the jobs that can be undertaken in winter, whatever the weather, is to check and maintain your tools.

Before you buy tools always look at them carefully and choose the best you can afford. Many are made from cheap pressed steel and will soon go blunt and frequently bend. This is particularly true of many makes of trowels, hand forks and hoes. Steel is the best material and stainless steel is the best of all. Avoid aluminium, especially in trowels, as it blunts very quickly and stains the hands when used. Second-hand tools can be a good buy if you are careful. You should be able to tell how well a tool is wearing, and if it looks as though it has had many years' use and yet is still in good condition it is likely to continue to be useful.

When you are choosing tools always buy ones that feel comfortable in the hand. Wooden handles can be modified so that the shape fits your hand comfortably. Always make certain that long-handled tools are, in fact, long enough for you to use it without undue bending.

BASIC TOOL KIT

Every gardener must have a spade. A stainless steel one is the best because it passes into the soil very easily, cleans easily and does not rust. A tread on the top of the blade adds to the expense but is a great deal more comfortable to use if you have a lot of digging to do. It is also easier when you are wearing shoes or boots because a non-tread model can dig into the soles. The shaft can be of wood or plastic. The handle can also be of either of these materials. Although it is not as common now, wood is preferred by many gardeners because the hands do not slip on it so readily when they are wet or coated with mud. A D-type handle is easier to work with than a T-shaped one. A general-purpose spade can be used for most work and, in a small garden, is likely to be sufficient. A keen gardener, however, might also want to buy a border spade, which has a shorter and narrower blade than the standard spade. It is also much lighter – it is also sometimes referred to as a lady's spade – and is very useful when you are working in confined areas such as between plants in a border.

There are several types of fork. As with the spade, there is a standard fork that all gardeners should have. This is used for digging, for lifting and turning compost and garden rubbish, and for other similar jobs. Of similar size but with broad, flat tines is the potato fork, which is, as the name suggests, used for lifting potatoes and other root crops. Its broader tines also make it useful for moving compost and manure. It is not, however, essential for the average gardener. Related to the border spade is the border fork, a smaller version of the standard fork. This is a very useful tool if you have borders or beds of any sort because it is much easier to wield than the larger version. It is perfect for working through a border, just teasing through the surface of the soil and removing weeds.

A set of a trowel and hand fork is essential. Again, if you can afford it, choose stainless steel. Avoid those tools on which the junction between the blade and the hand is pressed steel (it appears to be folded), because it will usually bend when under pressure. If you can, choose a trowel and hand fork that have forged sections. These are usually cranked – that is, they are set off from the blade – and are easier and more comfortable to use. Hand forks and trowels are ideal for weeding and close work in the border. In a small garden these may be all you need, but several other types of small hand-tools are useful for weeding. Whether you have these additional tools is a matter of preference: some gardeners have several, but others do not bother with any.

A rake is essential. A bolstered one, in which the teeth look like nails, will be sufficient for most tasks if you are restricted to just one. It will be capable of breaking down soil as well as raking it level and cleaning up rubbish. As a more expensive alternative, one with flat, rounded teeth is well worth having, and you will be able to find versions with wider heads than the bolster variety. In large gardens a wooden rake, like the old-fashioned hay rake, can be very useful for clearing up grass and other coarse rubbish. The other main type of rake, the spring-tined rake, is used on lawns and for raking up leaves. The most useful kind has thin, wiry tines , but you can also get ones with rubber or plastic teeth.

You will need at least one hoe, although keen gardeners may find that they acquire a whole battery of them over the years. Possible the most useful is the draw hoe. This has a near vertical blade and can be used for cutting down weeds and for loosening the soil. Its sharp corners can be used for removing stubborn weeds and for drawing out seed drills. A curved neck makes the tool easier to use and also explains one of its older names, 'swan-necked' hoe. You use a draw hoe by pulling it towards you. A Dutch hoe, on the other hand, is used by pushing it away as you work. This has a horizontal blade, which is pushed either on or just below the surface of the soil to loosen it and to cut off weeds.

Another type of hoe, not essential in the basic kit but very useful to have, is a cultivator. This has three (or sometimes five) curved prongs, which you draw through the soil to loosen it. A miller or star-wheeled cultivator consists of a series of spiked disks that push through the soil to break it up into a fine tilth. A Canterbury hoe, a heavy hoe with three strong prongs, is also useful for breaking down soil as well as for various other tasks. They are not often seen now, but most older gardeners still use them, and second-hand ones can frequently be found. There are several other types of hoe with different shaped heads – combination hoes, for example, have two blades. Rather than buy several different hoes, it is possible to by one shaft with interchangeable heads, which saves a lot of storage space.

A pair of hand shears is essential if you have got grass or hedges. Even if you use a mower and a hedge trimmer, you will always need shears for trimming those odd, awkward places. They can also be used for trimming the edge of a lawn, but if you can afford to duplicate tools, a pair of long-handled edging shears will save a lot of bending and effort.

A garden line is something that can made. At its most basic it is two sticks with a piece of string between them. More sophisticated ones use rot-proof plastic string and can be tensioned.

The final item of basic equipment is a pair of secateurs. As with all tools, buy the best quality you can afford. There are several different types, all having their own merits. Look at them and, if possible, think about your own requirements and the ways in which you will be using them. Remember, too, always to buy secateurs that are comfortable for you to hold and grip.

NOT-SO-BASIC TOOLS

Many other tools have their place in the gardener's armoury. Although they are not as essential as those described above, they are none the less still very useful. If you have a lot of shrubs and trees, either ornamental or fruiting, a saw will be useful. Although you can buy rigid pruning saws, one of the small folding models is ideal for most gardens. They fold up safely and are easy to store. A pair of loppers for cutting thicker stems is also very useful. For tree work a tree pruner, which is like a pair of secateurs on a long pole, can make life much easier. The handles are of wood, although there are versions with metal handles that can be taken apart in sections, allowing for easy storage.

Plants can be planted with a trowel, but a dibber can earn its keep in the vegetable garden for planting brassicas, leeks or onion sets. Rather than buy a special tool, you can use a pointed piece of wood or a stick. It is, however, easier and more comfortable to use if the dibber has a T- or a D-shaped handle. They can be bought or simply made, possibly from an old broken spade or fork handle. A bulb planter is another tool that is indispensable when it is actually in use, but lies unused for the rest of the year. The same goes for the old-fashioned potato planters. You can use a hand trowel for both tasks.

Metal watering cans are much more expensive than plastic ones, but they will far outlast their plastic counterparts. Those with long spouts are essentially for use in the greenhouse, but they are also useful for watering areas beyond easy reach.

SAFETY EQUIPMENT

As we all, quite rightly, become more safety conscious in the garden, so more equipment becomes available to keep us out of harm's way. Few people would have dreamed of gardening in gloves in days gone by, but now most gardeners use gloves for at least some of the time. Choose either an all-purpose pair or have different gloves for different purposes – tough ones, such as those made of leather, for pruning roses, and softer ones for more delicate jobs.

Ear muffs should always be worn when you are using noisy machinery, and goggles are essential when power saws or strimmers are used. Wear a protective helmet if you are cutting trees or working in situations where you could bang your head. Wellington boots will keep your feet dry, but it is worth remembering that they are very vulnerable to being pierced by tools, such as forks. Boots and gardening shoes with reinforced toecaps are much safer.

COLOURED TOOLS

A minor point but one of great value if you are a bit forgetful: buy tools that are brightly coloured or paint the handles in a bright colour. This means that if you leave them in a border, for example, you will easily find them. This might not matter so much with a rake, which is more easily seen, but a small trowel can easily get lost.

TREES AND SHRUBS

WINTER-FLOWERING SHRUBS

Winter can be a barren time, but there are a surprising number of shrubs that flower in winter and bring nothing but pleasure to those who grow them. Although some plants, like hazel (*Corylus avellana*), are wind pollinated, many are pollinated by insects. Because not many insects are around in winter, the shrubs tend to advertise their presence by a strong scent. There is, therefore, double value in many of these winter shrubs: they offer both flower colour and scent.

The winter honeysuckles (*Lonicera*) are a good example of this. They start flowering in early winter and often go right through to early spring and even beyond. On a warm day their lovely scent travels a long way and can perfume the whole garden. Scents vary considerably. The Christmas box (*Sarcococca*) has a very sickly, cloying perfume, whereas the cornelian cherry (*Cornus mas*) and witch hazels (*Hamamelis*) have very clean, pure scents.

Winter-flowering shrubs are no more difficult to grow than any other shrubs and need no extra looking after. If there is space in a large garden, winter-flowering shrubs can be planted near a path where they can be easily appreciated. In a smaller garden they can be planted at the back of a border where they can be seen and their fragrance appreciated in winter but are out of the way for the other months of the year when they do not have a great deal to offer other than foliage.

The winter honeysuckle, *Lonicera fragrantissima*, goes on flowering through all the frosts, perfuming the air for a great distance around.

WINTER-FLOWERING SHRUBS

Abeliophyllum distichum
Chimonanthus praecox
Corylus avellana
Cornus mas
Daphne mezereum
Erica carnea; *E. × darleyensis*
Hamamelis
Jasminum nudiflorum
Lonicera fragrantissima; *L. × purpusii*; *L. standishii*
Mahonia
Sarcococca
Viburnum × bodnantense; *V. farreri*; *V. tinus*

ATTRACTIVE WINTER BARK

Another way of brightening up the garden in winter is to plant trees and shrubs with attractive bark. At this time of year, when the trees are bare, the trunks and stems can be more easily seen and appreciated. Some, such as the birch-bark tree (*Prunus serrula*), with its shiny, copper-coloured bark, look at their best in the low winter sun. They positively glow.

The shiny bark of *Prunus serrula* brightens up many a dull winter's day.

TREES *and* SHRUBS
with ATTRACTIVE WINTER BARK

> *Acer capillipes* (tree); *A. griseum* (tree);
>   *A. pensylvanicum* (tree)
> *Betula ermanii* (tree); *B. utilis* var. *jacquemontii* (tree)
> *Cornus alba* 'Sibirica' (shrub); *C. stolonifera*
>   'Flamiramea' (shrub)
> *Corylus avellana* 'Contorta' (shrub)
> *Eucalyptus* (trees)
> *Prunus serrula* (tree)
> *Rubus cockburnianus* (shrub); *R. thibetanus* (shrub)
> *Salix alba* 'Britzensis' (tree)

 # VEGETABLES

On the whole, the soil is too cold for sowing many vegetables this month. However, in warmer areas broad beans can be sown (see below). Traditionally in some areas shallots are planted in late December (p. 185), but, except in warmer areas, most gardeners prefer to wait until at least this month. Rhubarb can be planted or transplanted now if the soil is not too wet or frozen (p. 177).

Continue to check that stored root crops (p. 165) are not being eaten by rodents or are otherwise deteriorating.

BROAD BEANS

Broad beans are the earliest beans to crop. Unlike other beans, it is normally only the seeds that are eaten and not the pods. However, immature pods are sometimes cooked and eaten, as are the tips of the shoots.

In order to get an early crop that can be harvested from late spring onwards, you can, in milder areas, make an early sowing in autumn or early winter. In mild areas, if the soil conditions allow, they can also be sown in late winter, but in most areas this will not be possible until the soil begins to dry out and warm up in early spring. However, if cloches are put over the ground in advance you may be able to sow at anytime in winter to get an early crop. It is also possible to start the beans off under glass in midwinter and then transplant them in early spring, after you have hardened them off.

Broad beans need a sunny position, but they are not too fussy about soils as long as they are reasonably fertile. They should be planted in a protected site, away from winter winds, and extra protection may be given by the use of cloches, at least until the plants grow too tall for

them. Dwarf varieties, such as 'The Sutton', are good overwintering types.

Broad beans are normally sown as a double row, the two rows being 23cm (9in) apart and the seeds the same distance apart in each row. Adjacent pairs of row are 30cm (12in) apart for dwarf varieties and 60–90cm (24–36in) apart for taller varieties.

The dwarf varieties will need no support, but taller ones will. Insert canes or posts at intervals along both sides of the row. Tie a length of string between the posts along both sides, with other pieces of string between the posts across the row to help prevent it from collapsing outwards. One of the worst pests is blackfly. These tend to go for the succulent tips of the stems, but they can be deterred if you remove the top 7.5cm (3in) or so of the shoots when the plant is in flower.

Harvest the beans when the pods have swelled. They can be used straight away or frozen. Some varieties are better for freezing than others, and in general the green-seeded varieties freeze better than the white-seeded forms.

RECOMMENDED VARIETIES *of*
BROAD BEAN

'Aquadulce Claudia'	'Jade'
'Bunyard's Exhibition'	'Jubilee Hysor'
'Express'	'Meteor Vroma'
'Hylon'	'Red Epicure': red seeds
'Imperial Longpod'	'The Sutton': dwarf

 # WILDLIFE IN
THE GARDEN

One of the great benefits of a mature garden is that it is likely to become a miniature nature reserve, and birds, insects and small mammals will make their homes there. Not all will be welcome, however – mice, moles and even birds can be a nuisance at times, but there are usually methods of deterrence available to the gardener that will prevent too much conflict between man and animal. Most gardeners take great pleasure in being part of nature and enjoy seeing the wildlife that they attract.

While wildlife will make a home in any garden, it is possible to increase a garden's potential and so encourage even more species. Creating a pond, for example, will introduce frogs and dragonflies into the garden as well as a host of pond insects. It will also attract other animals, which come to drink and bathe. As bushes, trees and

A good crop of early broad beans can be had by sowing in winter. In cold, damp areas, however, it is best to wait until the soil warms up and becomes workable.

gardens will attract a few, but if you grow the right plants, the air can be filled with these delightful creatures (p. 142). Bees will appreciate the same plants and many others, and the hum of bees is a quintessential part of a summer day for many people, while to those who gather honey any increase in the bees' supplies of nectar is welcome (p. 94).

Although it is not strictly gardening, one way that many gardeners like to attract birds is to provide them with nesting sites in the form of nestboxes, fixed to trees or buildings. These are easy to make from scraps of materials that cost nothing, but they can give a great deal of pleasure.

PLANTS SUPPLYING BIRD FOOD

Aster (Michaelmas daisies): seedheads
Corylus avellana: nuts
Cotoneaster: berries
Crataegus (hawthorns): berries
Cynara: seedheads
Dipsacus fullorum (teasel): seedheads
Echinops: seedheads
Hedera helix (ivy): berries
Ilex (hollies): berries
Lonicera (honeysuckles): berries
Malus (crab apples): fruit
Prunus (plums): fruit
Pyracantha (firethorn): berries
Quercus (oaks): fruit
Sambucus nigra (elder): fruit
Sorbus (rowans): berries
Taxus baccata (yew): berries
Viburnum opulus (wayfaring tree): berries

hedges mature, they provide nesting sites, refuge from the weather and feeding stations for a large number of birds and animals.

Birds are particular favourites with many gardeners. While they tend to look after themselves during the warmer months, in winter they can always do with a helping hand. One way to do this is to plant shrubs that produce edible fruits or seeds. As well as providing food, these are often decorative in their own right and frequently look their best when the rest of the garden is beginning to shut down for winter. If you have space, try planting a few of the shrubs and other plants listed below. Nuts trees for example, will bring a whole new range of birds to your garden.

If you are in no hurry to cut down the old vegetation from the previous year, leave at least some of the perennials that are in seed. Michaelmas daisies, for example, have seedheads, and there will be plenty of insects hiding among the dead stems and leaves for the birds to feed on.

Another form of wildlife that is appreciated in summer is butterflies. Most

Shrubs with berries not only bring colour into the winter garden, but they also provide birds and small mammals with food.

FEBRUARY

Although the weather is still likely to be at its worst, there are plenty of signs in the garden that things are beginning to wake up: bulbs are breaking through the soil and many are already blooming; the buds on many trees and shrubs are beginning to swell; and the birds are sensing the change and are singing their hearts out as they call for mates. All this activity begins to affect the gardener, and it is about now that impatience begins to set in. Everybody is anxious to set to work. Yet, if you can be patient, it is wise to wait for just a little while longer.

There are, however, still plenty of jobs to do, even if the real spring tasks, such as sowing seeds and getting the lawn under control, are best left until the weather improves. There is little point in sowing seeds into cold, wet soil – they will not germinate and are likely to rot, giving you the expense and trouble of re-sowing – and more harm than good can be done if you tackle the lawn too soon.

The best place to be at this time of year is in the greenhouse, which is just as good at keeping the gardener warm as it is the plants. Even in the greenhouse, however, you should not be in too much of a hurry. If you start your annuals too soon, they will have a long time to wait in their trays and pots before they can be planted outside. This means they not only have to be looked after but are likely to get drawn.

CHECKLIST

General

- Shred all prunings and old herbaceous material (p. 23)
- Keep water pipes drained or lagged (p. 150)
- Continue clearing up when conditions allow (p. 173)
- Continue digging when soil conditions allow (p. 25)
- Plan next year's ornamental display (p. 124) and vegetable crops (p. 26)
- Order seeds and plants (p. 185)
- Thoroughly clean and oil any tools used in winter (p. 22)
- Avoid walking on wet or sticky soil (p. 25)

Annuals and Tender Perennials

- Sow half-hardy annuals (p. 20)
- Check that overwintering annuals have not suffered wind-rock or frost upheaval (p. 50)
- Deadhead winter-flowering containers (p. 134)
- Bring chrysanthemum stools into growth for cutting material (p. 134)
- Take chrysanthemum cuttings (p. 134)

Bulbs

- Bring dahlia tubers into growth under glass for cutting material (p. 53)
- Lift and divide snowdrops as they finish flowering (p. 21)
- Deadhead early-flowering daffodils (p. 34)

Fruit

- Prune blackcurrants and other fruit bushes (p. 154)
- Plant new fruit trees and bushes when the weather and soil conditions allow (p. 162)

- Winter prune fruit trees and bushes (p. 10)
- Keep netting over trees and bushes to prevent buds being stripped by birds (p. 53)
- Knock snow from netting to prevent it from breaking (p. 187)
- Check stored fruit (p. 168)

Greenhouse

- Sow greenhouse tomatoes, cucumbers, aubergines, melons and peppers (p. 55)
- Sow early vegetables for planting out (p. 55)
- Start sowing tender annuals (p. 20)
- Finish pruning vines (p. 157)
- Bring dahlias into growth for cutting material (p. 53)
- Protect plants from frost if necessary (p. 37)
- Regularly check heating arrangements (p. 158)
- Water plants only when in growth (p. 122)
- Ventilate except in cold weather (p. 77)

Lawns

- Lightly mow if conditions are right (p. 38)
- Remove fallen leaves and debris (p. 23)
- Prepare ground for laying lawns in spring (p. 141)
- Turf new lawns on previously prepared ground (p. 182)
- Finish servicing lawn machinery and tools (p. 22)

Perennials

- Continue maintaining beds when conditions allow (p. 173)
- Continue preparing new beds for planting when conditions allow (p. 25)
- Shred and compost discarded material (p. 23)
- Continue sowing seeds (p. 39)
- Spread a general fertilizer around plants (p. 39)

- Mulch borders with well-rotted organic material (p. 172)
- Pot up or heel in bare-rooted plants that arrive from nurseries (p. 162)
- If conditions are right, start planting (p. 39)

Rock Gardens

- Prepare new beds (p. 63)
- Continue sowing seeds (p. 41)
- Prick out seedlings (p. 20)
- Carefully water plants under glass as they come into growth (p. 63)
- Order seeds from catalogues (p. 101)
- Order plants from nurseries (p. 101)
- Protect plants that dislike winter wet with panes of glass (p. 189)
- Protect delicate early flowers with glass (p. 144)

Trees and Shrubs

- Protect marginally hardy shrubs and climbers with hessian in cold spells (p. 186)
- Check stakes and ties (p. 41)
- Remove snow before it breaks or disfigures trees and shrubs (p. 187)
- Protect flowering trees against bud loss due to birds (p. 53)
- Finish pruning trees (p. 27)
- Prune clematis (p. 27)

Vegetables

- Sow vegetables under glass (p. 55)
- Chit early potatoes ready for planting (p. 44)
- Sow parsnips in mild areas (p. 68)

SOWING ANNUALS

Late winter to early spring is the time to sow most half-hardy annuals. In mild areas they can be sown now, but in colder areas it may be more sensible to wait until next month. If they are sown too early, the plants will become drawn and leggy long before it is possible to plant them out. Seeds sown a few weeks later will almost certainly quickly catch up with seeds sown now, and so the time and effort spent looking after premature plants is wasted. In areas where there are likely to be late frosts, delay sowing until late March or even April. Wherever you live, do not be in too much of a hurry to sow annuals.

Seeds can be sown in either pots or trays. For most uses a 9cm (3½in) pot is sufficient – it will easily produce forty or more plants, which are usually ample for most garden needs – although if you are planning large bedding schemes use a tray. However, bear in mind that pots require less propagator space and less compost.

Fill the pot or tray with a moist sowing compost (p. 24) and *lightly* press down; tapping the pot on the bench will often be sufficient to settle the compost. Spread the seeds thinly across the surface of the compost. There is no need to use all the seeds in the packet if there are a lot, unless you feel you can use all the resulting plants. Cover the seeds with a thin layer of sifted compost and water with a fine-rosed watering can or by standing the pot or tray in a pan of water.

Larger seeds, such as those of sunflowers, can be sown individually into pots so that pricking out is not necessary and the roots are not disturbed. Alternatively, they can be sown directly into cellular packs. Pelleted seeds can also be treated in this way.

Cover the pot or tray with a sheet of glass or polythene film to prevent it from drying out. The seeds must be kept at a temperature of 13–21°C (55–70°F). The ideal place is a heated propagator, but they can be placed on

Sowing seeds

Level off the compost in the seed tray by tapping it on a bench or using a board.

Scatter the seeds evenly across the surface of the compost.

Cover the seeds by sieving over a thin layer of compost.

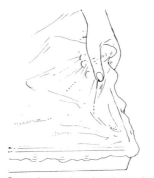

Cover the seeds with a sheet of glass or a piece of polythene so that the compost does not dry out.

an open bench in a heated greenhouse or, if you have space, you can even place them on a windowsill indoors as long as you do not draw the curtains at night so that they are affected by the falling temperature next to the glass. An airing cupboard can also be used, but remember to remove the pot or tray at the first signs of germination.

Once they have germinated, the seedlings must be kept at least at the lower end of the temperature range until they are ready to be pricked out. They should also be given adequate light, but shaded from direct sunlight. Keep watered.

PRICKING OUT

Once seedlings are big enough to handle and have at least one pair of true leaves, they can be pricked out.

Using a stiff plant label or a thin stick, carefully dig up one seedling at a time. Make a small planting hole in the compost and, holding the seedling by its leaves between your finger and thumb, carefully lower the roots into the hole. Gently firm the seedling with your fingers.

HALF-HARDY AND HARDY ANNUALS

Half-hardy annuals are tender and will be killed or badly damaged by frost. They therefore need protection in their early growing stages and should not be planted out until after the threat of frost has passed.

Hardy annuals are frost hardy and will stand a winter outside. For early flowering they can be sown in the autumn.

Some short-lived perennials are treated as annuals or biennials. Wallflowers and sweet williams are well-known examples. Biennials are sown in the first year in which they become established. They flower, set seed and die in their second year.

BULBS

Snowdrops and crocus are two of the best loved winter and early spring flowers. The sight of their heads popping up into the winter dreariness is a sure sign that spring and warmer weather are not far away.

SNOWDROPS

The delicacy and purity of snowdrops make them very popular bulbs, and the fact that they appear in winter, when there is so little else about, makes them doubly welcome. One tends to think of their appearance, but many snowdrops have a scent, which is particularly marked on a warm day. Probably the one with the strongest scent is *Galanthus nivalis* ssp. *imperati* 'Ginns'. The scent travels a long way and can pervade a whole garden. A more common scented variety is *G.* 'S. Arnott'. Its scent is less strong but is very noticeable when the flowers are picked and taken indoors.

There are more than two hundred varieties of snowdrops, many exhibiting only minor variations, although enough to satisfy enthusiasts. Most are easy to grow and are happy with a range of soils and conditions. A position in light shade suits them best. Avoid buying dried bulbs, because these are difficult to establish and may have been taken from the wild. Always buy nursery-grown stock. They can be bought either growing in pots or 'in the green'. The latter are often offered by specialist nurseries and large garden centres, which dig up the snowdrops from the nursery beds just after flowering and sell them straight away. Once planted they need not be moved for several years, but they can become congested and so it is a good idea to split them from time to time. The best time to do this is, again, just after flowering.

CROCUSES

Crocuses belong to a very large genus. Most gardeners are familiar with the large Dutch varieties, but there are many small species that can be grown and enjoyed. Many of these will grow in the open garden, preferably on rock

Even snow cannot dim snowdrops (*Galanthus*), which are one of the joys of winter.

gardens where they can be looked after, but some need to grown in special conditions and are usually cultivated in a bulb frame or in pots in an alpine house.

As well as the spring-flowering species, there are many autumn-flowering varieties (p. 154).

Most garden crocuses are easy to grow. They are not fussy about soil conditions as long as they are not too wet, and they will grow in sun or in light shade. The large varieties are strong enough to be naturalized in lawns and other grassy areas. Unlike snowdrops, these can be purchased as dried bulbs, but should come from a reputable source. Winter- and spring-flowering varieties should be planted in autumn, autumn-flowering ones in spring.

CYCLAMEN

Most people think of cyclamen as the colourful florist's cyclamen that are frequently given as presents at Christmas. These are tender and must be kept inside, but there are a number of perfectly hardy cyclamen. Different species flower at different times, and there is almost a cyclamen for every month. In the late summer and autumn *Cyclamen hederifolium* makes a splendid display. This is followed in the depths of winter by *C. coum*, with its deep magenta flowers and wonderfully marked leaves. In spring *C. repandum* puts in its appearance.

Cyclamen like a lightly shaded position and a woodland-type soil. They will also grow in quite dry and shady positions, even under horse chestnut trees. Always buy plants that are growing in pots, never dried specimens. Once planted, they need little attention and will soon seed themselves around to form large colonies.

BULBS *in* FLOWER *in* LATE WINTER

Crocus (crocuses)
Cyclamen coum
Eranthis (winter aconites)
Galanthus (snowdrops)
Iris reticulata (bulbous iris); *I. unguicularis*
    (winter iris)
Narcissus (daffodils)
Scilla (squills)

EQUIPMENT

There is an increasing number of machines available for the gardener. Some of them are so useful that we would be lost without them – lawnmowers, for example – but some are gimmicky and are of no real value. There is a third group and that is of machines that are very useful but the amount of use to which they are put is not great enough to justify the expense of buying them. Lawn aerators, for instance, are expensive and are likely to be used only once a year. Rather than buying one of these machines, it is more cost effective to hire one when you need to.

Always clean machinery before you put it away and always have it professionally serviced at least once a year. Winter, when the machines are not in use, is the traditional time to have machines serviced but do not leave it too late or there will be a queue and you may not get your machines back before you need them.

LAWNMOWERS

Although it is still possible to buy manual lawnmowers, most people prefer those that at least have the blades turned by power, whether in the form of electricity or petrol (solar-powered machines are beginning to appear, but at the moment are little more than a novelty). Electric machines are relatively quiet and convenient, but the main drawback is that you have to be connected to a power source via a long cable. Petrol-driven machines are noisy but are more powerful and independent of cables.

Cylinder mowers are the most expensive but they produce a very good cut, and, when fitted with a rear roller, they produce the stripes on the lawn that many gardeners like. They can also produce a tighter cut than rotary machines. Rotary mowers are less expensive, but they do not produce such a good finish. On the plus side, they are more versatile as they can cut much longer grass, and some models have rear rollers, so a stripe can be achieved. Most models now have grass boxes. Hover machines are very useful for getting under overhanging plants, but they do not produce a particularly good finish and leave the cuttings on the lawn. One of the major developments has been the increase in the number of tractor models. These are an extension of the old 'sit-on' mowers, and they can now be used to pull small trailers as well as operate leaf-gatherers and even snowploughs.

STRIMMERS

The main functional part of a strimmer is a fast-rotating length of nylon cord. This cuts long grass. The weaker electric models are used for trimming round trees and shrubs and the edges of lawns, but heavier, petrol-driven machines are capable of cutting really rough grass, and those versions with a blade rather than cord can cut even brushwood and scrub. Special machines for cutting the edges of lawns are available for those gardeners who have not got the patience to use long-handled shears.

Strimmers can be dangerous, and you should always wear protection for your eyes, feet and hands.

ROLLERS

Rollers are less used than they once were, partly because of the widespread use of mowing machines that incorporate them. Heavy metal rollers can still be purchased, but light plastic ones that are filled with water to provide the necessary weight are probably more convenient.

OTHER LAWN EQUIPMENT

There are powered machines for aerating, slitting and scarifying lawns as well as for clearing up leaves. These are all efficient, but they are worth owning only if you have a large amount of lawn. For the amount of use that an average gardener will get from these machines, it is far more economical to hire them as and when necessary. Buying a fertilizer spreader is more debatable – a small, hand-pushed model is not too expensive, but again, the more sophisticated versions can be hired.

WHEELBARROWS

There is a wide range of wheelbarrows available. Those with blown-up tires are the easiest to move around the garden and do far less damage in wet conditions. Those with solid wheels are cheaper, but they do cut into the ground when it is wet, making them difficult to push, and they mark the ground. However, they do not get punctures.

The cheapest of all barrows are those bought from builders' merchants. These are heavy and are liable to rust, but they have a good carrying capacity and, if treated with care, will last for years. Painted steel barrows will last for years if they looked after, but if left outside, they will rust after a few years. Those with galvanized steel bodies are far more expensive but will last much longer. Plastic barrows are also long lived. There are a number of other types of barrow, including two-wheeled versions, which are useful for people with large gardens.

SHREDDERS

Until recently the only ways to get rid of woody material, such as hedge trimmings, the dried remains of herbaceous plants and the tough stems of plants such as those of cabbages, was either to burn them or take them to a refuse tip. Now it is possible not only to get rid of them within the garden itself but also to put them to good use. They can be shredded into small pieces that can be composted for three months and then spread back on the garden as a valuable, weed-free mulch.

As with so much garden machinery, there are two types: one powered by electricity, and the other driven by a petrol engine. The electric machines are much cheaper, and although they are more suitable for amateur use, they are often underpowered. Always choose the most powerful machine you can afford.

The petrol-driven shredders are generally much more powerful, but, as one would expect, they are much more expensive than the electric equivalent.

Always wear protective goggles, earmuffs and clothing whatever type of shredder you use.

VACUUM CLEANERS

Garden vacuum cleaners are really effective only with dry leaves. Any dust or fine debris is blown straight through the mesh of the collecting bag and anything heavier is not picked up, which is, perhaps, a good thing otherwise it might lift soil from the beds as well as gravel from paths! While leaves can be fairly easily raked up from the lawn, the vacuum comes into its own when the leaves are scattered across borders and among plants. Most models can be used as 'blowers' and are used for blowing the leaves into heaps, which can then be picked up by hand. Some machines can be used only in this way and are no use at all for picking up leaves. Unfortunately, most kinds do not work very well on wet leaves or leaves that have become packed down, and another disadvantage is that the collecting bags can fill up very quickly.

HEDGE TRIMMERS

Hedge trimmers make light of work of what can be one of the most tiring jobs in the garden if done by hand. Electric machines are light but have not got the power to cut through anything large; they can, therefore, be used only for trimming a hedge, not for renovating one. A petrol-powered machine can be used on much thicker wood, but even so, it cannot cope with a hedge that has become seriously overgrown. The only problem with petrol-driven trimmers is that they are very heavy and noisy. There are now rechargeable electric trimmers that do away with the necessity of long cables, but their power is even more restricted and they do not operate for long before they need to be recharged.

ROTAVATORS

Powered cultivators have been around for a long time, and they have now become sophisticated and are available with a range of attachments, such as potato lifters. The basic machine is a petrol motor that turns a series of rotors, which sink through the soil to dig it and break it up. On heavy ground some gardeners initially dig by hand and then use the rotavator to break up the clods. The motive power of the better machines is through the wheels, while cheaper models are pulled along by the rotors as they cut into the soil. None of the rotavators is cheap, and because they are mainly used for digging they are of little use in the small garden. Nevertheless, they can be invaluable if several gardeners, such as a group of allotment holders, band together.

THE GREENHOUSE

COMPOSTS

One of the problems that exercises the minds of many gardeners is which of the wealth of different types of compost on offer at the local garden centre they should use. To carry out the various tasks successfully gardeners should really have a selection of different composts, each of which can be used for a different purpose. This is often far from feasible, however, simply because there is nowhere to store the separate bags and, in addition, buying several different types is expensive. There are several general-purpose composts that can be used whenever compost is required, and a potting compost can be used as a general-purpose growing medium.

The chief difference between the various kinds of compost is that some are soil-less while others are soil- or loam-based. The main constituent of the soil-less composts is peat or a peat substitute, such as coir, with added sand to help with drainage and fertilizer to feed the plants. Peat composts are lightweight, which means that full pots are easy to carry but can be easily blown over, especially when the compost is dry. When they do dry out, these composts are very difficult to re-wet because the water tends just to run off the top and down the sides of the pot.

Soil-based composts are made up of different ratios of loam, peat and sand or grit. The loam adds body to the compost as well as providing a certain amount of nutrient. They are heavier to carry about, but are more stable than soil-less composts. They are easier to re-wet and hold water for longer, but, at the same time, they are not as easy to waterlog. Every gardener seems to have his or her personal preference – often with very strong feelings on the matter – but most plants seem to grow happily in either, and it is more the preference of the gardener than the plant that seems to matter.

Potting composts are produced for plants that are already in growth and have their own roots. Because some plants need more nutrients than others, the composts are sometimes supplied in different strengths. For example, the soil-based potting composts are usually based on the formula devised by the John Innes Institute, with JI Potting Compost No. 1 have the least amount of fertilizer and No. 3 having the most.

Seed composts are made to a slightly different formula of various proportions of peat and sand or of loam, peat and sand. The seeds provide their own food, and the compost is really just something to keep the emerging seedlings upright and a 'sponge' to hold the water. Only a small quantity of fertilizer is required. Once the seedlings start to grow, they will need more nutrients and can be transferred to a potting compost.

A compost that is designed for cuttings is similar in its make-up to a seed compost and is, in effect, little more than equal proportions of peat and sharp sand. Until recently it was deemed that no fertilizer was required, but now it is thought that a small quantity is needed. Again, when roots have been formed and nutrients are required, the cuttings should be transferred to a potting compost.

There are also special growing mediums, such as ericaceous compost. This is formulated to contain no lime so that it can be used for lime-hating plants, such as azaleas. Other special composts are made orchids and for water plants.

There is no reason you cannot make your own composts, particularly if you have a source of good loam. You will need a sterilizer to clear the soil of harmful bacteria, although many gardeners would say that soil should not be sterilized because the process removes a lot of beneficial bacteria as well and, on balance, all the bacteria should be kept. The problem with not sterilizing the soil, however, is that weed seeds are not killed. Use either peat or a peat substitute and a sharp sand or grit as the other two components in the proportions listed below. Special formulated chemicals can be purchased to add to the composts; if you use one of these, follow the manufacturer's instructions on the packet.

Compost	Loam	Peat	Sharp sand
Potting composts:			
soil-based	7 parts	3 parts	2 parts
soil-less	none	3 parts	1 part
Seed composts	2 parts	1 part	1 part
Cutting compost	none	1 part	1 part

(all parts are by volume)

SOIL STRUCTURE AND FERTILITY

If conditions permit, autumn and winter are the times to prepare the vegetable garden for the coming season. Your main concerns must be, as elsewhere in the garden, with the condition and fertility of the soil.

The principal task is to dig the soil. When you are cultivating a plot for the first time and from time to time thereafter it is a good idea to loosen the lower soil by double digging. Double digging involves digging two spits deep – a spit is the depth of a spade's blade – but the bottom layer of soil, which is usually of relatively poor quality, is not brought to the surface and mixed with the top layer. Once the soil has been broken up, single digging will suffice for a number of years before it is advisable once again to break up the bottom layer, which is probably beginning to become hard and compacted.

In order to improve the structure of the soil it is essential that plenty of well-rotted organic material (p. 172) is added. This will help to break up the soil and add nutrients to it, and organic material has the additional advantage of helping to hold moisture in the soil. As well as using well-rotted material, many gardeners like to use a 'green manure' – that is, a crop that is grown especially as a manure and is then dug straight back into the soil (p. 30).

Most vegetables and border plants require what most gardening books describe as 'a well-drained and moisture-retentive soil'. This is not a contradiction. Well-drained means that excess moisture should be able to drain away freely, while moisture-retentive means that sufficient moisture is held in the fibrous organic material to meet the plants' needs. Very few plants like to be waterlogged, but they all need moisture. If the site is wet, particularly if there is water lying around, a proper drainage system must be installed. This can lead to a convenient ditch, to a soakaway or possibly to a pond that is specially created to take it. The soil's drainage can be improved by adding grit. In addition to holding water, humus breaks up the soil and helps with the drainage.

Light, dry soils, on the other hand, tend to lose moisture too rapidly. This is useful after a storm or rainy period, because you can soon get back onto the land, but it frequently leaves plants without any moisture. Again, well-rotted organic matter helps to supply the plants' roots with moisture. Light soil, through which water passes rapidly, loses much of its nutrients in the water. It

Single digging

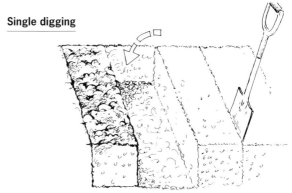

Remove the soil from an area one spit deep and about 30–38cm (12–15in) wide and put in a pile at the other end of the border.

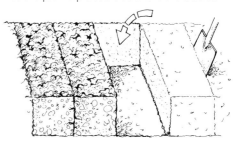

Move the soil from the next strip forwards into the area you have just dug out. Continue doing this until you reach the end of the border, and put the first batch of soil into the strip you dig out.

Double digging

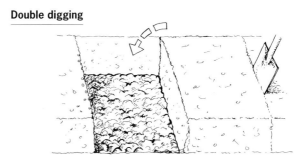

Remove the soil from a strip of ground to a depth of one spit and pile it near the other end of the area you area digging. Fork or dig over the base of the first area to a spit's depth, removing stones and weed roots and adding compost if you wish. Move the top layer of soil from the next strip to the top of the strip you have just dug.

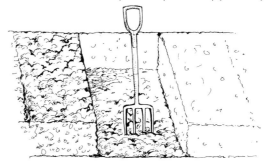

Fork or dig the lower layer in the second strip, again removing roots and stones and adding compost. Continue along the area, each time breaking up the lower level of soil but not bringing it to the surface, until you fill the final strip with the soil removed from the first.

is, therefore, important to replenish this and, yet again, organic material will help, partly by slowing down the leaching process and partly by supplying nutrients.

Another important aspect of soils is their relative acidity and alkalinity. Vegetables prefer a slightly acidic soil. In the ornamental garden, however, some plants need an alkaline soil, while others will die if they do not have acid conditions. If a soil is too acid it can be modified by adding lime (follow the instructions on the packet). Acidity is difficult to increase in extremely alkaline conditions, but it can be modified in more marginal situations by adding organic material to the soil. Rotted pine needles are a good additive.

Simple soil-test kits are widely available, and these not only tell the acid/alkaline condition of the soil (known as its pH), but they will also tell if there are any other deficiencies that can be put right with fertilizers.

the third is for permanent crops such as rhubarb. The other method, which is more usual, is to have five beds, four rotating while the fifth is, again, a permanent bed.

Work out the crops you will be growing next year and add anything you may grow in subsequent years and draw up a table as below. Divide the vegetable garden into plots and plant each section according to your plan.

It is not as complicated as it seems and once the rotation is set in motion it becomes automatic to move everything on one plot for the next year. The one thing that might cause a slight problem is the fact that some crops are still in the ground when the next year's rotation begins. Purple sprouting broccoli, for example, is not finished until April, and it can be a nuisance if it is right in the middle of the plot. Remember to plant them to one side so that you can work around them until it is time to dig them out and use the ground for later sown crops.

ROTATION OF CROPS

One important aspect of soil management is the rotation of crops. The idea behind this is that crops are not grown on the same part of the vegetable garden for two years running. There are two main reasons for this. First, if crops are grown on the same ground year after year there is the distinct possibility that soil-borne pests and disease will build up. If you move the crop on, these pests will die without their host. The second reason is that while some crops can be grown in freshly manured ground, others prefer to grow in ground that was manured the year before. So in the first year you manure an area and grow crop A in it; the next year you move crop A to a new piece of freshly manured ground while you move crop B onto the old-manured plot vacated by crop A and so on.

There are two forms of crop rotation. One involves using four plots, three of which rotate while

Four-year rotation

Plot 1	Plot 2	Plot 3	Plot 4	Plot 5 (permanent)
Peas	Cabbage	Bulb onions	Potatoes	Rhubarb
Broad beans	Brussels	Spring onions	Parsnips	Asparagus
French beans	sprouts	Shallots	Beetroot	Globe
Runner beans	Calabrese	Leeks	Carrot	artichoke
	Broccoli	Garlic	Salsify	Jerusalem
	Kale	Sweet corn	Scorzonera	artichoke
	Radish	Marrow	Celery	Seakale
	Swede	Lettuce	Celeriac	Perennial
	Turnip		Tomatoes	herbs
	Kohl rabi			

Three-year rotation

Plot 1	Plot 2	Plot 3	Plot 4 (permanent)
Peas	Potatoes	Cabbage	Rhubarb
Broad beans	Parsnips	Brussels sprouts	Asparagus
French beans	Beetroot	Calabrese	Globe artichoke
Runner beans	Carrot	Broccoli	Jerusalem
Onions	Salsify	Kale	artichoke
Leeks	Scorzonera	Swede	Seakale
Sweet corn	Tomatoes	Turnip	Perennial herbs
Marrow		Kohl rabi	
Lettuce		Radish	

TREES AND SHRUBS

PRUNING TREES

Ornamental trees in general need very little pruning apart from removing dead wood. The lower branches might, occasionally, need to be removed so that light can penetrate to the beds and borders below or because they are rubbing against the house or some other structure. Winter is a good time to carry out this work.

Cut off the branches cleanly and neatly with a saw, first making an upward cut to stop the branch splitting if it is a heavy one. It is not now considered either necessary or desirable to apply a protective coat to the wound.

PRUNING CLEMATIS

Clematis can be divided into three main groups according to when they need to be pruned. Specialist clematis nurseries or the labels on the plants themselves should be consulted before any plant is pruned.

Group 1 consists of vigorous plants, such as *Clematis montana*. This needs little or no pruning, although dead wood should be removed. From time to time it is worthwhile reducing the tangle of stems, if for no other reason than to reduce the weight that the plant's supports have to carry.

Group 2 consists of the large, early-flowered varieties, such as *C.* 'Lasurstern', which flower on shoots produced during the previous year. First, remove all dead wood and then cut out all weak growth, cutting shoots back to a pair of strong buds. If they are tangled, separate the remaining wood and tie in to the supports.

Group 3 clematis are those large- and small-flowered clematis that flower on new growth. The group includes, for example, *C.* 'Hagley Hybrid' and the *C. viticella* cultivars. These should be pruned almost to the ground in midwinter, so that all the previous year's growth is cut back almost to the base, just above a pair of sound buds.

PERMANENT STRUCTURES

There is time in winter to consider the various structures in the garden. Some of the most decorative of these are those that support climbers. These may be tunnels, such as arches and pergolas, or areas for sitting, such as arbours.

ARCHES

The value of arches is that they act as a link between two different areas. Arches are usually inviting, showing a glimpse of what lies beyond, and no matter how much you are enjoying the part of the garden you are in, you are

Pruning clematis

Group 1 clematis need pruning only when they are overgrown or to remove dead wood.

Prune Group 2 clematis by removing dead or damaged stems before new growth begins.

Group 3 clematis, which produce flowers on the current year's growth, should be cut back almost to ground level, just above two healthy buds, in late winter or early spring.

Clematis montana needs little or no pruning, except to remove dead material. It provides a magnificent display in spring each year.

The second aspect to consider is that the arch should be wide enough. When you are erecting an arch it is easy to think that there is plenty of room for a person to pass both through and under it. However, it is vital that you take into account that it will narrow considerably once it is covered with climbers.

A wide range of climbing plants can be used. Roses are the classic accompaniment to an arch, but do remember that people are going to walk through the arch, and stray branches of thorns can be uncomfortable as well as dangerous. If you do choose roses, select a thornless variety such as 'Zéphirine Drouhin'. Avoid at all costs those with vicious thorns such as 'Albertine', however enticing the scent may be.

Another advantage of roses such as 'Zéphirine Drouhin' is that they flower over a very long season. An alternative is to choose two or more climbers so that you have a succession of flowers and scents. You could, for example, use an early honeysuckle followed by a clematis. Fruit, too, can be grown on archways. Some varieties of pear, for example, can be trained over an arch and will provide blossom in spring, green leaves in summer, fruit in late summer and autumn-tinted leaves later in the year.

Archways need not be made from wood or metal but can be living. The hedge on either side of a gap or gateway can be grown upwards and over to create an arch. This is not difficult to do and yet it can transform the appearance of the entrance.

somehow inevitably drawn to the arch to see what is on the other side.

Arches can be filled with gates or they can be open. Similarly, they can be unadorned or they can be covered with climbers. There are places where the arch should be unclothed, but in most gardens where space is at a premium it seems sensible to use the opportunity of the arch to grow even more plants. One advantage of this from the visual point of view is that it helps take some of the planting up into the air, away from the ground, thereby creating a new dimension. This makes the garden a much more interesting place.

There are two criteria to bear in mind when building an arch: it must be stable and it must be wide enough. An unclothed arch need not be heavy, but one covered in climbers becomes very heavy indeed. The shrubs that go over it are subject to the full force of the wind, adding even more pressures on the arch. Metal is the best material, but it is expensive and is less easy to make yourself. Wood is a much easier material to work with, but it may rot after a few years. If you decide on wood, use sound material and treat all the timber with a preservative (but not creosote, which will kill the climbers). Make certain that the arch is well supported by burying the underground part deeply and firmly.

PERGOLAS

Pergolas are, in effect, a series of archways joined together. They are not necessarily the entrance to anywhere, however, but are more a covered walkway. The most effective pergolas need space, but, with a little ingenuity, they can be used to great effect even in a small garden – and they often make the garden appear bigger than it is.

The cool greenness of an arbour or pergola enhances any garden, providing an inviting area to walk or sit.

The use of iron or steel is very expensive in a large structure like this, and most pergolas are built of wood. If you are working on a grand scale, it is possible to use brick piers to support the top of the arch. Whatever material is used, the pergola should be built to last. Some of the most successful and attractive pergolas or walkways are covered with very ancient plants, such as wisterias, which give a sense of history and stability to the garden and add to the atmosphere of tranquillity and peace.

The strictures about stability and width, mentioned in regard to arches, apply equally to pergolas. Because this is a walkway and people like to walk in pairs, the structure should be even wider than the normal archway. This will cause problems if space is limited, not only because of the amount of ground it will take up but also because its size may well visually unbalance the rest of the garden.

The same comments apply to the use of plants as were mentioned under archways – and do beware thorns. It is, however, easier to accommodate roses in a wide pergola than over a narrow archway.

One fascinating form of pergola is that created from pleached trees, where the pleaching has continued across the top between the two rows of trees (p. 129). Pergolas can also be a good place to grow fruit trees, such as apples or pears, the sides and 'roof' being created by the use of espaliers (p. 12).

ARBOURS

Arbours are vital constituents of all gardens, providing shady areas in which to sit and relax. The simplest arbours are made from a framework that forms a box, one side of which is left open. This framework is then clothed in whatever climber you like.

The arbour should be large enough to take at least one seat, preferably a double one. Better still, however, it should be large enough to accommodate several seats and a table. On the whole, the arbour should be sited at the edge of garden or of an area of the garden, although they can sometimes become the focal point if they are sited in or near the middle. An arbour in the centre of the garden is likely to be rather more flamboyant than the rather more discreet structures near the edges of the plot.

Any climbers can be used, but because this is somewhere that you will sit and relax, it is a good idea to use fragrant plants. If you are likely to sit there in the evening, plant a climber that produces it perfume at that time of day – jasmine, for example. Another possibility is to cover the framework with a grape vine, either a decorative one or a productive one, which produces a wonderful dappled shade that is just perfect for eating under.

Arbours need not be created from frameworks and climbers, they can be 'carved' from solid bushes. Grow a hedge around and over the proposed area or hollow out an existing bush to make a lovely secret arbour, worthy of an amorous tryst.

PLANTS *for* ARCHES, ARBOURS *and* PERGOLAS

> *Clematis*
> *Hedera* (ivy)
> *Humulus lupulus* (hop)
> *Jasminum officinale* (jasmine)
> *Lathyrus odoratus* (sweetpea)
> *Lonicera* (honeysuckle)
> *Rosa* (roses)
> *Vitis* (grape vines)
> *Wisteria*

🍃 VEGETABLES

GREEN MANURES

The use of green manures is an invaluable way of increasing the fertility of your soil. As well as increasing both the nutrient and fibre levels of the soil, it also acts as a groundcover, keeping down weeds and helping to prevent the leaching of existing nutrients from the soil. It can be applied to complete plots or it can be used in ground temporarily left vacant by the harvesting of a crop.

Several crops can be used, but among the most valuable are members of the pea family, such as lupins, clovers or beans, which fix nitrogen from the air into the soil. Mustards are good green manures, but they should not be used on ground just cleared of, or about to be used for, brassicas because there is the risk of spreading club root.

Green manures can be used at any time in the growing season that the ground is vacant, and if the area will soon be needed for another crop, choose a fast-maturing kind.

Sow the seeds in shallow drills or broadcast them over the area and rake them in. Whatever crop you use, do not let it get past its flowering stage or it will seed and cause problems later on. Similarly, do not let it become too woody or it will not rot down. Low-growing crops can be dug straight into the ground – make certain that they are buried – but taller crops need to cut first and then dug in.

GREEN MANURE PLANTS

Broad beans (or fava beans): nitrogen fixing
Buckwheat
Italian ryegrass: quick-growing
Lupins: nitrogen fixing
Mustard: quick-growing
Phacelia: quick-growing
Red clover: nitrogen fixing
Winter tare: nitrogen fixing

CAULIFLOWERS

Cauliflowers are not the easiest of vegetables to cultivate, and being able to grow them gives not only the pleasure of producing something good to eat but also the satisfaction of achievement.

There are cauliflowers for harvesting at most times of the year. Winter is the most difficult time, although increasingly varieties are being bred to cover this gap, at least for milder areas. Summer cauliflowers are sown outside in the early spring or they can be sown under glass from midwinter onwards. Autumn and later varieties are sown in late spring. When planting out, space summer varieties at about 50cm (20in) apart and autumn ones at 75cm (30in) apart.

Cauliflowers need a sunny aspect, but they do not grow well in high temperatures. It is also important that the soil is moisture-retentive, because they do not like to be checked, and lack of rain may do this. Dig in organic material in the previous autumn. Firm down the soil well both before and after planting out.

Sow either in a seed bed or in trays under glass. The seeds can also be sown *in situ* and then thinned to the appropriate distances. This method helps prevent any check that may be caused by transplanting, and it is particularly important for autumn varieties.

The most important thing is to keep them moist in summer droughts. Cauliflowers suffer from a number of pests and diseases that are common to all brassicas (p. 130).

Once the curd begins to develop and reaches the size of a tennis-ball, bend over some of the outer leaves so that they protect it, and harvest when the curd is large enough. Cauliflowers can be kept for a short while if the whole plant is lifted and hung upside down in a cool place, and most types can be frozen.

RECOMMENDED VARIETIES *of* CAULIFLOWER

Summer varieties
'Alpha'
'Montano'
'Snow Crown'

Autumn varieties
'All Year Round'
'Autumn Glory'
'Dok Elgon'
'Castlegrant'
'Violet Queen'
'Wallaby'

Winter varieties
'Arcade'
'Cappacio'
'Early Feltham'
'Jerome'
'Purple Cape'

MARCH

This is a month of great excitement in the garden. The weather is beginning to get warmer, and there are signs of spring everywhere. It is a month when gardeners are at their keenest, just waiting for the soil to dry out so that they can get on.

There is plenty to be done, but do not be in too much of a hurry. Let the soil dry out a bit, because working on wet ground causes it to compact, which makes it difficult for water and air to penetrate as well as doing permanent harm to the structure of the soil. In many areas little purpose will be served by getting into the garden. The seeds of many vegetables will not germinate until the soil warms up, and any seeds lying in damp, cold ground are liable to rot, meaning that you will have the expense, in both time and money, of re-sowing.

Do not be too anxious to get on with sowing annuals. If you start too early the plants may well become very drawn while they are waiting to be planted out after the threat of frosts has eventually passed. You will also have to look after them.

In spite of these warnings about rushing into things, there is still a lot that can be done this month, and the more of the routine chores that are done now, the more time you will have next month, when things really do get busy.

General

- Prepare seed beds (p. 50)
- Hoe and weed all borders and beds (p. 50)
- Finish spreading organic material (p. 172)

Annuals and Tender Perennials

- Continue sowing tender annuals under glass (p. 20)
- Prick out those that have germinated (p. 20)
- Pot on cuttings of chrysanthemums, dahlias, felicias, pelargoniums and so on (p. 37)
- If the soil is dry enough, sow hardy annuals outside (p. 50)
- Plant out sweetpeas (p. 180)

Bulbs

- Lift and divide snowdrops as they finish flowering (p. 21)
- Deadhead unless seeds is required as flowers go over (p. 76)
- Plant summer-flowering bulbs (p. 110)

Fruit

- Finish pruning fruit trees (except plums) (p. 155)
- Graft trees (p. 36)
- Prune blueberries, gooseberries and redcurrants (p. 154)
- Plant new strawberry beds (p. 138)
- Protect emerging buds from birds with netting (p. 53)
- Feed trees and bushes (p. 53)
- Mulch trees and bushes (p. 53)
- Check stakes, wirework and cages for winter damage (p. 35)
- Hand pollinate early fruit trees (p. 35)

Greenhouse

- Start watering regime, especially if weather hot (p. 122)
- Continue sowing greenhouse tomatoes, cucumbers, aubergines and peppers (p. 55)
- Plant tomatoes, aubergines, peppers and cucumbers in heated greenhouses (p. 55)
- Continue sowing tender annuals (p. 20)
- Sow peas, beans and leeks ready for planting out (p. 55)
- Pot on cuttings of chrysanthemums, dahlias, felicias, pelargoniums and so on (p. 37)
- Ventilate during the day, but watch for night frosts (p. 77)

Lawns

- Remove thatch and open up the grass by raking the lawn with a spring-tined rake (p. 59)
- Roll if frost has lifted the turf (p. 38)
- If the weather is warm and soil dry, start mowing with high-set blades (p. 38)
- Feed lawns (p. 60)
- Sow or turf new lawns if weather right (p. 39)
- Re-sow or re-turf patches of worn grass if weather right (p. 39)

Perennials

- Finish cutting back and tidying borders (p. 173)
- Finish preparing borders for new planting (p. 25)
- Plant perennials (p. 39)
- Divide and re-plant existing perennials (p. 40)
- Feed borders (p. 39)
- Mulch new and existing borders (p. 172)
- Sow in pots (p. 39)

Rock Gardens

- Remove winter protection from plants (p. 41)
- Plant new plants and beds (p. 41)
- Divide clump-forming plants (p. 41)
- Feed and top dress beds (p. 41)
- Re-pot alpines growing in pots (p. 41)

Trees and Shrubs

- Finish planting bare-rooted deciduous trees and shrubs (p. 162)
- Finish pruning roses (p. 42)
- Remove any frost- or wind-damaged branches or twigs (p. 27)
- Check staking after winter winds (p. 41)
- Check ties and ease if necessary (p. 41)
- Tie in climbers (p. 64)
- Prune shrubs that will flower on new growth (p. 65)

Vegetables

- Prepare beds (p. 43)
- Earth up potatoes and cover shoots if frosts threaten (p. 44)
- Start sowing hardy vegetables if soil is warm enough (p. 44)
- Plant onion sets, shallots, mid- and late-crop potatoes and Jerusalem artichokes (p. 46)
- Plant permanent crops, such as asparagus and globe artichokes (p. 47)
- Give spring cabbages a nitrogenous feed (p. 130)

BULBS

The rush is on as large numbers of bulbs come into flower. Remove the deadheads of those that are over so that energy is not diverted from the bulb to producing seedheads. Do not remove the leaves, however.

The best time to transplant snowdrops is as the flowers fade (p. 21), which in some species is now.

DAFFODILS

Daffodils will be moving to their climax as the month progresses, but the early ones will already have finished flowering. In order to encourage good flowering next year, remove the dead flowers as soon as they appear. This prevents the bulb from wasting a great deal of its energy in producing seed. However, do not remove the leaves until they naturally die down. The bulbs are not harmed by picking flowers for the house.

RECOMMENDED VARIETIES *of* DAFFODIL

'Cheerfulness': tazetta, white/yellow, double
'Desdemona': large-cupped, white
'Dutch Master': trumpet, yellow
'February Gold': cyclamineus, yellow
'Geranium': tazetta, white/red
'Ice Follies': large-cupped, white/yellow
'Mount Hood': trumpet, white
Narcissus bulbocodium (hoop petticoat): species, yellow
N. pseudonarcissus (wild daffodil): species, white/yellow
'Old Pheasant Eye': poeticus, white/orange
'Peeping Tom': cyclamineus, yellow
'Salome': large-cupped, white/yellow
'Spellbinder': trumpet, yellow
'Sun Disc': jonquilla, yellow
'Suzy': jonquilla, yellow/red
'Tête-à-Tête': cyclamineus, yellow
'Unsurpassable': trumpet, yellow

BULBS *in* FLOWER *in* EARLY SPRING

Anemone blanda; *A. nemorosa* (wood anemone)
Chionodoxa (glory of the snow)
Crocus (crocus)
Eranthis (winter aconites)
Galanthus (snowdrops)
Leucojum vernum (spring snowflake)
Narcissus (daffodils)
Puschkinia (puschkinia)
Romulea (romulea)
Scilla (squills)
Tulipa (tulips)

FRUIT

Early spring is a busy time in the fruit garden, especially if you have not kept on top of things in the winter months. There is still time to finish pruning apple and pear trees (p. 155) as well as blackcurrant and other bushes (p. 154). It is also time to start training newly planted stone fruits. In some cases – peaches, for example – pruning also takes

Deadheading daffodils helps the bulbs build up energy for next year. Do not remove their leaves until they have died down naturally.

The range of plums offered in shops is limited, but for the gardener there are many delicious varieties available, including 'Merton Gage', seen here.

place at this time of year, but it is essential not to start pruning plums too early or they are likely to develop silver leaf; wait until summer, which is the best time for pruning them.

By now the worst of the winter weather should be past, and it is time to check and rectify any damage that wind, snow and frost may have caused to supports and cages. The snow may have stretched and broken the top net that covers the cage, while the wind may have loosened stakes protecting trees or posts that support the wirework for cane or trained fruit. The posts holding the netting for the fruit cage may also have worked loose, and wooden posts may have rotted or been broken. Strengthen or replace all damaged items.

Strawberry beds are best planted in the late summer or autumn, but if this is not possible, early spring is the next best time. However, these later plants will not be strong enough to bear fruit in the first year, and any blossom that appears should be removed.

Bullfinches seem to be at their hungriest at this time of year, and they can quickly strip a tree or shrub of all of its emerging buds. Trees can be protected by cotton or fleece, but netting is the most effective method. Once blossom begins to appear, remove the netting to allow pollinating insects free access.

HAND POLLINATING

In milder areas fruit trees that are protected by walls may come into blossom before their pollinating insects are active. These should be pollinated by hand to ensure a good crop.

Choose flowers that are in bud and just about to open (this is important, because no insect will have visited them yet). Open each flower and rub the anthers of the pollinating flower onto the stigma of the one you are pollinating. Cover the flower with a net bag or remove the petals to discourage further insect pollination.

TYPES OF FRUIT

BUSH FRUIT
white-, red- and blackcurrants, gooseberries and blueberries

CANE FRUIT
raspberries, blackberries, loganberries and tayberries

SOFT FRUIT
all the above bush and cane fruit plus strawberries

STONE FRUIT
plums, damsons, gages, cherries, nectarines, peaches and apricots

TENDER FRUIT
lemons, oranges, persimmon, pomegranates, avocado pears and pineapples

TREE FRUIT
apples, pears, medlars, quinces and figs, plus all stone fruit above

VINE FRUIT
grapes, passion fruit and kiwi fruit
(Chinese gooseberries)

Scion grafting

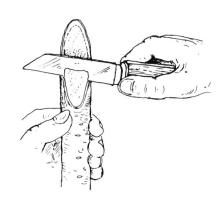

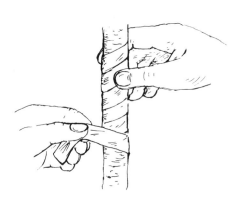

Prune the rootstock to 20–25cm (8–10in) and make a sloping cut. Make a nick in this to create a tongue.

Make a matching cut in the scion and slip it over the rootstock.

Make certain that the cadmium layers of both scion and rootstock are in contact before holding them firmly together with adhesive tape.

An alternative method is to pick up some pollen on a fine, soft brush and transfer it to the stigma. Sterilize the brush between plants. Label the flowers you have pollinated so that you collect the correct seed.

GRAFTING FRUIT TREES

Late winter or early spring is the best time for carrying out the scion grafting of fruit trees. Bud-grafting, however, is best undertaken in midsummer (p. 111). The most common method of this type of grafting is whip-and-tongue. It works best for apples and pears, but it can also be used for stone fruits, although budding is a better option for these.

The scion from the chosen variety is grafted onto rootstock that is at least one year but preferably two years old. Choose the rootstock carefully because this will affect the final size and vigour of the tree (see below). The scions should be selected and cut in midwinter. The wood selected should be healthy and taken from the previous year's growth. Cut lengths of about 23cm (9in), each containing at least three buds. Heel them into a well-drained soil in a sheltered position until they are required.

Just before bud-break, prune back the rootstock so that it is 20–25cm (8–10in) above the soil, removing any side shoots that may have developed. Make an upward cut, removing part of the bark and wood in a sloping cut. Make a nick in the slope about two-thirds of the way up, creating a tongue. Trim a scion to about three or four buds, and then make corresponding mirror-image cuts in its base so that it will marry exactly with the rootstock. Taking care that you do not touch either of the cuts with

your hand, place the groove of the scion over the tongue on the rootstock, making sure that the two cadmium layers are well in contact. Bind the two firmly together with a grafting tape. Once a callus has formed and the two have grown together, remove the tape.

ROOTSTOCKS

Apples

M27: an extreme dwarfing stock (bush, dwarf pyramid, cordon)

M9: dwarfing stock (bush, dwarf pyramid, cordon)

M26: semi-dwarfing stock (bush, dwarf pyramid, cordon)

MM106: semi-dwarfing stock (bush, spindlebush, cordon, fan espalier)

M7: semi-dwarfing stock (bush, spindlebush, cordon, fan espalier)

M4: semi-vigorous stock (bush, spindlebush)

MM4: vigorous stock (standard)

M2: vigorous stock

MM111: vigorous stock (half-standard, standard, large bush, large fans, large espaliers)

M25: vigorous stock (standard)

MM109: vigorous stock

M1: vigorous stock

Pears

Quince C: moderately dwarfing stock (bush, cordon, dwarf pyramid, espalier, fan)

Quince A: semi-vigorous stock (bush, cordon, dwarf pyramid, espalier, fan)

Pear: vigorous stock (standard, half-standard)

Plums, gages and damsons
 Pixy: dwarfing stock (bush, pyramid)
 Damas C: moderately vigorous stock
 St Julien A: semi-vigorous stock (bush, fan, pyramid)
 Brompton A: vigorous stock (half-standard, standard)
 Myrobalan B: vigorous stock (half-standard, standard)

Apricots, peaches and nectarines
 St Julien A: semi-vigorous stock (bush, fan)
 Brompton A: vigorous stock (bush)

THE GREENHOUSE

Although the weather outdoors may still seem cool and even wintry, inside the greenhouse things are already on the move. Plants can quickly use up the moisture in their pots, especially on warm days when the greenhouse can get surprisingly hot. Keep an eye on the pots and trays and water when necessary, but take care that you do not overwater, especially plants that are still dormant.

Provide as much ventilation as possible, especially in warm spells, but close down at night unless it is exceptionally warm. Cold greenhouses can be left open except when frosts threaten.

Sowing seed can continue for tomatoes, cucumbers, aubergines and peppers, which will be grown in a cool or cold greenhouse later in the year. Plants from already sown tomatoes and other crops are ready to be planted out in warm greenhouses.

In most areas, tender annuals are best sown this month (p. 20), but do not be in too much of a hurry, or it might be difficult to look after them without their becoming drawn and leggy well before the weather allows you to plant them out. Vegetables, too, can be sown inside so that they are ready to plant out as soon as they are large enough. This will get crops such as peas, beans and leeks off to a good start.

Cuttings taken from stools of chrysanthemums or dahlia tubers will be ready for potting up, as will any tender perennials that have been overwintered as cuttings. Continue to pot them on so that they become healthy, decent sized plants by the time the passing of the frosts makes it possible for you to plant them out.

GREENHOUSE CLIMATES

COLD GREENHOUSE
There is no heating, and the temperature is allowed to fluctuate. In extreme weather some insulation may be provided for the whole greenhouse or for individual plants. Such a greenhouse is used for summer crops or for overwintering plants that will suffer in extreme cold or that dislike winter wet.

COOL GREENHOUSE
Minimal heating is provided to prevent frost entering the greenhouse. The heating is set to come on when the temperature is likely to fall below 2°C (35°F). The greenhouse is used for summer crops and for overwintering tender garden plants that do not require warmth but that should not be subjected to temperatures below freezing.

TEMPERATE GREENHOUSE
Warmer than the cool greenhouse, this has a minimum night-time temperature of about 7°C (45°F). It is used for growing winter vegetable crops as well as for overwintering tender plants and cuttings. Many houseplants can be kept in these conditions. A heated propagator is required for seed germination.

WARM GREENHOUSE
The temperature is maintained at 13°C (55°F) or more. It is used for growing houseplants as well as for raising seeds and cuttings without the need for a propagator. It is likely to be too warm for overwintering many tender garden plants, which may well come into premature growth.

POTTING UP CUTTINGS

It is essential that cuttings are potted up as soon as they have developed a strong root system. If they are left in the pot in which they were struck, along with all the other cuttings, they will become starved and drawn. Such cuttings soon become unhealthy and rarely develop into first-class plants.

The promise of things to come. Young seedlings pricked into individual containers, protected from frosts by the greenhouse. They are standing on wet gravel, which helps keep the air buoyant around the plants.

Do not pot them up into too large a pot, because the compost beyond the reach of the roots will remain damp and become sour, possibly allowing rot to develop. When it is in a pot that is the correct size, a plant will regularly use up all available moisture. Place a little potting compost (p. 24) into the base of the pot and suspend the cutting in the centre of the pot by holding it between your finger and thumb while steadying your hand by resting your little finger on the rim of the pot. With the other hand, pour compost around the roots. The cutting should be planted to the same depth as it was in the original pot.

When the pot is full of compost, tap it smartly on the bench or *lightly* firm down the compost with the fingers. Do not ram it down. Water the pot either from above with a watering can or stand it in a water bath so that the compost absorbs water through the holes in the bottom of the pot.

Once the roots have filled the pot, move the plant on to a larger size pot so that it is able to develop into a healthy, well-grown specimen.

Do not allow the pots to dry out completely and feed once a week as long as the plants are in continuous growth. If there is a prolonged cool period with little active growth, reduce watering and stop feeding.

 LAWNS

Unless they are well-drained it is best to avoid using lawns or grass paths in the winter months. Once spring weather appears, however, lawns should begin to dry out, allowing access once more.

If the frost has lifted the lawn or made it uneven, lightly roll it as soon as you can get on it without compacting the underlying soil. If you do not have a roller, the roller on a cylinder or rotary mower will do. Set the blades high so that they do not cut the grass or, if they do, they remove only the very top.

The warmer weather will also start the grass into growth and the mowing regime will have to begin. If you delay, the grass may grow too long, making it difficult to cut and leaving the resulting sward an unsightly yellow or brown colour. As soon as the lawn is dry enough, give it a light trim, setting the mower's cutters above their normal cutting height. Gradually lower this over the next month or so until the grass is cut to its summer length.

If the lawn has been damaged during the winter while the soil was wet and soft, now is the time to repair the damage. This can be done either with turves or seed, the former being the easier. Cut out the damaged piece of grass, removing slightly more than the area that has been damaged. Lightly fork over the soil beneath, raking it level and gently firming it down. Place the new turf over the area and cut it to size. Place it in the hole, firming and levelling it.

To repair a damaged section of edge, cut a far larger piece than is damaged. Cut off the damaged portion and replace it so that it forms the new edge, packing it with soil if necessary so that the edge is level. If the damage is not too severe, place the remaining turf back in the hole, filling

Repairing lawns

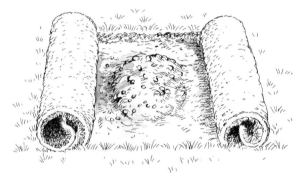

Damage to the edge of a lawn can be repaired by cutting an area larger than the damaged section and moving it so that the damage can be cut off to create a new edge. The gap can be filled with a strip of new turf or sown with grass seed.

To repair sunken areas of lawn, peel back the affected area, rather than remove it altogether, add some sifted compost and replace the turf.

any gaps with sifted compost and sowing fresh grass seed into it. If it is beyond repair, replace it with a new turf.

Sunken areas of lawn should also be repaired. Cut a cross in the turf, with the centre in the middle of the depression. Carefully peel back the turf so that a square hole appears where the sunken area is. Loosen the earth inside the hole, add some sifted compost and lightly firm down. Fold back the turves and firm again. If the level is still not right, raise the turves again and adjust the level of the soil beneath.

SOWING GRASS SEED

If new turf is not available to replace any damaged areas, seed should be sown. Remove the damaged turf and dig over the underlying soil. Fill the hole with a good loam/sand mix. Firm down and add more of the loam and sand if necessary until the soil is level with the lawn. Rake over the top to loosen it and then sow the seed. If possible, choose a seed that is the same as or that is a near equivalent to the original lawn. If the area that is being replaced is at the edge of a lawn, either cut out a piece of

turf further into the lawn and use this to repair the damage and then re-sow the area from which you have removed a section or temporarily place a length of wooden batten along the side of the lawn so that the soil can be built up without it crumbling away. Once the seed has germinated and the lawn has firmly re-established itself, the batten can be removed.

PERENNIALS

As soon as you are able to get onto the soil without damaging it, finish removing all the dead material that remains from last year. Tidy up the border, removing any old supports, leaves and weeds. Lightly dig over the surface so that air and water can enter, and if possible fork in some well-rotted organic material. As long as it is weed free, this can also be spread over the border as a mulch, but before mulching, apply a general-purpose fertilizer, following the instructions on the packet.

Spring is a good time for dividing perennials and planting new ones. New borders should have been prepared last autumn (p. 143), but they can be finished now if they are not yet complete, and old borders can be dug out and the soil rejuvenated, ready for replanting.

Seeds of perennials can be sown in pots and left in a sheltered place to germinate. Although the germination of many perennials can be speeded up by a little warmth, they will all germinate perfectly well without any heat at all, although they may take a bit longer in some cases.

SPRING WORK

The amount of work that you can do on the perennial borders depends on your soil and on the weather. If the soil in your garden is heavy, it is important that you do not tread on it until it has dried out. If it is compacted in winter and early spring, air will be unable to enter the soil and later in the year moisture will run off without penetrating. Both these factors will adversely affect the performance of the plants in your

GREEN TIP *Mulching*

Mulching a border in spring with a 10cm (4in) layer of organic material helps to conserve moisture in the soil and will help to reduce the need to water in summer.

borders. If it is really essential to get onto heavy soils, work from a plank or piece of board, so that your weight is spread.

If the weather is very wet this month, even comparatively free-draining soils are likely to compact, and so working them should be avoided, too. Work can begin once the drying winds of spring have removed a lot of the excess moisture and you can venture onto the borders without doing any harm. Even then, however, it is advisable to dig over any areas on which you have walked so that the soil is open.

In some years you may be lucky enough to have had sufficient dry spells in late autumn and winter to have got on top of maintenance work, but there is usually still some left in the early spring. If it is at all possible to get onto the borders it is essential that you do so. Removing any weeds and digging over the borders at this time of year will save immeasurable amounts of time later in the year. If you leave the weeding until the warm days of early summer, you will find that not only have the weeds been growing for a couple of months or more, but it is now more difficult to get at them as the herbaceous plants begin to grow. Weeding can then become an uphill struggle, with the weeds often emerging as the winner. If all the weeds are removed by late spring, only a light, easy weeding is usually required for the rest of the year.

DIVIDING PERENNIALS

There are two reasons for dividing perennials. The first is that clump-forming or spreading perennials tend to become tired and woody in the centre, often dying back. By dividing them and replanting the young growths, the plant is rejuvenated and will produce much better flowers than the old clump. Second, dividing perennials is one way of increasing your stock, so that you have extra plants to use, sell or give away.

Dig up the plant and divide it into small pieces. Discard the woody central portion and use the young outer growth either to replant or to pot up. Some plants, such as sisyrinchium, will easily fall apart, while others are more difficult. The easiest method is to insert two forks back to back in the plant and prise them apart.

A less strenuous method and one that does less damage is to hold the plant in your hand and shake off the soil, at the same time manipulating it apart into separate crowns with your fingers. For more difficult plants try this in a bucket of water – it is surprising how easily many plants separate into individual sections.

Dividing perennials

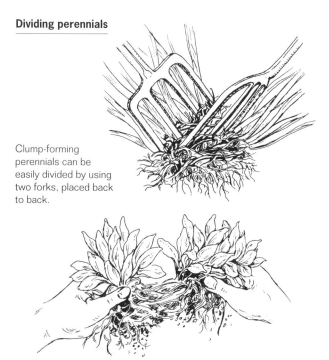

Clump-forming perennials can be easily divided by using two forks, placed back to back.

Some perennials can be divided into separate crowns with your fingers.

You may have to use a knife to cut through some perennials clumps. You should then find that you can separate the crowns with your fingers.

For really tough plants, such as hostas and hellebores, wash off all the soil with a hose pipe and then divide off the individual crowns with a sharp knife, finally working them apart with the fingers.

The crudest method is simply to chop the plant into sections with a spade, but this, apart from its ease, has little to recommend it as it not only produces many wounds through which infection can gain a hold but it also wastes a lot of material. However, if you are not very strong it may be the only way you can cope with large, tough plants such as hostas, which you may not be able to lift, let alone separate, by hand. If you do chop clumps up, remove any severed roots to lessen the chance of infection. Replant all divisions immediately, before they dry out.

ROCK GARDENS

Many rock plants come into flower in the early spring, and the rock garden and alpine house can be the most colourful parts of the garden at this time of year. It is a joy to tend the beds and pots because there is so much to look at. Weeding can never be so delightful as at this time of year.

Now is the time to remove the panes of glass and polythene covers that have been protecting the more fragile plants in winter months. Alpine plants like to have plenty of fresh air blowing round them, and the sooner they are open to the elements the better.

Most rock garden plants are sold in containers so they can be planted at any time, but the most favoured time is in spring. New beds that were prepared in the previous autumn (p. 127) can now be planted up, and replacements can also be planted now.

Some of the clump-forming or spreading herbaceous plants can be divided at this time of year. If they are spring flowering, divide them once they have finished flowering or wait until the autumn. If possible, divide them by shaking off the soil and manipulating them with your fingers. Doing it in a bucket of water will make this a simple job in a surprising number of cases (see Dividing Perennials, p. 40).

Keep a constant eye out for weeds and remove them on sight. Once they are allowed to get established in a rock garden they are often very difficult to remove.

Alpines should not be overfed. In the wild, nutrients are supplied by decomposing detritus, and this usually becomes available only in small quantities. The best method is to scrape back the top dressing of gravel or stone chippings and to fork through the soil, adding a small quantity of well-rotted organic material such as leaf-mould. Replace the stones and top up with fresh ones if necessary. This needs to be done only every two or three years. An easier alternative is to apply a sprinkling of general fertilizer at the rate of a quarter of the quantities recommended on the packet.

PLANTING ALPINES

Alpines can be planted in mid-autumn, although if you have a newly built rock garden (p. 127) the planting is better completed now. Place the plants in their pots on the rock garden, so that you can get some idea of what they will look like, moving them around if necessary until the overall effect looks right. Set the plants in the ground to the same depth they were in their pots. Some, such as *Ramonda* and *Lewisia*, prefer to be planted on their sides so that water does not lodge in their crowns. Plant these in vertical crevices. In tight places, remove the plant from the pot and gently squeeze the rootball into a more elliptical shape. Even narrower crevices can be planted by washing all the soil off the roots, wrapping them in damp tissue and carefully inserting them, trickling in compost on top. Keep this type of planting watered until the roots are established. Another way of dealing with cracks in crevices is to place some seeds on the palm of your hand and, using a drinking straw, blow them into the gap.

Once all the plants are in place, top dress the bed with gravel or small stone chippings. This will not only create an attractive background for the plants but it will prevent soil being splashed onto the low flowers. The top dressing also helps to improve the drainage and keeps the roots of the plants cool.

When you need to replace a dead or unwanted plant in an existing border, loosen the soil around the area with a fork, adding a little well-rotted organic material. If the soil has become compacted, the addition of some grit or gravel will help to keep it open. Plant the new plant at the same depth as it was in its pot. Cover the exposed soil with gravel or stone chippings.

TREES AND SHRUBS

Early spring is the last opportunity you will have for planting bare-rooted shrubs and trees. After this, the plants come into growth and the roots will find it difficult to cope with both the plant's growth and its efforts to become established. It will, however, be possible to continue to plant out container-grown plants because the roots are not disturbed.

Now that winter is finally over it is time to check and rectify any damage that may have been caused. First, check that gusting winds have not rocked any trees or shrubs, causing the roots to snap and holes to develop around the trunk. Re-stake any loose plants and fill in the holes with soil or compost (p. 163). Check all ties, replacing any that have worked loose and slackening those that are cutting into the bark.

Remove any dead wood and cut out any branches that have been damaged by the wind, snow or frost.

Now is the best time to prune roses. It is also time to prune those shrubs that flower on new growth (see also Pruning Clematis, p. 27).

PRUNING ROSES

Opinions vary as to when is the best time to prune roses. It should certainly be while the bushes are dormant – that is, between leaf fall and bud break the following spring. In windy areas it is useful to remove at least some of the top growth in early or mid-autumn, even if the final pruning is left to spring, which is the time favoured by most gardeners. One reason for waiting until spring is that in cold winters the tips of stems may become frosted, and if you have already pruned you will have to do it again. Waiting until spring means that you can do it all in one operation. Whenever you prune, avoid doing it in frosty weather. See p. 128 for pruning rambler roses.

All Roses

To start with, remove all dead wood and then take out any thin or weak growth. Any stems that cross through the bush or rub against others should also be removed. This usually reduces the volume, leaving you with the framework of a healthy, productive plant. It also allows you to see what you are doing when you make the final prune. All cuts should be just above a bud, sloping away from it.

Hybrid Teas (Large-flowered Varieties)

From the basic framework described above, cut back the main stems to lengths of 20–25cm (8–10in).

Floribundas (Cluster-flowered Varieties)

After cutting back the stems to a basic framework, prune the main shoots to 30–45cm (12–18in) and reduce the length of any remaining side shoots by half.

Bush Roses

It is important not to prune bush roses in the same way as you do hybrid teas, because most flower on two-year-old wood (which is pruned out in hybrid teas and floribundas). Apart from basic pruning, no other action is required except to take out some of the oldest wood each year so that new, vigorous shoots are promoted. Any old flower stems should be removed if the bushes were not deadheaded in the previous season.

Pruning roses

When pruning roses, make the cut at an angle above a bud.

Good cut – just above a bud and angled away from the bud.

Bad cut – too far from the bud and causing die back.

Bad cut – sloping towards the cut and possibly causing rot.

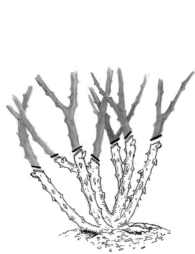  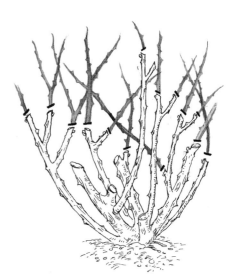

After you have removed dead and crossing stems, prune all the stems to leave a neat, balanced framework.

The main stems of hybrid teas should be cut back to 20–25cm (8–10in).

Floribunda roses should be pruned so that the main shoots are 30–45cm (12–18in) long and side shoots are reduced in length by about half.

Miniature Varieties

These can be pruned hard back as the floribundas above or by simply thinning out some of the basic framework to produce a more open plant.

Ramblers and Climbers

These are pruned in late summer or autumn (p. 128).

SPRING-FLOWERING TREES *and* SHRUBS

Amelanchier	*Magnolia*
Berberis	*Mahonia*
Camellia	*Pieris*
Cercis	*Prunus*
Chaenomeles	*Rhododendron*
Corylopsis	*Ribes*
Cytisus	*Salix*
Daphne	*Spiraea*
Exochorda	*Viburnum*
Forsythia	

Rhododendrons are one of the glories of spring, although flowering can be cut back by frosts. If frost threatens, drape the plant with fleece, which will help protect the buds and flowers. This variety is *Rhododendron* 'Bow Bells'.

PLANTING CLIMBERS

Bare-rooted climbers should be moved or planted any time between late autumn and mid-spring. If they are container grown, they can be planted at any time, provided the weather permits and you are able to keep them well watered.

Prepare the ground thoroughly by adding plenty of well-rotted organic material. Dig a hole that is larger than the rootball of the plant, place the plant in position and spread out its roots. Refill the hole and water well.

Climbers can be supported over arches, pergolas or arbours, or they can be trained up through trees or bushes. They can also be grown over a trellis, either a free-standing construction or one fixed against a wall. Always plant the climber a short distance from the pole or wall, if necessary training it up one or more canes until it reaches the trellis.

VEGETABLES

Now is the time when things begin to get busy in the vegetable garden. No matter how keen you are to get started, however, it is important not to get onto the beds until the soil has dried out a bit and will not compact under your weight. More harm than good will be done by beginning too early.

When it is possible to get down to work, fork or rake through the beds that were prepared last autumn and winter (p. 165). The frosts and rain should have broken up the soil, which should be easy to reduce to a fine tilth. Remove any weeds that have germinated in milder spells in winter and dig in any organic material that remains from autumn mulching. If the beds have not already been dug or if they have been compacted by winter weather, dig them over again. The digging of vegetable beds on light soils is, in any case, best left until spring, when well-rotted organic material should be incorporated.

Another reason for not starting work too early is that it is also important to allow the soil to warm up before you start to sow seed. Many vegetables – carrots, for example – are perfectly hardy but they will not germinate until the soil has warmed up to 7°C (45°F). If they are sown before this temperature is reached the seeds will lie dormant or, worse still, will rot and have to be replaced.

If you are anxious for earlier crops, you can cover the ground with black polythene or with cloches. These will help not only to dry out the soil but also to raise its temperature. Some vegetables – peas and leeks, for example – can be started in pots in the greenhouse or coldframe and planted out once the weather and soil conditions improve. Both the use of cloches and the pre-germinating of seeds are useful techniques in areas where the effects of winter linger.

Mid- and main-crop potatoes, onion sets and shallots can be planted out when the beds are in the right conditions. Early potatoes, which could well have been planted last month or at the beginning of this month (see below), are likely to be pushing up through the soil. Keep earthing them up so that the new leaves are covered and protected from the frosts.

Peas

Peas do not seem to be as popular with gardeners as they once were, possibly because they take up quite a lot of space and, with modern gardens being smaller, gardeners prefer to devote the vegetable plot to more productive crops. Even so, many people still manage at least one row. In fact, peas are a crop that all gardeners should try to grow. Fresh peas straight from the garden are like nothing you can buy. One reason often given for not growing peas is that they all tend to mature at around the same time – there is a glut and then they are over. But with the modern possibility of freezing any excess, this argument is not really valid. If you want peas but not a glut, grow shorter rows and sow successionally so that you get a smaller but constant supply.

If you have a fairly small garden grow the shorter varieties, which use up less space although they do not so crop heavily as taller varieties. Choose the appropriate pea for the season, earlies usually being the most appreciated. Mange-tout, sugar or snap peas are eaten whole, shell included, before the peas are fully swollen. Wrinkled varieties have a sweetish taste. Round peas are hardier than wrinkled peas but not as flavoursome. Petit-pois are small, round peas

A well-drained but fertile, moisture-retentive soil is required in a sunny position. Sow in drills 23cm (9in) wide, placing the seeds about 5–7.5cm (2–3in) apart. Some of the shorter varieties do not need support, but taller varieties do. This can be in the form of traditional peasticks or wire or plastic netting. Alternatively, they can be grow in blocks and grown up wigwams of sticks.

Keep the ground weeded and water once the flowers have set. Protect the plants from birds, especially in the initial stages of growth.

RECOMMENDED VARIETIES *of* PEA

Round peas
'Bountiful': early, tall
'Douce Provence': early, short
'Feltham First': early, short
'Meteor': early, short
'Pilot': early, medium

Wrinkled peas
'Alderman': main-crop, tall
'Early Onward': early, tall
'Hurst Beagle': early, short
'Hurst Greenshaft': main-crop, short
'Little Marvel': main-crop, short
'Miracle': main-crop, tall
'Onward': main-crop, short
'Top Pod': main-crop, medium

Petit-pois
'Darfon': main-crop, short
'Minnow': main-crop, short

Mange-tout
'Herault': early, tall
'Honey Pod': early, short
'Nofila': early, short
'Norli': early , short
'Oregon Sugar Pod': main-crop, medium
'Sugar Short Sweet Green', main-crop, medium

Potatoes

Like peas, potatoes are not as widely grown as they once were. This is partly because commercially grown potatoes are very cheap and easily available, and partly because growing them takes up quite a lot of garden space. However, as with all vegetables, if you grow your own you will have a much greater choice of varieties, giving a wide range of flavours as well as allowing you to grow special sorts for baking, roasting and so forth.

When you buy seed potatoes always choose certified stock that is free from virus diseases. Do not go for the biggest potatoes – ones that are about the size of a large hen's egg are best. About four weeks before you plan to plant, place them in a tray with the 'eyes' uppermost in a light, frost-free place to chit. When the potatoes have produced shoots that are approximately 2cm (¾in) long, they are ready to plant.

There are three basic groups of potatoes. First earlies are planted in early to mid-spring; they mature quickly and are usually ready for digging by early summer. They are not usually used for storing. Second earlies are planted in mid-spring and harvested from midsummer onwards. Again, they are not usually used for storing. Main-crop potatoes are planted in mid- to late spring. They are lifted in early autumn and can be stored for winter use.

Planting potatoes

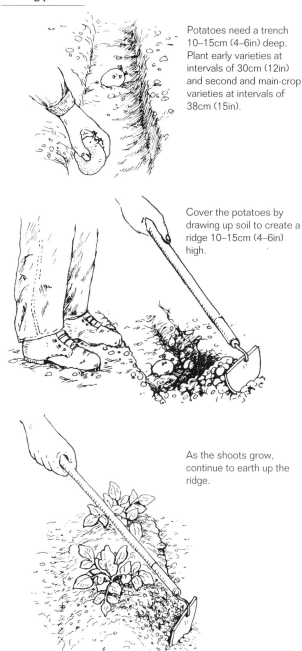

Potatoes need a trench 10–15cm (4–6in) deep. Plant early varieties at intervals of 30cm (12in) and second and main-crop varieties at intervals of 38cm (15in).

Cover the potatoes by drawing up soil to create a ridge 10–15cm (4–6in) high.

As the shoots grow, continue to earth up the ridge.

Potatoes need a deep, free-draining but rich soil, preferably in an open position. Add plenty of well-rotted organic material at the time of digging. Dig out a trench 10–15cm (4–6in) deep and place the potatoes in it at 30cm (12in) intervals for earlies and 38cm (15in) for second earlies and main-crop. Place them with the eyes or shoots uppermost. Cover the trench with a low ridge of soil. Allow 60cm (2ft) between rows.

As the shoots emerge, draw up more soil onto the ridge. This helps to keep the roots moist as well as keeping the growing potatoes covered and away from the light. An alternative to earthing up is to grow the potatoes under black plastic – make a series of holes in the plastic and plant a tuber through each hole. Potatoes turn green and poisonous if exposed to the light. Keep the rows well watered in dry spells.

Dig earlies and second earlies as they are required. Lift main-crop in the autumn, leaving them as long as possible in the ground. About two weeks before lifting, cut off the haul (top growth) about 5cm (2in) above the ground. Lift the potatoes and leave them lying on the ground in the sun for the skins to harden for a couple of hours. Store the potatoes, preferably in hessian or paper sacks, in a dark, cool, but frost-free place.

Slugs and wireworms are the worst pests. Wireworms, which tend to be more of a nuisance in newly cultivated land, can be removed by hand from the soil when it is dug. The worst disease is potato blight, a fungal infection that is difficult to control once it has broken out. Be sure to choose resistant cultivars and use a different area of the garden each year to prevent the disease from taking a hold. Do not plant potatoes in ground in which tomatoes were grown the previous season, because they suffer from the same disease.

RECOMMENDED VARIETIES *of* POTATO

Early varieties

'Arran Pilot': white skin; early, heavy cropper

'Epicure': white skin; high yield; popular old favourite

'Foremost': white skin and waxy yellow flesh; good flavour

'Maris Bard': white skin and waxy texture; very early, heavy cropper

'Pentland Javelin': white skin and waxy flesh; last of the earlies to crop

'Ulster Chieftain': white skin and floury texture; heavy cropper

Second early varieties

    'Estima': white skin and waxy, yellow flesh; good
        cropper

    'Kondor': red skin and yellow flesh; heavy
        cropper; good boiler

    'Marfona': white skin; heavy cropper; good for
        baking

    'Maris Peer': white skin and waxy texture; heavy
        crop of small tubers

    'Wilja': white skin and waxy, yellow flesh; heavy
        cropper; good salad potato

Main-crop varieties

    'Cara': pink skin and white, floury flesh; heavy
        cropper but late

    'Desirée': pink/red skin and waxy, yellow flesh;
        heavy cropper; good for baking and chips

    'King Edward': pink and white skin and creamy,
        floury flesh; good for baking

    'Maris Piper': white skin and floury texture; heavy
        cropper; good for baking

    'Pentland Dell': white skin and floury
        texture; heavy cropper; good for baking and
        roasting

    'Pink Fir Apple': pink skin and yellow, waxy flesh;
        wonderful flavoured salad potato

    'Ratte': white skin and yellow, waxy flesh;
        excellent flavoured salad potato

    'Romano': red skin and firm, white flesh; heavy
        cropper

ONIONS

Onions are one of the most indispensable of vegetables, not only as an ingredient in numerous dishes but also as a vegetable that can be eaten on its own, hot or cold. The onion family is very large, with many ornamental varieties as well as culinary ones. The mainstay of the kitchen onion is the bulb onion, but shallots (p. 185) are becoming increasingly popular for cooking. Spring onions (or bunching onions) are mainly used as a salad vegetable, but they are also used as an ingredient in other dishes. The family also includes pickling onions, which are used, as their name suggests, for pickling, and garlic, with its distinctive flavour (p. 165). There are also Welsh onions, which are like a large spring onion but will stand through the winter, and Japanese onions, which are also winter hardy and can be used as a slender form of bulb onion during a time when the latter are scarce. Leeks are also a form of onion.

Bulb Onions

Bulb onions are grown either from sets or from seed. Sets are small bulbs, grown from seeds during the previous season. They should be grown in a sunny position in a fertile, well-drained soil. Dig the bed in the autumn, adding organic material at the same time. Onions like firm ground, so leave it to settle over winter. Sets are planted 10cm (4in) apart in rows that are 25–30cm (10–12in) apart. Push them into the soil, making a shallow hole with a dibber if necessary, and cover with soil so that the top of the onion can be seen. You may need to cover them with netting until they are established, because birds have a habit of pulling them up.

Bulb onions from seeds are sown this month or next. Sow in shallow drills at 25–30cm (10–12in) intervals. Sow thinly and thin seedlings to 10cm (4in) intervals. If you want large show onions sow them in trays under glass in midwinter and transplant them into the open ground in early spring after hardening them off. Some onions can be sown in autumn to give a longer growing period.

Keep the onions free from weeds but avoid damaging them with the hoe. Once the necks of the onions begin to turn yellow and collapse, lift the onions slightly from the ground with a fork to loosen the roots. Lift after a week or so, removing any soil and allowing the bulbs to finish drying in a dry sunny position. Tie into ropes or store in net bags in a cool, but frost-free place.

RECOMMENDED VARIETIES *of* BULB ONION

    'Ailsa Craig': spring/late-summer-sown
        seed

    'Albion': spring-sown seed

    'Autumn Gold': sets

    'Bedfordshire Champion': spring-sown seed

    'Buffalo': spring-sown seed

    'Dobie's All Rounder': sets

    'Giant Fen Globe': sets

    'Hygro': spring-sown seed

    'Mammoth Red': winter-sown seed

    'Red Baron': sets

    'Red Torpedo': late-summer sown

    'Rocardo': sets

    'Sturon': sets

    'Stuttgart Giant': sets

Spring Onions

Spring or bunching onions are grown in the same conditions as bulb onions. They should be sown in spring in shallow drills at distances of 15–20cm (6–8in) apart. Thin the resulting seedlings to about 2.5cm (1in) apart, although if they were sown thinly there should be no need to do this. Harvest when ready and required. They do not store. Sow every two or three weeks to get a regular crop throughout the summer. In late summer sow an overwintering variety, which should be protected with cloches during bad weather.

RECOMMENDED VARIETIES *of* SPRING ONION

'Guardsman'	'Savel'
'Hikai Bunching	'White Knight"
'Ishikura'	'White Lisbon'
'Santa Claus	'Winter White Bunching"

Pickling Onions

Pickling onions should be grown in the same way as spring onions. Sow in mid-spring and harvest once the foliage has died down.

RECOMMENDED VARIETIES *of* PICKLING ONION

'Barletta'
'Giant Zittau'
'Paris Silver Skin'
'The Queen'

ASPARAGUS AND GLOBE ARTICHOKES

Permanent vegetables, such as asparagus and globe artichokes, can be planted out this month. The beds should be thoroughly prepared: remove all weeds and dig in plenty of well-rotted organic material. Permanent vegetable beds are difficult to clear of perennial weeds once they become established, so be certain to remove every trace of them.

Asparagus should be planted in a light, free-draining, but moisture-retentive soil. A trench about 30cm (12in) long and about 20cm (8in) deep, with a 7.5–10cm (3–4in) ridge running down the centre, is ideal. The plants are set on the ridge, with the roots spread evenly down each side. Set the plants about 45cm (18in) apart. Cover the crowns with 5–7.5cm (2–3in) of soil. Gradually pull the remainder of the soil over the trench in the course of the summer. Do not cut any asparagus in the first summer and only a few spears in the next. From the third summer onwards – for up to twenty or more years – a full crop can be harvested.

Globe artichoke divisions or young plants are planted in holes to the same depth as they were before dividing. Set them about 75cm (30in) apart. A few heads may be cut in the first year, but cropping really starts in the second year.

Globe artichokes are easy to grow, and they produce one of the most delicious of vegetables.

APRIL

The soil is beginning to warm up and more work can be carried out in the garden. This is one of the busiest times of year, and, if possible, every spare moment should be spent in the garden. The more that is done this month the easier it will be for the rest of the year. One way of reducing the amount of work later is to mulch as many of the borders as you can. This will help to keep down the weeds as well as save time spent on watering because it will also help to retain moisture in the soil.

Weeds are growing apace, and they should not be ignored. Seedlings are also growing fast and should be potted up as soon as possible before they get too large. Pests are also beginning to wake up after their winter's rest. Keep an eye out for these and take appropriate action.

Despite everything that has got to be done, make some time to enjoy the profusion of plants that is beginning to unfold. In addition to the bright colours of the bulbs and the early perennials, the new shoots and leaves that are appearing everywhere provide a wealth of different greens, worthy of any artist's palette.

One word of warning: the sun may not seem hot, but it is very bright, and spending long hours outside can lead to sunburn and even skin cancers. Apply appropriate creams to skins that have paled over winter.

CHECKLIST

General

- Hoe and weed all borders and beds (p. 50)
- Mulch all borders and beds (p. 172)
- Watch out for pests and take relevant action (p. 103)

Annuals and Tender Perennials

- Prick out those annuals that have germinated (p. 20)
- Pot on any that have outgrown their original containers (p. 37)
- Pot on cuttings of chrysanthemums, dahlias, felicias, pelargoniums and so on (p. 37)
- Start to prepare containers and hanging baskets inside (p. 51)
- Sow hardy annual seeds in situ (p. 50)

Bulbs

- Deadhead as flowers fade unless seeds are required (p. 52)
- Remove foliage as it begins to die back (p. 52)
- Divide dahlia tubers and plant (unless in leaf) (p. 53)
- Plant gladiolus corms (p. 53)
- Water bulbs in pots until they die back (p. 52)
- Continue to plant summer- and autumn-flowering bulbs (pp. 110, 154)

Fruit

- Protect early blossom from frost (p. 53)
- Protect blossom from birds but allow access to pollinating insects (p. 53)
- Hand-pollinate early-flowering fruit (p. 35)
- Prune plum trees (p. 169)
- Weed and then mulch between bushes (p. 53)

Greenhouse

- Allow for plenty of ventilation, except when frosts threaten (p. 77)
- Shade when necessary (p. 96)
- Prepare beds and supports for tomatoes and other crops (p. 55)
- Plant tomatoes in unheated greenhouses (p. 55)
- Plant aubergines, peppers, cucumbers and melons in heated greenhouses (p. 55)
- Sow tender annuals, such as runner beans, ready for planting out (p. 55)
- Prepare hanging baskets and containers ready for the end of the frosts (p. 50)
- Watch for early pests and diseases (p. 55)

Lawns

- Increase the number of mowings as the grass grows more quickly (p. 59)
- Feed lawns if not already carried out (p. 60)
- Apply selective weedkillers if not contained in lawn feed (p. 59)
- Continue to water newly laid lawns if weather is dry (p. 59)
- If necessary, fill in gaps in newly laid turf lawns (p. 59)
- Sow (p. 141) or turf new lawns (p. 182)
- Re-sow or re-turf patches of worn grass and damaged edges (p. 38)

Perennials

- Finish border maintenance and preparation (p. 25)
- Complete planting of borders (p. 39)
- Complete the lifting and dividing of overcrowded perennials (p. 40)
- Prick out seedlings as they germinate (p. 20)
- Pot on developing seedlings (p. 37)

- Begin to stake perennials (p. 80)
- Take basal cuttings (p. 61)
- Sow perennials directly into the soil (p. 60)
- Apply a mulch if not already done (p. 172)

Rock Gardens

- Deadhead flowering plants where seeds are not required (p. 101)
- Cut back plants that have sprawled too much (p. 101)
- Remove any weeds on sight (p. 63)
- Keep an eye out for pests and diseases and take appropriate action (p. 63)
- Finish planting new plants in new beds (p. 41)
- Keep new plantings watered if weather dry (p. 41)
- Take basal cuttings (p. 101)

Trees and Shrubs

- Finish pruning shrubs that will flower on current year's growth (p. 65)
- Prune shrubs that have finished flowering (p. 65)
- Tie in climbers (p. 64)
- Check staking after winter winds (p. 41)
- Check ties and ease if necessary (p. 41)

Vegetables

- Continue sowing hardy vegetables (p. 44)
- Plant onions (p. 46), shallots (p. 185), asparagus crowns and globe artichokes (p. 47) and final potatoes (p. 44)
- Sow tender vegetables under glass ready for planting out (p. 55)
- Earth up potatoes and cover if frost threatens (p. 44)
- Put up supports for peas and beans (p. 55)

ANNUALS

Depending on when you sowed the seed for your annual plants, this month is likely to be a busy one as you prick out the resulting seedlings (p. 20). Do not leave them too long in their original pots or trays, or they are likely to become very drawn. They will also soon run out of nutrients and become starved.

Continue to sow annuals. In many areas this month is the best time to sow tender annuals. If they are sown earlier they may be difficult to keep inside until the passing of the final frosts allows you to plant them out. There is rarely any need to be too much in a hurry because later sown annuals usually catch up those sown earlier and are often far healthier. If you have started your annuals early and they are already filling their pots or trays, pot them on into larger containers so that there is no hold up in their development.

Similarly, rooted cuttings of chrysanthemums and dahlias should be potted up if you have not already done this. Any that have already been potted up should be checked to see if they need moving on to the next size of pot. Bedding fuchsias, pelargoniums and any other tender perennials that are continued each year by overwintering cuttings – argyranthemums and helichrysum, for instance – should be potted on if they are becoming cramped in their pots.

Outside displays of tender annuals cannot be planted out until towards the end of next month in most areas. However, if you have some space in the greenhouse or conservatory where you can prepare hanging baskets and other containers, by the time you are able to put them out they will be in full flower. The middle of this month is the time to start preparations. If you do not have any spare space, they can just as easily be prepared in the open, but they will take a while to settle down and come into flower.

Hardy annuals can be sown in the open soil this month.

If you haven't planted out sweetpeas (p. 180) there is still time to do so. Indeed, it is often a good idea to sow and plant them out in several stages, including some next month, so that you have a succession of blooms, lasting through to the first frosts.

SOWING HARDY ANNUALS

For early flowering, some hardy annuals, such as antirrhinums, can be sown in the autumn, but the main flush can be sown in the open in mid- and late spring.

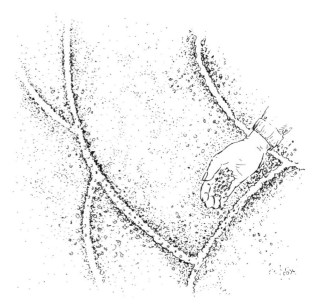

Use a fine trickle of silver sand or a pointed stick to mark the areas for sowing annual seeds.

Annuals can be sown between perennials or shrubs or they can be combined with other annuals to make a colourful bed. Whether the planting is to be just a small area or a larger bed, the preparation is the same. The first task must always be to prepare the bed thoroughly, removing any weeds and incorporating well-rotted organic material. Break down the soil into a fine tilth suitable for sowing seed.

The seeds can be sown in parallel rows and the resulting seedlings thinned to give the impression of a random distribution, or they can be broadcast over an area forming a block of plants. In a bed or where you are going to sow more than one variety, it is a good idea to mark out the various sowing areas on the ground before you begin. This will help to get the arrangement right as well as preventing gaps or areas where sowing has accidentally overlapped. Scratch out the outlines of the various areas on the soil with a pointed stick. A clearer way is to fill a plastic bottle with silver sand and allow it to trickle onto the ground around the edge of each different planting area.

HANGING BASKETS

Although it is not possible to put out hanging baskets containing tender perennials until the threat of frost has passed, they can be prepared this month if you are able to keep them under glass or even under the shelter of a porch, which will provide sufficient protection if the threat of frost is not too great.

The appealing faces of pansies, *Viola* x *wittrokiana* 'Maxim Marina', which have been raised from seed. Usually these would be planted out before they started flowering, but here the complete tray makes a beautiful display in itself. The velvety flowers of the auricula, *Primula auricula* 'Argus', are the perfect foil.

Hang the basket at a reasonable working height in the greenhouse or stand it in a bucket on the bench. First, insert a liner of some sort. There are quite a number from which to choose, of which black polythene is the cheapest and most readily available. However, if the basket is not covered with plants, the plastic shows, and it is not very attractive. Moss looks the best, but it also possible to get liners in pressed paper or fibre that are coloured green, and these do not intrude into the planting scheme too much.

If you are planting into the side of the basket, puncture holes in the appropriate places. Partly fill the basket with a potting compost and slip in the side plants before continuing to fill the basket, lightly pressing the soil around the roots of the side plants. Plant the main set of plants on the top of the basket, firm down and water.

Leave the basket hanging in the greenhouse or conservatory where it is protected from frost until it is safe to put outside. Even at this time of year there is sufficient sun to dry out the basket surprisingly quickly, so water daily if necessary. Add a liquid feed to the water once a week, following the directions on the pack.

Baskets containing non-tender plants, such as pansies, can be hung out as soon as they have been hardened off.

CONTAINERS AND WINDOW BOXES

Containers and window boxes can be prepared in much the same way as hanging baskets if you have space to store them. It must be borne in mind, however, that both can be very heavy when they are filled with compost, and it is often more practicable to wait for a few weeks and plant them *in situ* after the frosts have finished. A possible approach is to plant up the display in a light plastic container, which can be slipped into the window box or formal container when the conditions are right. Boxes and containers of non-tender plants can, of course, be planted out now.

ANNUALS *and* TENDER PERENNIALS *for* HANGING BASKETS

Alonsoa

Argyranthemum

Begonia

Bidens ferulifolia

Brachycome iberidifolia (Swan River daisy)

Chlorophytum comosum 'Variegatum' (spider plants)

Convolvulus tricolor

Fuchsia

Helichrysum petiolare

Impatiens (busy lizzie)

Lobelia erinus

Pelargonium (geraniums)

Petunia

Plectranthus coleoides

Senecio cineraria

Tolmiea menziesii 'Taff's Gold' (pick-a-back plant)

Tropaeolum (nasturtiums)

Verbena × hybrida

Viola × wittrokiana (pansies)

 # BULBS

Bulbs are at their best this month and next. Daffodils and tulips, in a multitude of varieties, are in flower, brightening up the most miserable of days. There are many other bulbs, however, some of them that are not as familiar, that do good service at this time of year (see below).

The advantage of most bulbs is that they require very little looking after. The main problem is that it is possible to dig them up accidentally when they are dormant. There can be very few gardeners who have not stuck a fork through hidden bulbs. It is a good idea to label them while they are above ground so that you know exactly where they are.

In order to keep the bulbs plump and healthy, remove the old flowers as they die back. This prevent the formation of seeds, which uses up a great deal of the bulbs' stored energy. On the other hand, the leaves should be left as these assist in producing new food stores.

Bulbs that are grown in pots in the greenhouse or coldframe should be watered until the foliage dies back. Water sparingly, however, because very few bulbs like to be waterlogged.

REMOVING FOLIAGE

Once the flowers have died, bulbs tend to lose all their charm. The leaves often look tatty and are rarely an asset to the garden. Many gardeners are tempted to cut them off at this stage, but this is something that ought to be resisted because the leaves are essential for photosynthesis, which is one of the processes involved in producing food. This is important, for although the bulb has finished flowering, it still must build up energy for the next season.

In order to neaten the plants some gardeners tie the leaves in knots, or bundle them up and secure them with an elastic band. This is almost as bad as cutting them off, because they are unable to function properly unless their surfaces are open to the light. The time to cut them off is when they turn yellow and their function is finished.

There are ways of reducing the eyesore of untidy leaves. One is to plant your bulbs among other plants, which will grow up and hide them. Another way is to plant them at the back of borders. In spring the borders are usually empty so that daffodils, for example, will show up well if planted at the back. By the time the daffodils are finished, the plants in front will be growing up once again to hide the leaves from view, while, at the same time, still allowing the light to fall on the bulb's leaves from above.

Another alternative is to dig up the bulbs and replant them somewhere where the leaves can be left to die back. Although this is frequently recommended, it does check the plants and reduce the amount of energy stored.

The leaves of naturalized bulbs also need to be left until they die back naturally. If you plant them in grass do not mow until the bulbs' leaves turn yellow.

SPRING-FLOWERING BULBS

Anemone blanda; *A. nemorosa* (wood anemone)

Chionodoxa (glory of the snow)

Crocus

Fritillaria imperialis (crown imperial); *F. meleagris* (snake's head fritillary)

Galanthus (snowdrops)

Erythronium (dog-tooth violets)

Hyacinthoides non-scripta (bluebell)

Hyacinthus (hyacinths)

Muscari (grape hyacinths)

Narcissus (daffodils)

Ornithogalum (star of Bethlehem)

Puschkinia

Tulipa (tulips)

PLANTING DAHLIAS

This month or next is the time to plant dahlia tubers. By the time the leaves reach above the soil the frosts should be over. If they already have shoots, which is likely if you leave it until next month, it is best to leave it until towards the end of the month when the frosts will have abated. Any foliage that is caught above ground by a frost will be burned off, so there is little advantage in planting them out earlier. If a late frost is expected and shoots are above ground, cover them with two or more sheets of newspaper.

Before planting, it is possible to divide the clumps of tubers into smaller sections. Cut away each tuber cleanly with a knife and make sure that each has a growing shoot. Dust the cuts with a fungicide to reduce the chance of it rotting. Pot up each tuber individually and plant out once the frosts have passed.

Put stakes in at the same time as planting so that you can do it while you can still see the tubers. Once they are covered with soil you might accidentally push the stake through one of them.

GLADIOLI

One of the most popular of summer bulbs is the gladiolus. There are a number of species that are grown in gardens, including the popular spring-flowering *Gladiolus byzantinus*, but the large-flowered hybrids are the most popular of all. They are not only colourful garden plants, but can also be cut for indoors and for showing. There is a vast number of hybrids, and new ones appear every year. As with other popular plants, such as chrysanthemums, gladioli can take over your life if you let them.

They need a sunny position and a well-drained but fertile soil. It pays to prepare the ground well. The corms are planted in mid-spring, about 10–15cm (4–6 in) apart and at a similar depth. When they are in flower they can be top heavy, especially the taller varieties, and so they need supporting with canes or posts, which should be inserted carefully into the soil so that the corms are not pierced. For safety they can be inserted at the same time as the corm is planted. Keep them watered during dry spells in the summer.

Lift gladioli in autumn, remove the stems and dry off the corms. Separate off any cormlets. Store in a dry, cool but frost-free place and replant in spring. The cormlets can be planted out, about 5cm (2in) deep, in a nursery bed to increase in size for flowering the following year.

 FRUIT

There is not a great deal to do in the fruit garden at this time of year, except to check that everything is well. One of the big problems in mid- to late spring is frost. It will not damage the trees or bushes, but it will knock out any blossom that is around. Most early-blossoming fruit should be planted against a wall, which not only provides protection by radiating warmth but can also support frameworks covered in polythene or hessian that can be placed in position at night.

In the open garden it is not so easy, especially if the blossom is on large trees. Netting, such as the close-weave variety that is used for shading, draped over the plants is usually sufficient as the frosts are generally not too severe. Lower growing plants, such as strawberries and small bushes, can be covered in newspapers, sacking or something like old curtains. Never leave covers on during the day, or even at night when they are not necessary.

Another form of protection that is required is against birds (see below). Bullfinches, in particular, can be a tremendous nuisance and can quickly strip a whole tree or bush of its buds.

By this month pollinating insects should be flying, but in cool periods it may still be necessary to hand pollinate some fruit trees (p. 35).

Keep the ground around fruit trees and shrubs free from weeds. If the ground was thoroughly prepared before they were planted, it should be possible to keep it clear of perennial weeds. If such weeds do gain a hold the only realistic way to deal with them is to use the appropriate weedkiller, because the trees' and bushes' roots make it impossible to dig them out. Once all weeds have been removed, mulch around the trees with well-rotted organic material. This will not only keep further weeds down but also feed the plants and improve the soil.

PROTECTING FRUIT

It is essential to protect ripening fruit from birds. Even in the most built-up areas there are sufficient birds around to make short work of strawberries or blackcurrants, for example. Even apples will be attacked, and once they have a few peck marks on them they will soon rot and are useless for storing.

It is no use relying on fluttering pieces of silver foil or the family cat, because birds are unlikely to take much notice of them when a feast is on offer. Netting is an effective

Fruit cages are essential for keeping out animals. They can be easily constructed or ready-made ones can be purchased.

deterrent, and a mesh of 2cm (¾in) will keep out the birds but allow pollinating insects to get through. However, even if you think you have completely covered the fruit with a net, the wily birds will invariably soon find a way underneath. Indeed, even if there is only one hole in a fruit cage, you can guarantee that the birds will soon find it.

Another way is to buy a proprietary fruit cage, which usually consists of an aluminium frame covered with plastic netting. It is cheaper, however, to make your own using wooden posts and either the readily available plastic netting or, for a more permanent job, wire netting. Even if you use wire netting, it can be a good idea to cover the top with plastic netting so that it can be easily removed. The reason for removing the top is that there are times when birds are an asset rather than a nuisance. They will eat a lot of insects pest, both from the plants and from the ground.

The most vulnerable part of the fruit cage is around the bottom, where the netting is frequently torn by being knocked by a lawn mower or by digging to remove weeds. Attaching a board right round the base not only protects it against damage but also makes a secure junction between the netting and the ground.

Strawberries can be protected by a low-level cage. Again, boards around the edge can be a great asset.

Fruit trees present a bit of a problem in that they are often too large to include in a cage. Cordon and fan-trained specimens can easily be covered, but the larger

trees are obviously more difficult. One way is to cover the tree with cotton, which deters the birds from landing on the branches. Unfortunately, this is unsightly and as often or not it is the gardener who becomes ensnared in it. Another is to use a thin fleece, but this looks even worse. It is possible to drape trees as big as spindlebushes with netting. If you have a constant problem with larger trees it may be worth considering removing them and replanting with one of the smaller types. Large apple trees will usually produce sufficient fruit that some, if not the majority, of the applies are untouched. However, you will need several acres of cherry trees before you can guarantee an undamaged crop. Fortunately, cherries can now be grown on dwarfing stock, which means that the resulting trees can be netted (p. 112).

Peach trees require particular care (p. 170). Protect the trees against frost once the blossom has started to form. A framework can be built against the wall, over which netting or polythene can be stretched, perhaps in the form of a roller blind. Peach curl, which is a serious disease, can be kept at bay by covering the trees with polythene frames, which keep the tree dry and thus reduce the chance that the fungal spores that cause the disease will germinate. Although the trees should be protected from the rain, leave plenty of ventilation.

GREEN TIP *Weeding*

If you do not like the idea of using any kind of weedkillers, it is possible, although it needs a lot of effort, to kill off perennial weeds by a war of attrition. Go around the affected area several times a week, removing any weed shoot that appears above ground. Eventually the weed will have used up all its stored energy and will die. If you allow leaves to appear for even a couple of days, the rootstalks will start be replenished and the weeds will gain the upper hand again. With persistence, even bindweed (convolvulus) can be subdued in this way.

THE GREENHOUSE

As the weather begins to warm up, make sure that the greenhouse is well ventilated. Cold greenhouses can be left open all the time, and cool ones need only be shut at night if there is the threat of frost (p. 37). Temperate and warm ones should be opened as much as possible without the loss of any heat.

Similarly, although one thinks of greenhouse shading as being something that is required in the summer, it may also be needed in periods of bright sunshine even at this time of year (p. 96).

If you want to produce early crops, sow tender beans, such as runner beans, under glass and move out the resulting plants as soon as it is safe to do so. Marrows, courgettes and outdoor (ridge) cucumbers can be treated in the same way. Sow seeds in individual pots so that they can be planted out with disturbing the roots. Marrow, courgette and cucumber seeds should be sown on edge.

Tomato plants should now be ready to plant in unheated greenhouses; they will already have been planted in heated ones last month. Aubergines, peppers, cucumbers and melons should be planted under heated glass this month.

Take advantage of the protection afforded by the glass and prepare hanging baskets (p. 50) ready for hanging out once the threat of frost is past. The advantage of this is that the plants should be in flower by the time you put them out. If there is room and you are able to move them when they are full, containers and window-boxes can be prepared in the same way (p. 51).

As the temperature rises, conditions become ideal for pests and diseases, so keep a watchful eye out and take appropriate action if any are seen.

GREENHOUSE TOMATOES

Tomatoes are one of the most popular crops for the greenhouse. They were traditionally grown in soil in the greenhouse border, and although this produces very good results for the first few years, the soil becomes tired and often sick, and yields are reduced. In order to ensure a regular good crop it is important to change the soil every year. This is not only a heavy chore but it is not always possible with small gardens to have a ready supply of fresh soil.

A simple solution to the problem is to use growing bags. These are plastic bags containing specially formulated

Cucumbers and tomatoes are often grown in the same greenhouse. When buying plants or seed, check carefully, because separate varieties of each are available for growing outside or under glass.

compost, which are placed on the floor of the greenhouse. Part of the upper surface of the bag is cut away and up to three tomatoes planted in it. In the autumn, when the crop is finished, the bags are discarded and fresh ones purchased for the following year. The spent compost is a good soil conditioner and can be dug into the garden.

Another method is to grow the tomatoes in large, individual pots, again stood on the floor. Until the advent of inexpensive growing bags one of the most popular 'non-border' methods was ring culture. This system involved placing a bottomless pot on gravel and filling it with compost. The tomato was then planted in the pot in the normal way. At first the ring is watered but once the roots have descended into the gravel, water is applied direct to this. When the fruit start to form, high-potash fertilizer is applied to the ring once a week.

Growing tomatoes

Tie in the tomato plants to a support as they grow.

Regularly pinch out side shoots.

RECOMMENDED VARIETIES *of* GREENHOUSE TOMATO

'Ailsa Craig': medium-sized variety

'Alicante': medium-sized variety

'Big Boy': large beefsteak variety

'Dombito': large beefsteak variety

'Gardener's Delight': cherry variety

'Golden Sunrise': yellow variety

'Mirabelle': yellow cherry variety

'Shirley': medium-sized variety

'Sungold': orange-coloured cherry tomato

'Tigrella': red and gold striped variety

CUCUMBERS

Although most gardeners grow tomatoes in their greenhouse as a matter of course, cucumbers are not so popular, although they are widely bought from greengrocers. There are three types of cucumber: those grown under glass, which are long and smooth; ridge cucumbers, which are grown outside and are small with rough, often prickly skins; and gherkins, which are much like the latter, except they are shorter, and which are used mainly for pickling.

The modern greenhouse varieties do not require pollination; if they are accidentally pollinated the fruit often tastes bitter. When you buy seeds make certain that you choose an all-female cultivar. Cucumbers require a high temperature – a minimum of 18°C (64°F)– and a high humidity. Sow seeds for indoor plants in early spring, two seeds to a pot, with each seed sown on its side. Place them in a propagator with a temperature of about 24°C (75°F). Once the seeds have germinated carefully remove the weaker plant. The seedlings can be planted into grow bags in a warm greenhouse as soon as they are large enough to be transplanted. Plant two per growing bag or at 75cm (30in) intervals if they are in a greenhouse border. Erect a framework of wires or canes above the plants (plastic nets are also very effective) and train the cucumber up this, spreading the side shoots horizontally and tying them in. Once cucumbers begin to appear, pinch out the tips of the side shoot two leaves beyond the fruit. Remove any male flowers if they appear. Water regularly and feed once every two weeks when fruits have started to appear.

Ridge cucumbers can be grown outside in a vegetable garden that has had plenty of well-rotted organic material added to it. Raise the seeds under glass and plant them out or, if you prefer, sow where they are to grow, covering each sowing point with a cloche or large jam jar. Do not sow or plant out cucumbers until the threat of frost has passed. Trailing types can be grown up supports in the same way as greenhouse varieties, but bush cucumbers should be allowed to spread over the ground. Pinch out the side shoots once six leaves have been formed and keep the plants well watered. Gherkins are grown in the same way.

RECOMMENDED VARIETIES *of* CUCUMBER

Greenhouse varieties

'Birgit'

'Fenumex'

'Pepinex'

'Petita'

'Telegraph'

'Telegraph Improved'

Ridge varieties

'Burpless Tasty Green'

'Bush Champion'

'Crystal Apple'

'Long Green Ridge'

'Masterpiece'

Gherkins

'Bestal'

'Venlo Pickling'

MARROWS/COURGETTES

This is one of the easiest and most productive of garden crops. Courgettes are really small versions of marrows, and it is possible to pick marrows at an early stage. However, it is more satisfactory to grow varieties that are specially bred as courgettes. The old-style trailing plants need a lot of space, but modern bush varieties are compact and yet still provide plenty of produce. They can be grown in any fertile garden soil to which plenty of organic material has been added. One way of saving space is to cover a compost heap with soil and to plant the marrows into this, breaking up the heap in the autumn, once the marrows have finished, for spreading on the garden.

Sow seeds under glass this month so that they are ready for planting out once the threat of frost is passed. Alternatively, they can be sown directly into the soil next month. Trailing varieties need to be 1.2–1.8m (4–6ft) apart or closer if they are grown up supports such as peasticks or netting. Bush varieties need be only 90cm (3ft) apart. Keep the plants well watered.

Pick courgettes while they are still small, even if you do not use them. If they are allowed to grow they will continue to do so until they are large marrows, preventing the formation of more courgettes.

Squashes and pumpkins can be grown in a similar way.

RECOMMENDED VARIETIES *of* MARROW

'All Green Bush'
'Badger Cross'
'Green Bush'
'Long Green Trailing'
'Tiger Cross'

RECOMMENDED VARIETIES *of* COURGETTE

'Ambassador'
'Early Gem'
'Gold Rush'
'Patriot'
'Sardane'
'Supremo'
'Zucchini'

RECOMMENDED VARIETIES *of* SQUASH

'Butternut'
'Custard White'
'Orangetti'
'Pyjamas'
'Tivoli'
'Vegetable Spaghetti'

RECOMMENDED VARIETIES *of* PUMPKIN

'Atlantic Giant'
'Crown Prince'
'Jackpot'
'Mammoth Orange'
'Spellbound'

BRUSSELS SPROUTS

No vegetable garden is complete without a supply of Brussels sprouts, and although it is often thought of as simply a winter vegetable, if you choose the varieties correctly, you can have a continuous supply of sprouts from mid-autumn through to the spring. There are three main types – early, mid- and late season – and if you can accommodate them, it is best to aim to grow a few plants of each. The only problem is that they do take a quite a bit of space. If space is a problem, grow some of the more compact varieties such as 'Peer Gynt'. A recent development is to produce red cultivars, although there does not seem to be any real merit in this in terms of flavour.

Like all brassicas, they need a sunny position and a well-drained but moisture-retentive soil that has been manured for a previous crop. Because they form tall, heavy plants, make sure that there is adequate protection from the wind. If the site is open, each plant may need staking.

Sow in a seed bed in the early or mid-spring. They can also been sown under glass and hardened off if you prefer to work this way. Thin the seedlings as soon as they are big enough to handle so that they do not become too drawn. When the plants are about 12–15cm (5–6in) high, plant them out in their final positions. Plant them in firm ground, placing them 60–75cm (24–30in) apart. They should be well firmed in. Water and keep watered until the roots are established.

The beds will need to be weeded because immature Brussels do not make very good groundcover and there is a lot of space between them. They are hungry plants and will benefit if a high nitrogen fertilizer is applied in late summer. Pick as soon as the sprouts are large enough and try not to leave them to become large and loose leaved. Brussels sprouts can be frozen, but it is best to choose a variety that is bred for this purpose.

A good crop of Brussels sprouts. Most varieties will withstand winter conditions and provide a ready crop whenever you want them.

RECOMMENDED VARIETIES *of* BRUSSELS SPROUTS

Early varieties
  'Lancelot'
  'Oliver'
  'Peer Gynt'

Mid-season varieties
  'Bedford Fillbasket'
  'Citadel'
  'Evesham Special'
  'Mallard'
  'Roger'

Late varieties
  'Fortress'
  'Icarus'
  'Sheriff'
  'Widgeon'

CELERY

This crisp vegetable can be eaten raw or cooked, and it can also be used as a flavouring. Tradition has it that it always tastes sweeter after the first frosts and this appears to be so. There two basic types of celery, trench celery, which is further divided into three sub-categories, white-, pink- or red-stemmed, and self-blanching, which is further divided into the white- and green-stemmed (also known as American green) kinds. When you are growing trench celery, the light must be excluded (by earthing up) to achieve blanched stems; self-blanching celery does not need to be earthed up.

Dig over the ground in winter, adding plenty of well-rotted manure. This month or last month, sow the seeds in the greenhouse in a temperature in the range of 10–16°C (50–60°F). Harden them off and plant out in late spring or early summer. For trench varieties dig out a trench, plant them at 30cm (12in) intervals and water. Self-blanching varieties can be planted in rows, but they do best when planted in blocks so that the accumulated leaves create shade and help with the blanching. They should be planted 23cm (9in) apart in all directions.

Celery must not be allowed to dry out, so keep it watered during dry spells. Tie the stems of the trench celery together and gradually fill up the trench as they grow. The same effect can be achieved by tying paper collars around them, adding more as they grow. Self-blanching varieties should blanch themselves, but they are improved if the light is further reduced by placing straw around the stems.

Self-blanching varieties are more tender than the trench and should be used before the frosts; trench celery will stand quite a bit of frost but should be covered with straw during extremely harsh weather.

RECOMMENDED VARIETIES *of* CELERY

Self-blanching varieties
  'Celebrity'
  'Golden Self-Blanching'
  'Ivory Tower'
  'Lathom's Self-Blanching'

Trench-grown varieties
  'Giant Pink'
  'Giant White'
  'Hopkin's Fenlander'
  'Martine'
  'New White Dwarf'

CELERIAC

This bulbous plant has much the same flavour as celery, and it is grown in the same way – that is, sown under glass at 10–16° (50–60°F) and planted out after the last frosts. Mulch around the plants after planting. It should not be allowed to dry out. A liquid feed once every two weeks is also beneficial. As they grow, earth up the bulbs slightly to keep them white and remove any roots that appear from the side of the bulb. In late summer remove some of the outer leaves to expose the crown. They can be left in the ground and used when required. Cover with straw during very cold weather.

RECOMMENDED VARIETIES *of* CELERIAC

'Balder'
'Giant Prague'
'Marble Ball'
'Monarch'
'Snow White'
'Tellus'

> GREEN TIP *Inter-crops*
> Sow another, quick-maturing crop – radishes or lettuces, for example – between the Brussels sprouts as soon as they have been planted. They will be harvested by the time the Brussels have grown large enough to cover their ground.

LAWNS

This can be a busy time for working on lawns because the ground is soft enough to carry out a number of processes with comparative ease and yet firm enough to allow you to get onto it without damaging it.

This month and the next are the ideal times for scarifying the lawn to remove thatch (see below).

> GREEN TIP *Lawn Clippings*
> One advantage of mowing regularly is that the length of the clippings will be quite short. Instead of collecting these in the grass box, leave them on the lawn. They will be taken down by earthworms and will decay, improving the structure of the soil and providing nutrients. Taking away the clippings only means that you are taking away the goodness that in nature would be returned to the soil. You will have to add fertilizer to the soil to replace it, but if you leave the clippings, the nutrients will be recycled. Avoid leaving long clippings on the lawn because these will soon smother the grasses, choking them and creating brown patches.

As the weather warms up, so the growth rate of the grass will increase and so will the number of mowings that is required. Gradually drop the height of the cutter until the grass is at your normal summer level. It will also be time to consider mowing new lawns laid down last autumn (pp. 141, 182).

The warmer growing conditions mean that now is the time to apply the first feed of the year (p. 60). Some fertilizers contain selective weedkillers. If the one you use does not, you will need to apply a weedkiller now to remove unwanted broad-leaved weeds. The same is true of moss-killers if you have not already applied them.

It is still not too late to sow and turf new lawns. Newly laid lawns should be kept watered and not allowed to dry out. If turves shrink, fill in the gaps with sifted soil or compost and sow the same or comparable seeds in it.

This is also a good time to re-sow or re-turf damaged patches of lawns or grass paths (p. 38).

SCARIFYING

Mid-spring is a good time to remove the thatch that has built up on the lawn in the autumn and winter. Thatch is the remains of dead grass and moss that, if it is not removed, will form a mulch over the lawn, stifling emerging grass. Removing the thatch also allows air to reach the soil.

Use a spring-tine rake to scarify the lawn.

It is a simple but tiring process. A spring-tined rake is drawn across the lawn in short sweeps so that the tines dig into the top of the soil. Scarifying pulls off the dead material and at the same time slightly opens up the soil. Work in one direction across the lawn and then again at right angles. If you have a large lawn it may make sense to hire a machine to carry out the work. These have the advantages of not only sparing your aching muscles but also of picking up the thatch as they go. If there is a lot of moss in the lawn, it should be treated with a moss-killer before the lawn is scarified.

Once scarified, the lawn can be mown to remove loose thatch and to restore its neat appearance.

FEEDING LAWNS

Although one does not often think of lawns as being made up of plants in the same way as, say, a perennial border or a vegetable garden, they are, in many respects, exactly the same. They are composed of living plants that need to be fed, watered and maintained in the same way as their more decorative counterparts. A lawn that is looked after will always be much more attractive than one that is neglected.

There are several types of lawn treatments available. Some are simply fertilizers, while others also contain a selective weedkiller, and yet others add a moss-killer as a third ingredient. A combined application is convenient as it saves a lot of time, but you may not need to apply the last two elements, so check before you buy to make sure you have exactly what you need. Do not automatically buy the triple pack.

Lawns are usually fed twice a year, once in spring or early summer and once again towards the end of the year, in early autumn. It is more important to stimulate growth in spring than in autumn, and so spring feeds contain a higher percentage of nitrogen (N). Many formulations now contain both fast-acting and slow-release fertilizers so that the grass does not only green up quickly but remains green for the season. In the autumn, if you want to green up the grass without encouraging it to make excessive growth, use a formulation that contains iron (Fe). Look through the lawn feeds that are available and choose the one that is most appropriate to your needs and to the time of year.

It is very important to follow the instructions given on the pack. It is a mistake to use more than the recommended dosage because far from making a better lawn, it is likely to cause problems by killing off areas of grass. It is also important to get an even coverage, because if some parts receive more than their share, the grass may, again, turn brown, while areas that are not treated will be undernourished and look pale.

Fertilizer can be broadcast by hand, but this method makes it difficult to get an even spread. Some brands come with a special applicator, which facilitates distribution. The most satisfactory way is to buy or hire a spreader, which distributes the fertilizer in even strips. To get a really even spread, distribute the fertilizer at half the recommended rate but go over the lawn twice, once in one direction then again at right angles to the first application. Make certain that adjacent strips do not overlap or have gaps between them.

NATURALIZED BULBS

Do not cut areas of lawn or meadow grass in which bulbs have been naturalized until their leaves have died down. If you cut the rest of the grass, leaving a well-defined area containing the bulbs, the lawn will still looked neat and cared for and should not detract from the appearance of the garden.

🍂 PERENNIALS

The warmer weather is bringing the perennials into growth, and hummocks of leaves are beginning to erupt in the borders. It is essential to finish any border maintenance before these get too big. In the first place it is difficult to work around growing plants and, second, the new shoots can be easily damaged. The worst situation is if you have not managed to cut back last year's stems before this year's lengthen. It is very difficult to get between the new growth to cut out the old without doing a great deal of damage. If you find yourself in this position, perhaps because of a wet late spring, cut off the old stems above the current height of the new and allow the continuing growth to hide the remains. Next year, or preferably this autumn, cut both years' stems right back to the ground.

Make sure that you finish weeding the borders this month because the growing plants will soon cover the border, making a living mulch. The darkness beneath close-growing herbaceous plants will prevent new weeds from germinating but will not stop any that are already on the move. A few hours spent weeding now will help save many hours later on.

As spring moves on and the days become hotter and the soil drier, it becomes more difficult for plants to establish themselves after planting or re-establish themselves after being moved or divided. It is, therefore, important to finish planting all new borders and renovating older ones before the end of this month unless it is a wet spring.

Seedlings from earlier sowing of perennials should be continuing to germinate. Pot these up before they become too large or they will soon become overcrowded and starved (p. 37). They will last longer in their initial pot or tray if they are sown thinly, so be certain to do this if you lead such a busy life that you might not be able to get round to things at the precise moment that they need attention.

Similarly, seeds that germinated in the autumn or earlier in the year and that have already been potted up, may well need potting on. Never neglect growing plants, or they will become starved and may never fully recover to become robust, healthy plants.

It is important to stake plants before they require it. A plant that has blown over and then been tied up, usually looks perfectly miserable. One that was staked at the correct time will happily grow away and the staking is unlikely to show. Stake when the plant reaches between half and two-thirds of its final height, depending on the strength of the stems (p. 80). The majority of plants require staking next month, but a few precocious ones may well need attention now.

Slugs can cause a lot of damage at this time of year. They can graze off young shoots and it is only later that you realize that something is amiss when you notice that the plant is missing. Delphiniums and heleniums, for example, are very prone to this problem, as are some nepetas, asters and many other plants. Take action now. Do not plaster the landscape with slug pellets – place one or two at strategic points in the clumps of growing plants, well away from the prying eyes of birds, and renew them every few days until the slugs have been reduced.

The new growth appearing on many perennials makes ideal cutting material and now is the time to take cuttings.

BASAL CUTTINGS

Cuttings can be easily taken from the new shoots that appear in spring around the edge of clumps of herbaceous perennials. The practice is well known to chrysanthemum growers, who remove the new growth from the old stools and strike these as cuttings. A large number of plants can be treated in the same way – the labiates (mint family), such as the nepetas, lamiums, monardas, mints, salvias and many others, are good candidates, as are violas and pansies. Asters, especially those that do not divide easily, such as the various cultivars of *Aster frikartii* or *A. amellus*, also come readily from this technique.

Choose fresh material that is not too drawn. Cuttings should be about 5cm (2in) long but can be shorter for violas and many smaller plants. Cut through the stem just below a node (where the leaf or leaves join the stem) and

Taking basal cuttings

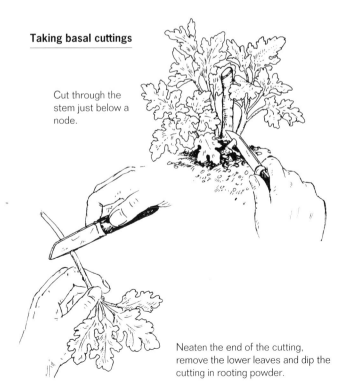

Cut through the stem just below a node.

Neaten the end of the cutting, remove the lower leaves and dip the cutting in rooting powder.

Brilliant blue hummocks of *Festuca valesiaca* 'Silbersee'. Move and divide grasses only in the spring, just as they come into growth.

cut off the lower leaves, leaving just one or two pairs at the top of the cut. Dip the cuttings in rooting powder and insert them around the rim of a 9cm (3½in) pot of cutting compost (p. 24). Place the pot in a propagator or in a polythene bag and leave until the cuttings have rooted, when they should be potted up.

Basal cuttings can be taken at any time of the year as long as there is fresh growth. Sometimes it is a good idea to stimulate this by sheering over the plant once it has finished flowering. This is a good technique with violas, aubrieta and nepeta, for example.

PERENNIALS *from* BASAL CUTTINGS

Achillea (yarrows)	*Euphorbia*
Anthemis	*Geranium*
Artemisia	*Helenium*
Aster (Michaelmas daisies)	*Lamium* (dead nettles)
Aubrieta	*Lupinus*
Campanula (bellflowers)	*Lythrum*
Chrysanthemum	*Mentha* (mints)
Crambe	*Mimulus* (monkey flowers)
Delphinium	*Monarda* (bergamots)
Diascia	*Nepeta* (catmints)

Perovskia	*Sedum* (stonecrops)
Phlox	*Solidago*
Physostegia	*Verbena*
Salvia	*Viola* (violas, pansies)

GRASSES

Ornamental grasses are well worth considering for the garden. They create elegant, statuesque shapes, they have a very long season, and they suffer from few pests and diseases. A few can be pests themselves as they tend to spread uncontrollably, but if they are planted where this does not matter or if they are restricted by, say, being planted between a path and a drive or being planted in a bottomless bucket, they are not a problem.

Grasses can be treated as other perennials. They will grow on a wide range of soils but do best in a moisture-retentive one. Most grasses prefer to be in a sunny position. They should be planted in mid-spring, just as they come into growth, and the main method of propagation, division, is also carried out at this time of year. Cut back the old growth to the base in late winter or early spring. Those grasses that self-sow – many of the annuals, for example – should be cut back before they shed their seeds.

GRASSES *for the* BORDER

Agropyron pubiflorum: medium, blue
Alepecurus pratensis 'Aureovariegata': low, yellow
Arundo donax: tall, green
Briza media: medium, green
Carex: low/medium, green/yellow/brown
Cortaderia: tall, green/yellow
Deschampsia caespitosa: medium, green
Hakonechloa macra 'Aureola': low, yellow
Milium effusum 'Aureum': medium, yellow
Molinia: low/medium, cream/green
Miscanthus: tall, green
Pennisetum: medium, green
Phlaris arundinacea var. *picta*: medium, white striped
Pleioblastus auricomus: medium, yellow
Stipa: tall, green
Carex: low/medium, green/yellow/brown
Deschampsia caespitosa: medium, green
Elymus hispidus: low, blue
Festuca: low/medium, blue
Leymus arenarius: low/medium, blue
Uncinia rubra: low, red/brown

🍂 ROCK GARDENS

From now on the work in the rock garden involves a continual assessment of current conditions and the taking of suitable action to remedy defects. Weeds should be removed as soon as they are seen and before they can take a hold. Similarly, any pests or diseases should be dealt with as soon as possible.

It is often assumed that because alpines like a free-draining soil, they do not need watering. This is not true: they do need water to stay alive and to grow, but they do not like to sit in damp soil. The best soil for rock garden plants is one that contains organic material, such as leaf-mould, which retains a certain amount of moisture, and grit, which allows excess water drain away. In spite of the leaf-mould, this kind of soil can dry out rapidly, especially if the plants are drawing up as much moisture as they can in hot or windy weather.

Once the drier weather starts and it is necessary to think about watering the garden, the rock garden should be considered as well. If you have plants in an alpine house or coldframe, do not forget them because they are likely to dry out very quickly under glass in sunny weather, and it is possible to lose quite a number of plants in a few days if you forget to water. In the growing season they will need to be checked, and very probably watered, every day, especially in hot, sunny weather.

Although many plants are in full flower, with many still to come, quite a number will have finished flowering already. Deadhead these as the flowers go over. This will help promote further flowering and help to conserve the plants' reserves because a lot of energy goes into seed production. If seeds are required, leave at least some of the dying flowers on the plant, so that the seeds are allowed to develop.

It is not too late to finish planting new beds as long as the weather is not too dry and hot. Those plants that have been grown in containers, where the roots will not be disturbed when they are planted, are the best to use. Bare-rooted plants have a bit of a struggled to get established and to survive from this month on. Water these and any others recently planted specimens because they are more susceptible to drought than established plants.

As in the perennial borders, this is a good time for taking basal cuttings (p. 61).

RAISED BEDS

Although rock gardens still have a place in contemporary gardens, they seem to be increasingly out of favour. This may be partly because it is not always possible to incorporate an imitation piece of mountainside in an urban garden without it looking incongruous, partly because of the cost of rock and partly because of the problems of maintenance, especially if weeds are liable to come in from the surrounding areas of the garden.

An alternative that is gaining in popularity is the raised bed. Although it looks quite different from the rock garden, it is based on the same theory – that is, the plants' need for a well-drained environment. Basically, it is a bed that is raised above ground level, surrounded by walls and filled with rubble and then a free-draining soil.

Choose a site that is in the open and away from overhanging trees. It should preferably get the sun all day, but as long as it gets sun during the majority of the day, this is usually sufficient.

The walls can be of any material that you like. Brick or concrete blocks are easy to work with and can be chosen to match those of the house or some other nearby walls or structures. Stone is ideal and creates a more natural setting for the plants. It can be used in the form of dry-stone walling, or the blocks can be cemented together. Wood is an inexpensive alternative, railway sleepers being particularly good. Wood, however, is not as long lasting as the other material, and although sleepers tend to last a long time, they have the rather nasty habit in hot weather of oozing the tar with which they were preserved. This inevitably gets on clothes and skin when you tend the bed.

Whatever the choice of materials for the walls, it is a good idea to use proper foundations. These can be

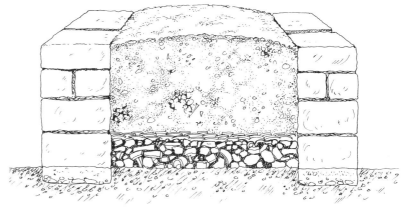

The base of a raised bed should be filled with a layer of rubble to improve the drainage. Cover this with a porous material before adding the compost.

skimped, as the walls are not frequently very tall, but usually at a later cost when the structure begins to sag. Brick walls should be built vertically but stone ones can lean inwards slightly so that the bed is narrower towards the top, like a traditional stone wall.

When you are building the wall leave a few small gaps at ground level to help excess water drain out of the bed. A few similar holes can be left higher up the walls to be used as planting holes for trailing plants and for those plants that naturally grow on the sides of rock so that water does not collect in their crowns.

The walls can be anything from 25–60cm (10–24in) high. From the plants' point of view the height is irrelevant, but a higher bed is more convenient for elderly and handicapped gardeners to attend without having to bend too far. Remember, however, that a deep bed will require more soil to fill it.

Fill the bottom of the bed with a layer of rubble to help with free drainage. This is then covered either with plastic with drainage holes in it (the type sold for mulching strawberries) or with upturned turves (make sure they are free of perennial weeds). This layer is needed to prevent the compost, which goes in next, from falling down between the pieces of rubble and clogging the drainage.

The remainder of the bed is then filled with soil or compost. Whatever it is it should be a mixture of two parts loam, one part grit and one part organic material, such as leaf-mould (all parts by volume). A John Innes potting compost can be used instead of the loam (p. 24). This mixture should be at least 30cm (12in) deep, although proportionately less in lower beds. In deep beds the bulk of the infill can be rubble if this is cheaper to obtain than the soil.

Once filled, allow the bed to stand for several months before it is planted. Remove any weeds that appear and top up with more compost as the surface sinks. Plant with whatever alpines or rockery plants you wish, planting some of the trailing types, such as aubrieta, in the holes in the sides of the wall. When the planting is complete, top dress with a layer of grit or stone chippings. Rocks can be used to give the surface character and will also provide a small amount of shade for those plants that require it.

Most alpines will appreciate a place on a raised bed, although, depending on its size, the smaller ones are probably the best ones to use. You should try to include a few dwarf shrubs, *Daphne cneorum* 'Eximia', for example, and conifers, such as *Juniperus communis* 'Compressa', to give height and structure as well as interest in their own right.

PLANTS *for a* RAISED BED

Aethionema
Androsace
Antirrhinum (small species)
Aquilegia (small species)
Armeria
Aubrieta
Aurinia (syn. *Alyssum*)
Campanula (small species)
Daphne
Dianthus
Draba
Erinus alpinus
Erodium
Euryops acraeus
Gentiana
Globularia
Helichrysum coralloides
Lewisa
Linaria alpina
Oxalis
Papaver (small species)
Phlox subulata
Primula
Ramonda
Saxifraga
Sedum (small species)
Sempervivum
Silene acaulis
Thymus
Verbascum 'Letitia'

🍂 TREES AND SHRUBS

By now all bare-rooted trees and shrubs should have been planted. It is, however, still possible to plant container-grown specimens as long as they are kept well watered. Avoid planting them during hot or dry, windy weather.

Re-check all trees and shrubs to make sure that recent winds have not loosened any stakes are caused root rock. Strengthen stakes and firmly fill in any holes around the base of the tree or shrub. If you have not already done so, check that ties are not too tight and cutting into the bark.

As climbers begin to put on growth, tie in any loose ends so that they do not whip about and become damaged or cause damage to other plants.

Finish weeding and mulching shrub borders before the plants come into leaf. Any perennial weeds, such as couch grass, should be carefully treated with a weedkiller as they come into growth. Once they are established in a shrub border, persistent weeds are very difficult to eradicate except by removing all the shrubs and starting again. The judicial and very careful use of herbicides can help to bring the situation under control. However, don't just do it once and forget about it, or the problem will soon be back again. Regularly check and treat until the weeds no longer reappear.

Mid-spring is the time to finish pruning shrubs that will flower on the current year's growth.

PRUNING SHRUBS IN SPRING

Some shrubs flower on the current year's growth. If they are left, the amount of new growth lessens as the shrub reaches its ultimate size and the amount of flowering also grows less. To keep the shrub vigorous and producing the maximum amount of flowers, it should be pruned each year in early to mid-spring.

As with all pruning, start by removing any dead or dying wood. At the same time remove any that is injured, bruised or diseased. The next step is to take out any stems that cross over, rubbing against others and causing congestion, and any weak growths.

This leaves a basic framework, which should now be pruned to improve this year's flowering as well as that of subsequent years, which is achieved by ensuring that the plant remains vigorous with plenty of young growth. Cut out several of the oldest stems, right to the base. This will promote the growth of new wood. You should attempt to remove about a third of the wood if it is possible to do this without destroying the shape of the bush, and this will mean that the whole shrub is renewed over a three-year period.

Next, reduce last year's growth on the remaining stems to within about two to three buds of the darker wood from the previous year.

Pruning shrubs

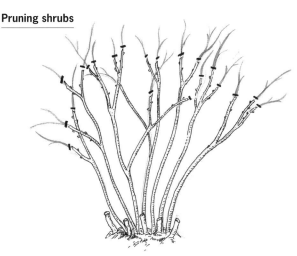

Spring pruning is carried out on shrubs that flower on the current year's growth to encourage new stems. The aim to remove about a third of the stems each year. Remove old, damaged or dead stems, cutting them at the base, and cut back the previous year's growth to about four buds on the older stems.

Buddleia can be cut back hard in spring but will still flower later in the year. Each year, aim to remove some of the oldest woody stems to ground level to keep the plant open in the centre. Cut back shoots that flowered the previous year to about three buds from the old wood.

DEALING WITH THE PREVIOUS YEAR'S GROWTH

There are a small number of shrubs – *Buddleja davidii* and the elder (*Sambucus*), which is grown for it foliage, being two of the most common – on which the previous year's growth needs to be back almost to the base. This looks rather drastic, but the shrub quickly grows back to its full size, with the buddleia flowering before the end of the summer. Leave it and the plant will become sprawling and untidy with small flowerheads. If you require flowers on the elder then only cut out about a third of the old material each year, but by cutting it back you will get large attractive leaves.

You can also cut back other trees and shrubs that produce attractive juvenile leaves. Eucalyptus, for example, will grow into a large tree, but if it is cut back regularly to almost the ground it will produce a very attractive foliage, much in demand for flower arranging.

Not all shrubs that are pruned in spring produce flowers later in the year. Some, such as forsythia or *Prunus triloba*, will have already flowered on the previous year's wood in late winter or early spring. These should be pruned after flowering to promote new growth for next year's flowering.

Another group of shrubs that require spring pruning are those that are grown for their winter bark, such as various cultivars and species of *Cornus albus*, *Salix* and *Rubus*. The stems of all these should be cut right back to the base because it is the new growth that produces the coloured bark; old wood is frequently just a dirty brown.

SHRUBS *to* PRUNE *in* EARLY *or* MID-SPRING

Aucuba	*Hydrangea*
Ballota	*Hypericum*
Buddleja (butterfly bush)	*Indigofera*
Buxus (box)	*Lavandula* (lavender)
Calluna (ling)	*Lavatera*
Caryopteris × *clandonensis*	*Perovskia*
Ceanothus	*Prunus triloba*
Ceratostigma	*Pyracantha* (firethorn)
Clethra	*Salvia* (sage)
Convolvulus cneorum	*Sarcococca* (Christmas box)
Cotinus (smoke bush)	*Sorbaria*
Datura	*Spartium* (Spanish broom)
Forsythia	*Spiraea*
Fuchsia (hardy varieties)	*Zauschneria*
Hibiscus	

VEGETABLES

By mid-spring work in the vegetable garden should be in full swing. If you have not already started sowing hardy vegetables, the soil and weather conditions are likely to allow you to make a start now. In favoured areas, where it was possible to start last month, it is time to make further sowings (see below).

Although it is still too early to sow outside the more tender vegetables, such as runner beans and courgettes, they can be sown under glass in pots towards the end of this month so that they will be ready to harden off and plant out as soon as the threat of frost is past. Several beans can be sown in one pot, but it causes less root disturbance when they are planted out if you have only

one per pot. Having said that, if you have plenty of seeds it is a good idea to sow two per pot and pull out the weaker if both germinate. Marrows, courgettes and ridge cucumbers can be treated in the same way.

In late springs or in wet areas where it is not possible to get onto the soil until well into the season, it is possible to sow other vegetables under glass and move them out when conditions improve. They can be sown in trays, or better still, into plugs or modules, which, again, will help them to be transplanted into the beds without too much root disturbance.

SOWING VEGETABLES

The ideal soil for sowing seeds is one that is moist but not too wet and certainly not sticky. If it is compacted when you walk on it, wait until it is drier or, if you must get on, work from a plank that will spread your weight. Break the soil down with a hoe and rake until it forms a fine tilth. If the soil is dry or is on the clay side, making it difficult to break down, shuffle up and down, breaking the clods with the soles of your boots and then rake it. In a wet season cover the area with cloches or polythene to help it dry out and warm up before you start to work on it.

Using a line to ensure that the row is straight, draw out a shallow drill using the corner of a hoe. The depth will depend on the plants. If the ground is very dry, water the

GREEN TIP *Slugs*

Although many consider slugs to be one of the gardener's worst enemies, an increasing number of people are becoming reluctant to use slug bait of any kind. There are many 'green' ways of dealing with the problem but most are not particularly effective. Putting ashes or grit around a plant, for example, is nowhere as effective as is often thought. By far the best way is to round them up by hand. Go out at night with a torch and you will see hundreds at work. Put them in a bucket or jar. After several nights of this, the slug population will be reduced to an acceptable level. The captured slugs can either be dispatched by putting them in water in which a little washing-up liquid has been added or, if you really can't bring yourself to kill them, taken elsewhere and released.

Station sowing, which involves sowing groups of three or four seeds together, makes it possible to sow fast-maturing crops, such as radishes, in the spaces between the main crops.

drill some time before you sow. On the other hand, if the soil is very wet and yet it is important that you get on with sowing, line the drill with a light sprinkling of sharp sand.

Sow the seeds thinly in the drill. With vegetables that will eventually be some distance apart, use a technique known as station sowing. This involves sowing groups of three or four seeds together, each group spaced apart by the distance of the eventual plants. Thus, sow groups of beetroot seeds at 10cm (4in) intervals. When the seedlings appear, remove them all except the strongest growing in each group.

Station sowing makes it possible to sow fast-maturing crops, such as radishes, in the spaces between the main groups. This is a particularly useful technique for plants whose seeds are slow to germinate. The radishes will quickly appear and act as a marker for the row of much slower germinating parsnips, for example.

When you sow the larger seeds, such as beans and peas, place each seed individually so that the spacing between the resulting plants will be right. Peas and broad beans and dwarf French beans can be sown in drills 15–20cm (6–8in) wide, in effect giving two rows close together.

Before you do anything else mark the end of the rows, either with sticks or, preferably, labels. If you do not do this at this stage, it is often difficult to remember where the row is once it is covered in. It is important to know where it is as you may have to how between the rows before the seedlings come up. Cover the drills with a thin layer of soil and lightly tamp it down with the back of the rake.

DISTANCES BETWEEN ROWS *of* SOWN VEGETABLES

Taller types of beans and peas need wider distances between rows.

beetroot	30cm (12in)
broad beans	30–90cm (12–36in)
carrots	20–25cm (8–10in)
dwarf French beans	30cm (12in)
fennel	45cm (18in)
kohl rabi	30cm (12in)
lettuce	30 cm (12in)
parsley	30cm (12in)
peas	60–90cm (24–36in)
parsnips	30cm (12in)
radishes	15cm (6in)
runner beans	90–120cm (36–48in)
salsify	25cm (10in)
scorzonera	25cm (10in)
spinach	30cm (12in)
spring onions	15–20cm (6–8in)
swedes	45cm (18in)
swiss chard	45cm (18in)
turnips	30cm (12in)

See also Planting Distances (page 88); Thinning Distances (page 85).

Sowing seeds

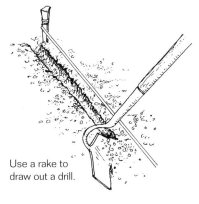

Use a rake to draw out a drill.

Sow the seeds thinly in the drill.

Rake the soil carefully over the seeds.

An alternative method is to broadcast seeds thinly over prepared ground.

If you are using the bed system or are sowing in blocks, it is possible to cover the area in short rows as already described or the seeds can be broadcast. Broadcasting means scattering the seeds over the bed and then gently raking them in. One way to facilitate this is to rake the fine tilth in one direction, with parallel impressions left behind by the rake's teeth. Sow into these and then rake again, this time at right angles, across the previous impressions.

CARROTS

This is another crop of which home-grown specimens are difficult to better, especially the first ones of the season, which have an exquisite taste. There are many different varieties available, some to be grown as earlies, with others as main-crop to be stored for winter use. There is an increasing tendency to produce varieties that are resistant to carrot root fly.

Carrots like a deep soil that is free from stones that will distort the shape of the roots. Add plenty of well-rotted organic material to the soil during the autumn. Earlies should be sown in early to mid-spring; main-crop from late spring onwards. Sow thinly so that the amount of thinning required is reduced. If possible, thinning should be avoided altogether, because the smell of bruised flesh and foliage attracts the carrot root fly, one of the most troublesome pests. Try to thin on evenings when the air is heavy and still, because the smell will not travel far then.

Lift early carrots as and when they are required. Although main-crop can be left in the ground in milder areas, they are best lifted and stored in the autumn. Lift the carrots, remove the tops and wipe off excess soil. Lay the carrots on a bed of sand in wooden box. Cover with sand and put another layer of carrots on top and so on, until the box is full.

RECOMMENDED VARIETIES *of* CARROT

Early varieties
  'Amsterdam Forcing 3'
  'Amsterdam Sweetheart'
  'Early French Frame'
  'Early Nantes'
  'Nanco'
  'Rondo'

Main-crop varieties
  'Autumn King'
  'Beacon'
  'Chantenay Red Cored'

  'Favourite'
  'Fly Away'
  'James Scarlet Intermediate'
  'Minicor'
  'Nantes'
  'Nantes Express'
  'St Valery'

ROOT CROPS

Once maligned as 'cattlefeed', root crops are once again returning to popularity. With proper cooking they are among the most delicious of vegetables and have the advantage that they can be used fresh even in the depths of winter. Many can stay in the ground through the frosts, while other can be lifted and stored in dry or slightly moist sand where their freshness does not deteriorate.

Some, such as beetroot, carrots, potatoes and swedes, are discussed elsewhere. The remainder of the more commonly grown are dealt with here.

Kohl Rabi

This is not so much a root but a swollen stem. It is a member of the cabbage family and, as such suffers, from many of the same problems. The swollen stem has the flavour of turnip, but it is more subtle in both taste and texture.

Kohl rabi likes a sunny site and a light, fertile soil. It will tolerate dry hot summers. It is sown where it is to grow in shallow drills set 30cm (12in) apart. Once they are large enough to handle, thin out the seedlings to about 20cm (8in). Sow at two to three week intervals to provide a succession of tender roots.

The best time to eat kohl rabi is when they are young and tender, so harvest when they are about the size of tennis balls. As long as they do not get too large, they can be left in the ground until they are required even well into the winter. In colder areas they can be stored like other root crops but they tend to shrivel.

RECOMMENDED VARIETIES *of* KOHL RABI

  'Green Vienna'
  'Kolpak'
  'Lanro'
  'Purple Vienna'
  'Rowel'
  'Trero'
  'White Vienna'

Parsnips

Parsnips are very good winter crops as they will stand quite a few degrees of frost and need not be stored inside except where conditions mean you cannot get them out of the frozen ground.

Grow in a deep, stone-free soil that has been fertilized for a previous crop. Always use fresh seed, and station sow at 15–20cm (6–8in) intervals in rows 30cm (12in) apart. Do not sow too early because the seeds germinate best in a warm soil. They are slow to germinate. Thin when the seedlings are large enough to handle.

Harvest when the parsnips are large enough to eat, although they do not develop their full taste until after the first frosts. Leave in the ground until required or store in trays of just-moist sand.

RECOMMENDED VARIETIES of PARSNIP

'Avonresister'
'Bayonet'
'Cobham Improved Marrow'
'Gladiator'
'Hollow Crown'
'Intermediate'
'Lancer
'Tender and True'
'White Gem'
'White King'
'White Spear'
'Hollow Crown'

Salsify and Scorzonera

These are two of the less often grown root crops. They are like small parsnips in appearance and have a delicate flavour (salsify is also known as the vegetable oyster). They are very similar in growth and requirements. The soil should be deeply dug and free from stones. It should have been manured for a previous crop. Sow in mid-spring in drills 25cm (10in) apart. Station sow at 15cm (6in) intervals or thin to that distance when seedlings have developed. Take care when weeding that you do not cut or bruise the roots.

Salsify and scorzonera like a long growing season but are ready when they are about the size of small parsnips. Be careful not to damage the roots when you are lifting them. They can be left in the ground over winter until they are required, or they can be lifted and stored in just-moist sand.

RECOMMENDED VARIETIES of SALSIFY

'Giant'
'Mammoth'
'Sandwich Island'

RECOMMENDED VARIETIES of SCORZONERA

'Habil'
'Russian Giant'

Turnips

The turnip is another of the so-called root crops that is related to the cabbages. Although similar to kohl rabi in some respects, turnips must have moist soil in which to grow. The soil should also be fertile, preferably manured for a previous crop. Sow in shallow drills about 30cm (12in) apart. When they are large enough to handle, thin out the seedlings to 15cm (6in) apart. Do not let the growing plants dry out. Harvest turnips before they go hardy and woody – small ones are best. In warmer areas they can be left in the soil in the autumn until they are required; elsewhere, put them into trays of just-moist sand or peat.

RECOMMENDED VARIETIES of TURNIP

'Golden Ball'
'Green Top Stone'
'Jersey Navet'
'Manchester Market'
'Orange Perfection'
'Purple Top Milan'
'Snowball'
'Tokyo Cross'

SUCCESSIONAL SOWING

Some vegetables – lettuce and radishes, for example – tend to be at their best for only a short time, and to ensure good crops throughout the summer and into autumn you will need to sow every two to three weeks. It is not necessary to sow complete rows each time, half or even a third of a row is sufficient to last until the next batch is ready. Successional sowing of this kind is preferable to sowing a whole row and then having to throw most of it away as it is past its prime, although if you have a freezer any excess can be stored.

Kohl rabi is a versatile crop, but it is not frequently grown, although it has been around since the sixteenth century. Harvest the stems before they get too large and tough.

Not all vegetables need to be sown successionally. Parsnips, for example, will remain in the ground from late autumn until spring without deteriorating and thus you might as well sow all you are likely to need in one go.

Sowing at different times is not the only way to get a variation of cropping times. The variety that you choose can have a lot to do with it. For example, you can choose three different varieties of Brussels sprouts that will provide sprouts in late autumn to early winter, in midwinter and in late winter to early spring. A few plants of each will ensure that you have a crop throughout the winter months. Choose only one and you will have a shorter season.

WATER FEATURES

Not much comes alive in ponds and damp borders until the water begins to warm up. A few plants, such as king cups and skunk cabbage, will be brightening up the scene, but generally the water gardens are the last feature of the garden to wake up.

Now is the time to start removing all the debris that has accumulated in the pond during winter. When you are removing leaves, sticks and so on, be very careful not to puncture the liner. If you use a rake to pull out the waste material, for example, it is very easy to snag the plastic liner and make a hole in it.

If you have a stream, remove any debris that has washed down during winter. Repair and reinforce any parts of the banks that have eroded when the stream was in full winter spate.

If there has been any appreciable loss of water during winter, check for leaks and make the appropriate repairs.

Check that the pump is working if you have a fountain or waterfall. Run it to clear out any sediment that has settled in it during winter. If you have stored it, check that it has not seized up before you put it back in the water. If there is any doubt, check that the electricity supply is sound, replacing cables and fitments if necessary.

Thin out oxygenating plants so that the pond is not congested.

CLEANING A POND

While it is necessary to remove any debris that falls into a pond, there is no need to drain it down and clear it every year – once every four or five years is perfectly adequate. If it is a large, natural pond there is seldom any need to clear it at all unless it silts up.

Make a temporary pond by draping polythene over a circle of blocks or a mound of earth that has been hollowed in the centre. Fill this with water and leave it until the next day to reach the same temperature as the pond and to release any gases, such as chlorine, that might be in the water.

Remove the plants and divide them, throwing away the old, central pieces, and keeping the young new growth. There is no need to keep all of the rapid-spreading oxygenators because a few pieces will soon spread once replanted. Carefully remove the fish and other pond life, and keep them in a bucket of old pond water or put them into the temporary pond.

Ponds need regular maintenance to ensure that they look good and to prevent a build-up of pests and diseases which will attack plants and fish. Do not allow plants to overcrowd the water – there should always be some clear water visible.

Carefully clean out the pond, removing any rotting vegetation and thick deposits of silt. Check that the side of the pond has not slipped, leaving part of the liner lower than the rest. Rebuild this if necessary. Repair any leaks using repair kits that can be obtained from garden centres or specialist nurseries. If there are cracks in a concrete pool, widen the crack with a hammer and cold chisel and refill it with cement. It will not seal properly if you simply try to fill the crack. Once filled, cover the crack with a sealing agent to prevent any toxic chemicals from seeping into the water. If the damage is extensive or difficult to repair, cover the concrete with polyester matting to mask any sharp pieces of concrete or stone and then cover it with a butyl liner.

Refill the pond and let it stand, preferably over night, so that the water reaches ambient temperature and, again, any unwanted gases can be given off. Replant the plants and replace the wildlife.

MAY

The garden is beginning to look more like a garden should after its long winter's rest. Lawns are mown and borders tended, with more and more plants coming into bloom every day.

Do not be lulled into a false sense of security, however. Nature is quite capable of delivering a neat blow below the belt. Frosts can suddenly appear at any time this month, and the later they appear, the more devastating they can be. If any frosts are forecast, cover all tender plants with whatever you have to hand – newspapers are usually sufficient. It is not only tender plants but also hardy ones, whose shoots are still tender, such as hostas, that need protection.

Weeding should, of course, be carried out throughout the year, but the weeds are growing at their fastest around now. If you put off the task of removing them, they will grow much larger, often running through other plants. A great deal of time can be wasted, and not particularly enjoyably at that, trying to renovate overgrown beds. Spend as much time now as is necessary to get the weeds under control while they are still young and you will have time to put up your feet later in the year.

CHECKLIST

General

- Water in dry weather (p. 92)
- Keep weeds under control (p. 92)
- Watch out for late frosts (p. 75)

Annuals and Tender Perennials

- Prick out (p. 20) and pot on (p. 37) late-sown annuals
- Harden off tender annuals (p. 75)
- Harden off hanging baskets and containers (p. 50)
- Plant out tender annuals and perennials once frosts are over (p. 74)
- Prepare supports for annual climbers (p. 74)

Bulbs

- Cut grass around naturalized bulbs as foliage begins to die back (p. 60)
- Collect seed (p. 76)
- Sow freshly collected seeds in pots (p. 76)
- Plant out dahlia plants after threat of frost has passed (p. 53)
- Remove spent foliage (p. 52)
- Lift tulip bulbs if necessary and store until late autumn (p. 94)

Fruit

- Protect blossom from late frosts (p. 53)
- Thin gooseberries (p. 76)
- Allow access to pollinating insects (p. 53)
- Prune and tie in fan-trained fruit trees (p. 10)
- Water if necessary (p. 76)
- Place a straw mulch under strawberries (p. 76)

Greenhouse

- Allow plenty of ventilation (p. 77)
- Shade the greenhouse (p. 96)
- Water at least daily (p. 122)
- Continue to sow bedding plants to use later in the year (p. 50)
- Prick out annual seedlings (p. 20)
- Harden off developed annual and perennial plants (p. 75)
- Plant aubergines, peppers, cucumbers and melons in the unheated greenhouse (p. 55)

Lawns

- Mow regularly (p. 78)
- Apply selective weed- and moss-killers later in the month (p. 79)
- Apply nitrogenous feed later in the month (p. 60)
- Take the last opportunity to sow new lawns (p. 141) or lay new turves if necessary (p. 182)
- Thoroughly water all lawns if necessary (p. 113)

Perennials

- Prick out seedlings as they germinate (p. 20)
- Pot on developing seedlings and plants (p. 37)
- Stake plants before they get too tall (p. 80)
- Deadhead early-flowering perennials (p. 79)
- Continue sowing perennials directly into the soil (p. 60)
- Control pests if necessary (p. 98)

Rock Gardens

- Collect seeds as they ripen (p. 101)
- Deadhead flowering plants if seeds are not required (p. 101)
- Water newly planted plants (p. 81)
- Pot on seedlings and developing plants (p. 63)
- Re-pot existing plants (p. 41)
- Keep an eye out for pests and diseases and take appropriate action (p. 63)

Trees and Shrubs

- Plant climbing plants (p. 43)
- Prune shrubs that have finished flowering (p. 65)
- Watch out for pests and diseases and take appropriate action (p. 63)
- Clip hedges if necessary (p. 82)
- Tie in new growth on climbers (p. 64)
- Take softwood cuttings (p. 82)
- Finish planting evergreen trees and shrubs (p. 184)

Vegetables

- Continue successional sowings of hardy vegetables (p. 44)
- Sow tender vegetables (p. 55)
- Plant out pre-sown tender vegetables after last frosts (p. 84)
- Plant out annual herbs after last frosts (p. 125)
- Water as necessary (p. 103)
- Take precautions against pests, especially on broad beans, carrots and cabbages (p. 84)

ANNUALS

Prick out and pot up late-sown annuals so that you have plenty of spare plants to set out as gaps appear in the borders when plants finish flowering. If you holding onto them for some time as spares for later in the year, be certain to pot them up in individual pots and not in trays, which do not provide enough root space, and the plants will soon become crowded, spindly and generally rather unhealthy looking.

Towards the end of the month harden off tender perennials so that they are ready for planting out once the threat of frosts has finally passed. Similarly, pre-planted baskets and containers can be hardened off and set in their summer positions.

Annual climbers should be well under way by now and it is time to start preparing their supports (see below)

SUPPORTING CLIMBERS

Climbers can be used to give height and structure to a border as well as being used to hide or decorate a wall or fence. Perennial climbers are, of course, fixed in one position, but the advantage of annual climbers is that they can be placed in different positions each year.

Against walls and fences it is best to have permanent supports, such as trellising or wires, but in the open garden temporary supports can be used, giving the option of moving them elsewhere for next year. If they are available, one of the simplest forms of support is peasticks. These are cut to the right height and pushed in the ground in a circle or straight line. Extra support can be obtained by tying the sticks together about 30cm (12in) from the top. When they are done with, shred both the sticks and the remains of the climber.

Make a longer lasting support, which can be used year after year, by wrapping wire netting around a strong post. For a row or temporary hedge, two or more posts can be used with the netting between them. Another alternative is a wigwam of canes with string wound between them to create a cone. Ready-prepared wigwams of woven willow can be purchased. These not only make good supports but are decorative in their own right. Not quite as attractive but certainly functional are the plastic supports that can be found in most garden centres.

Cobaea scandens, which is sometimes known as monastery bells and the cup and saucer vine, seen here supported on a willow framework, is a climbing annual that can easily be grown from seed.

ANNUAL CLIMBERS

Asarina
Cobaea scandens (monastery bells)
Convolvulus tricolor
Eccremocarpus
Ipomoea
Lablab purpureus (syn. *Dolichos lablab*)
Lathyrus odoratus (sweetpeas)
Rhodochiton
Thunbergia alata (black-eyed Susan)
Tropaeolum (nasturtiums)

BUYING ANNUALS

One advantage of growing your own annuals is that seed merchants offer a far greater range of plants than if you buy them ready germinated from your local nursery or garden centre. A look through just one seed catalogue will show the enormous range of annuals that is available, not only in terms of different species, but also in the number of cultivars and hybrids there are for each species. For example, you will probably have a choice of up to fifty different varieties of sweetpeas, pansies or petunias, whereas if you buy them as plants you may well be restricted to one variety of mixed colours. However, not everybody has either the facilities or the time to raise their own seed and the convenience of buying plants may far outweigh the wider choice of seed.

When you are buying annuals as plants, do not buy them too early, or you will have to look after them until it is time to plant them out. This month is early enough. The best plants are those that are not too crowded in their containers and are not too drawn or anaemic looking.

Always choose healthy plants, and remember that biggest is not always best – smaller plants that look as though they are full of potential are better and will soon catch up and overtake the bigger ones, which often take longer to settle down. Plants that are flowering furiously are not the best choice. Choose those that are still to flower. On the other hand, if you are seeking particular colours and have doubts as to which plant will produce which colour, go for those that have either one or just a few flowers open so that you can check the colour.

If the plants you buy are under cover at the nursery, harden them off when you get them home before you plant them out.

HARDENING OFF

Tender annuals that are have been grown in the greenhouse or have been recently purchased from nurseries where they were kept under cover will have to be hardened off before they are planted out. This process allows them to adjust gradually to the harsher climate in the open, where the temperature, especially at night, is lower than they are use to, and they have to get use to a drier atmosphere and to winds.

A coldframe is ideal for hardening off plants, but it is not essential. If you have a frame, open it slightly to start with, shutting it at night and then gradually, over a fortnight, open it further and for longer periods until the lights are left off completely.

If you have no coldframe, simply take the plants out into the open, returning them to the greenhouse or conservatory at night. Gradually leave them in the open for longer periods until they are able to stay outside all the time without showing signs of stress.

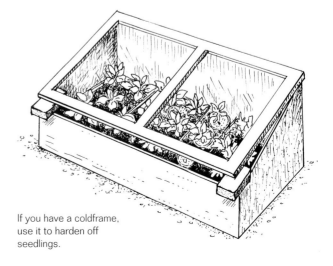

If you have a coldframe, use it to harden off seedlings.

BIENNIALS

Although it may seem a long way off, now is the time to sow seeds for next year's biennials, such as wallflowers and sweet williams. They should be sown in rows, in a seed bed if you have one, but the vegetable garden or a spare piece of ground will do. They can be sown in pots but because they will soon need planting out you might as well sow them directly into the soil – it will involve far less trouble. Thin as the seedlings appear and plant into their flowering position in the autumn, by which time they should be decent sized plants.

BULBS

Once the leaves on bulbs that have been planted in grass start to turn yellow and die back, it is time to mow the grass. Until then, leave that part of the lawn or meadow so that the leaves help the bulb to create stored energy for the following year.

Continue to remove foliage as it dies back. Lift tulips as they die back and store them away from the predations of mice until the autumn. Unless you need the ground, it is less trouble to leave them where they are.

If you want to raise more bulbs from seed, collect it as soon as it ripens. If you delay too long the seeds may well be shed.

If you did not plant dahlia tubers last month, do so now (p. 53).

GROWING BULBS FROM SEED

Unlike most other plants, bulb seedlings remain in their original pot for at least a year and often two or more years. This means that it is best to select a wide pot or a tray so that there is plenty of space in which to spread out the seed. Use a potting compost rather than a seed compost so that there is some fertilizer present, because the compost will not be changed until the seedlings are eventually potted on or planted out.

The seed of most bulbs is best sown while it is still fresh, so, in the absence of information to the contrary, sow all species as soon as you get it. Make certain that it is spread thinly over the surface of the compost, with plenty of space between each seed. The majority of bulbs produce large seeds, so this is not difficult to achieve. Cover the seeds with a 2mm (⅛in) layer of grit and, after watering, place in an open coldframe, preferably in the shade.

Do not allow the compost to dry out and make certain that, when the seedlings appear, you keep them growing by watering and feeding about once every three weeks. Leave the seedlings in the same pot until the bulbs have developed to a reasonable size, which is likely to take at least a year and probably longer. If you treat them like other plants and transplant them as soon as the seedlings appear, you will probably lose them. If you are likely to be planting the resulting bulbs into the open soil, after the first year it is possible to transfer the whole pot, without separating or disturbing the roots of the bulbs to the ground, but if you want to get big bulbs, keep them in the pot and keep watering and feeding.

One important point to remember when growing bulbs from seed is that cultivars of daffodils and tulips are unlikely to come true to the parent. Species, unless it is a variable species, will produce similar bulbs but the named varieties of the more popular bulbs are likely to be quite different. However, you never know your luck: while the majority will be inferior to the parent, occasionally you might be lucky and get a vastly improved form.

BULBS *in* FLOWER

Allium (decorative onions)
Camassia leichtlinii
Cyclamen repandum
Erythronium (dog-tooth violets)
Hermodactylis tuberosa (black widow iris)
Hyacinthoides non-scripta (bluebells)
Iris
Leucojum aestivum (summer snowflake)
Ornithogalum (star of Bethlehem)
Trillium grandiflorum (wake robin)
Tulipa (tulips)

FRUIT

Late frosts can still be a problem, especially as more fruit is coming into blossom this month. It is difficult to protect tree fruit but it is sometimes possible to throw netting or fleece over the smaller trees to save the blossom. Wall fruit is easier to protect using the methods described for last month (p. 54).

If fruit trees and bushes are inside a fruit cage, make certain that pollinating insects can get through the netting mesh. If necessary, remove the top or sides of the cage so that insects can enter freely. By this time bullfinches should not be causing too much damage.

Gooseberries (p. 168) are one of the first fruits to be produced, and some varieties are often big enough to pick by the end of this month. However, in years when the crop is prolific it is often a good idea to thin out some of the berries so that those that remain can fill out properly. Thin when the fruit is quite large, removing the largest of the berries, which can be cooked.

Towards the end of the month prepare strawberry beds by placing fresh, clean straw under plants to protect the fruit from the soil. If slugs are a problem put a little bait under the straw. Alternatively, use strawberry mats, which are slid under the plants. A more permanent arrangement can be made by laying polythene over the empty bed and planting the plants through slits, but this needs to be done when the bed is first created.

There should still be enough moisture in the soil from the winter and spring rains, but should the weather have been dry or if winds have dried out the soil, be prepared to water fruit bushes and trees from this month.

THE GREENHOUSE

Things should be beginning to warm up in the greenhouse, so make certain that there is plenty of ventilation (see below).

As the sun increases in its intensity, shading is also necessary from this month (p. 96). The heat from the sun and the flow of air will dry out the plants, so you must be sure that you water at least once a day from this point on. Occasionally, in overcast damp weather, it might not be necessary, but get into the habit of checking daily. If you are not at home during the day, an automatic irrigation system may be a help (p. 122).

Although it may seem late in the season, continue to sow a few annuals, because these will be very useful for filling gaps later in the year. Continue to prick out and pot on annuals and perennials sown earlier, and harden off plants that are ready to be moved outside (p. 75).

Aubergines, peppers, melons and cucumbers can now be planted in unheated greenhouses.

VENTILATION

When you are buying a greenhouse do not skimp on the number of opening windows. There are rarely enough in the standard models, and the cheaper ones often having only one. However, because modern greenhouses are modular, it is usually possible to buy extra opening lights. The usual form is a panel that opens upwards and is held on a stay. A modern alternative is louvred slats of glass. These have the advantage that they tend to keep pests out of the greenhouse, whereas they can often gain access through ordinary lights. Make certain that all the windows fit snugly because you do not want cold air entering on frosty nights when the lights are shut.

The windows may be positioned in the walls, at the end or in the roof of the greenhouse. In larger greenhouses there may be a door at each end, which will allow a through airflow. A combination of low side vents and high ones in the roof allows a constant flow of cool air in at the bottom and hot air out at the top. Not all the vents need be used at once – depending on the weather, use a combination that allows a free flow of air without creating gusting draughts.

Automatic opening devices can be attached to most types of vent. These can be adjusted to open at a particular temperature, which is very useful if you are not at home all day and are not, therefore, around to deal with a sudden change in weather conditions.

Animals and birds can be a nuisance in the greenhouse. Blackbirds will tear pots of alpines to shreds as they search for grubs and will soon put paid to a crop of grapes. Cats can find the warmth a great attraction and will snuggle down on top of your favourite plants. To deter unwelcome visitors, wire netting, attached direct or on wooden frames, can be fixed across all opening lights. Frames can also be made up for the doors if they are left open. It is often possible to hang a netting door opposite the main door so that it can be shut when the other is open.

The main types of greenhouse ventilation

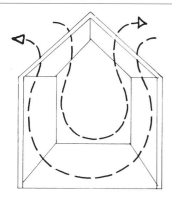

Vents in the roof permit air to circulate and escape.

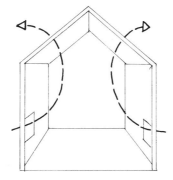

If there are windows in the sides, warm air will escape through vents in the roof while cooler air is drawn in lower down.

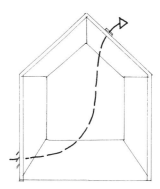

A more sophisticated system is to use fans to draw in cool air and extract warm air. The benefit of using such a system is that it can be fitted to a thermostat.

Peppers can easily be grown in a greenhouse, but given a warm spot they may also be grown outside. They can be grown in growing bags or in pots containing a good-quality potting compost.

AUBERGINES AND PEPPERS

Aubergines are tropical and subtropical plants and so need warm conditions in which to grow. They should not be planted out in the greenhouse until the temperature is constantly about 16–18°C (60–65°F). In heated greenhouses this can be earlier in the year. The seeds should be sown in early spring after being soaked in water for a day. Sow the seeds in a tray or in individual pots and place them in a propagator at about 18–20°C (65–8°). When they reach 10cm (4in) high, they can be planted into beds, 20cm (8in) pots or growing bags.

Pinch out the tops when they reach about 30–60cm (12–24in) high depending on variety, and support the plants with canes or strings if necessary. Water regularly and feed with a high-potash liquid fertilizer every two weeks once the fruits begin to form. Spray the plants once, preferably twice, a day with warm water to reduce the risk of red spider mites. Alternatively, keep humidity high by drenching the floor of the greenhouse with water once a day.

Sweet peppers and chilli peppers are grown in a similar way. These tend to be taller plants and should be stopped when they reach about 60cm (24in). Both types of pepper can be picked and used at either the green or the following red stage. Sweet peppers can also be yellow. Chilli peppers become hotter as they mature.

RECOMMENDED VARIETIES *of* AUBERGINE

'Bandera': white skin with maroon stripes
'Black Beauty'
'Black Enorma'
'Easter Egg': white skin
'Mini Bambino': small fruit
'Slice-Rite'

RECOMMENDED VARIETIES *of* SWEET PEPPER

'Ace'
'Big Bertha'
'Californian Wonder'
'Canape'
'Early Prolific'
'Gypsy'
'Jingle Bells': mini-pepper
'Jumbo Sweet'
'Minibelle': mini-pepper

RECOMMENDED VARIETIES *of* CHILLI PEPPER

'Anaheim': mild
'Chili Serrano': very hot
'Hero': very hot
'Hot Mexican': hot

LAWNS

The top priority from now on through to the autumn is mowing. Try to establish a regular routine (p. 97).

If you did not feed the lawn last month do it now. This is the month to apply weedkillers. A combination fertilizer/herbicide can be used or you can use separate applications (see below).

It is getting a bit late, but there is still time to sow or turf lawns, provided that any new area is kept well watered. Avoid using either method in hot sunny spells or when there are strong drying winds. If a period of a few damp, overcast days is forecast, take the opportunity to sow (p. 141) or to lay turves (p. 182).

In most areas there should not be any need to water, but in dry regions it may be necessary to start watering lawns this month. Never just give the lawns a light sprinkle; always water thoroughly, applying at least 2.5cm (1in).

LAWN WEEDS

This is the time of year when weeds are growing vigorously and are most receptive to the use of weedkillers. Lawn herbicides can either be granular or liquid. The granular form is mainly used in conjunction with lawn fertilizers and is spread at the same time. Liquid varieties are used on their own. If there are problems with just one kind of weed, it is most effective to use a liquid selective weedkiller that eradicates just that type of weed.

Whatever type you use, always follow the instructions on the bottle or packet. Most require at least six hours' dry weather after the application so that rain does not wash off the chemicals before the leaves have absorbed them, so always check the weather forecast before applying. Do not apply immediately after mowing the grass – wait for a few days for the leaf surfaces to develop again – and do not mow for several days after the application. Always apply evenly and do not over apply in the hope that the chemical will be more effective – the opposite is likely to be true. Use strings across the lawn to act as guides when you are applying the weedkiller. Sprayers can be hired for large areas, but for the average lawn the use of a watering can with a dribble bar is sufficient. Keep and mark the can for weedkiller applications only. You may need to re-apply the herbicide next month to be sure of exterminating the more persistent weeds, and if they are really stubborn, you may even require third or fourth applications.

When the weeds are in large patches it may be necessary to re-sow with seeds after the chemical has had its effect. Coarse grasses and larger weeds can be removed by hand.

DISCOLOURED PATCHES

Dogs urinating on grass will cause brown patches where the urea has burned and killed it off. Bitches have a stronger concentration of urea in their urine and are, therefore, more prone to leaving ugly scars on a lawn or grass path. There is little that can be done, except to train the dog to use other areas of the garden or to take it for regular walks so that it gets accustomed to urinating outside the garden. If you notice a dog urinating on the grass, apply water to the area immediately to prevent discoloration. Once the patch has been burned and the grass killed, you will have to cut out the offending patch and replace it, either by re-sowing or by laying a new piece of turf.

PERENNIALS

One of the most important jobs at this time of year is to make certain that any plants that are vulnerable to the wind are well supported. A few minutes spent now will save a lot of time later, as well as making a much better job of it because the plants will grow up and disguise the supports.

Perennial seeds will still be germinating from sowings made earlier in the year. Prick out the seedlings when they are large enough to handle. Those that have already been pricked out are likely to need potting on if they are fast growing. There is no need to keep perennials under glass longer than necessary, so harden them off at the earliest opportunity and move them outside. Under glass they are liable to get drawn and out of character, and they are also likely to be more prone to pests and diseases.

There is still time to sow perennials directly into the soil. This is a good method for plants of which you want large numbers.

Early-flowering perennials will be going over now, and it is time to begin what is, for many, one of the most tedious aspects of gardening – deadheading. Unless you want to collect the seeds, it is important that you remove any old flowerheads. This helps to keep the plant flowering over a long period and to preserve the plant's strength because seed production takes up a lot of energy.

GREEN TIP *Hand weeding*

The larger and more unsightly weeds, such as dandelions and plantains, can be removed by hand. Use a long pointed tool to dig out as much of the tap roots as possible. These plants are quite big, and a large bare patch will be left where each is removed. Fill the resulting hole with some loose soil, capping it with a small piece of matching turf. If you have no turf, fill the hole with soil, firm it down and then sow with grass seed.

STAKING PLANTS

Not all plants need staking, and in a well-protected garden it might be possible to get away with using virtually no supports at all. Planting close together also helps, as one clump of plants supports the next and prevents the wind finding an opening. However, if you wish to grow the full range of herbaceous perennials, it is likely that at least some staking will be inevitable.

The art of supporting plants is to apply the supports before they are needed. Once a plant's weight or the wind has made it flop over, it can never be propped up in a natural way. Another key to success is to do the staking early enough that the supports are covered by foliage and do not show. The basic idea is to put the support above the growing plant so that it grows through it in a natural way rather than putting the support around the already-grown plant, forcing all the stems into an unnatural clump, a bit in the manner of a corn stook.

There are a number of supports that can be used. Unfortunately, not everybody has access to peasticks, but if you can find a source, they make ideal supports for herbaceous plants. Place three or four around the edge of the emerging plant and bend over the twiggy top part to form a mesh about two-thirds of the eventual height of the plant. The twigs can be interwoven but the structure is more stable if it is tied together with string. The plant will grow up through the mesh and out through the sides of the sticks, so that the framework cannot be seen.

There are several ways of creating a similar effect. You can buy metal hoops that have a grid across them and wire supports that are pressed into the ground. The hoop should, again, be about two-thirds up the eventual height of the plant. For large areas you can push wooden stakes into the ground and support a wide mesh wire netting between them. Stakes with a cat's-cradle of string woven between them achieve the same effect. Another proprietary device is an inverted L-shaped piece of plastic-coated wire. A series of these shapes can be linked into a circle around the outside of the plant. To provide better support, a few can be linked across the circle.

All of the above methods allow the stems of the plant to move in a natural manner but at the same time restrict movement sufficiently to stop the stems being bowed over by the wind, weight of rain water or heavy flowerheads.

The stems of tall plants, such as delphiniums, can be individually supported by canes, sticks or proprietary plastic or metal posts to which the stem is tied directly. Some proprietary methods involve a plastic loop that goes

round the plant, but discreetly tied string is often best. Push the post in behind the stem so that it is at least partially hidden and avoid using posts that are longer than the ultimate height of the stem.

Staking plants

Before the plant starts into growth, press the legs of a proprietary ring stake into the ground so that the shoots and foliage will grow up through, and eventually hide, the grid.

Link stakes are L-shaped pieces of metal that can be joined together to accommodate quite large plants.

A single cane is suitable for a tall-stemmed plant such as a delphinium.

Peasticks or a circle of canes can be linked by garden twine to provide support for plants that would otherwise flop over.

SHORTENING PLANTS

If you find that some plants grow too tall for your garden or for a particular border, then, strange as it may seem, it is often possible to shorten them. By this time of year plants such as Michaelmas daisies (*Aster*) may have grown to 30cm (12in) or so. If they are cut to the ground now they will start to regrow, but they will flower at the usual time, by when they will not have regained all the growth they have lost and will be much shorter. Not all perennials will respond to this treatment, but a surprising number will.

SOME PERENNIALS *that* NEED STAKING

Achillea (yarrow)
Alcea rosea (hollyhock)
Aster (some)
Campanula (bellflowers)
Centaurea
Eryngium (sea hollies) (some)
Geranium (some)
Helenium
Heliopsis
Knautia macedonica
Leucanthemella × *superba* (shasta daisy)
Nepeta (catmints)
Paeonia (peonies) (some)
Papaver orientalis (oriental poppy)
Sanguisorba (some)
Sedum (stonecrops) (some)
Solidago (golden rods)

Keep an eye on pots of seeds and prick out any that germinate. Pot on any that have already been pricked out and that have outgrown their container.

TUFA

Tufa is a porous rock that has a special place in the rock garden because plants can be planted directly into it, and it creates an environment within which the most delicate and often most difficult plants can be grown. Many alpine gardeners believe that it can form one of the most attractive features of a garden.

The rock is formed when mineral-rich water pours over moss. The minerals coat the moss with a 'scale', rather like the inside of a kettle. The moss is killed, but another layer grows on top, which, in turn, filters out the minerals, and so on until large rocks are formed. It is a limy rock but the lime seems to be bound up as quite a number of lime-hating plants will grow in it. Tufa is usually sold by weight, so buy it in dry weather or you will also have to pay for all

🍃 ROCK GARDENS

Although it may seem early in the year, seeds are already ripening on some plants – anemones, for example – and a careful eye must be kept out if you wish to collect them. The process will go on right through to the autumn. It takes a little time to collect and clean seeds, but the effort is usually worth while, especially since seeds of many alpine and rock garden plants are not available from the usual seed merchants (p. 101).

If you do not require seeds, deadhead the flowers as they go over. This not only preserves energy as seeds are not formed, but it also prevents rotting flowers being left on the plant, which, especially with cushion plants, can cause further parts of the plant to rot and die. Some plants, such as aubrieta and alyssum, can be clipped over with your shears to remove the lanky growth and neaten the plants.

Because they are free-draining, rock gardens can dry out very quickly, so remember to water regularly in any prolonged period without rain.

A rock garden bearing a colourful spring display of plants, including *Aubrieta*, *Aurinia* (syn. *Alyssum*) and miniature *Phlox*. The shrubs provide a permanent structure.

the rain water it has absorbed. When it is dry it is surprisingly light and a large lump can be easily carried.

Position it so that the base is in contact with soil and preferably with up to one-fifth of it buried. This will help to keep moisture in the rock. Drill or carve holes with an old chisel in a few selected places. Ease a seedling into the hole and trickle compost in around the roots. Keep watered until the plant is established.

PLANTS *for* TUFA

Androsace

Arenaria tetraquetra

Campanula fenestrellata; C. piper; C. tommasiniana;
    C. zoysii

Dianthus

Edrianthus pumilio

Eritrichium nanum

Paraqualegia anemonoides

Physoplexus comosa

Ramonda nathaliae

Saxifraga

Viola cazorlensis; V. delphinantha

 # TREES AND SHRUBS

A number of shrubs will have finished flowering by now, and these should be pruned (p. 65). Hedges are coming into full growth and may begin to start looking a bit unkempt (p. 83).

If the weather is still mild and damp at the beginning of the month, there is time to finish planting trees and shrubs. However, once it starts getting hot and the winds are drying, it is certainly too late for bare-rooted trees and shrubs, and, even though container shrubs can still be planted, they should be given plenty of aftercare to ensure that they get off to a good start.

Pests, like gardeners, appreciate the increasingly pleasant weather and their numbers start to build up. Keep an eye out for problems and take the appropriate action to deal with them.

Softwood cuttings can be taken from the tips of new wood of some shrubs. This is the equivalent of taking basal cuttings from perennials (p. 61). Take the top 5–10cm (2–4in) of the soft growth and remove all but the top two leaves. Cut through the stem just beneath a node (where the leaf joins the stem). Place it in a pot of cutting compost, which should be put into a heated propagator if you have one or in a polythene bag kept in a warm, light place. Harden off and pot up once the cutting has rooted. Firmer cuttings, known as greenwood cuttings, can also be taken at this time of year. Instead of still being soft, these cuttings are beginning to harden at the base. Treat as for softwood cuttings.

Climbers are beginning to romp away as the conditions warm up. Many have tendrils and will become self-clinging, but others need to be tied in as they grow, otherwise they will thrash around in the wind and damage not only themselves but also other plants.

SHRUBS *from* SOFTWOOD *and* GREENWOOD CUTTINGS

Abelia

Abutilon

Calluna

Caryopteris

Ceratostigma

Cestrum

Cotinus

Daphne × burkwoodii

Enkianthus

Erica

Forsythia

Fuchsia

Hydrangea

Lantana

Lavandula

Lavatera

Perovskia

Philadelphus

Potentilla

Salix

Salvia

CLIPPING HEDGES

There are several reasons why it is essential to cut hedges regularly. A neat hedge always contributes greatly to the overall appearance of a garden. Let it grow untidy and immediately the garden will also look unkempt, even if it is not. Once a hedge is allowed to grow away, it is very difficult to restore it, and if a hedge does outgrow its original size, it often opens up, leaving gaps for both animals and wind to enter, as well as losing its ability to create privacy.

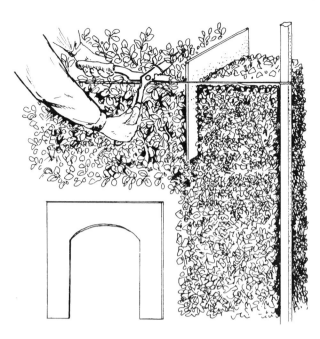

It can be helpful to use a template when you are cutting a hedge so that you achieve an even profile throughout the length.

Regular clipping amounts at most to three cuts a year, and possibly only one if the hedge is of yew, beech or hornbeam.

Shears, hedge trimmers or secateurs can be used. Shears are used where greater control is needed, especially if there are shapes to cut round. Secateurs are to be preferred for large-leafed shrubs, such as laurel. An electric hedge cutter is limited by the length of its power lead but it is possible to run them off small generators or to have petrol-driven machines. The latter are heavier than the electric models, but they tend to be more powerful when dealing with overgrown hedges.

Shape the hedge so that it is thinner at the top than at the bottom. This will help with stability, preventing wind or snow from opening up the top and permanently damaging it. If you want to have a really formal look to the hedge, use lines and a template to create a perfect shape each time. Use self-supporting steps rather than a ladder to reach high hedges, because the pressure of the ladder will deform the hedge and make it impossible for you to obtain a regular shape. For a very high hedge, use a ladder with a plank fastened across it to spread the load.

Use secateurs to cut large-leafed hedges, removing one stem at a time. If you use shears or a hedge trimmer you will cut leaves in half, which leads to the hedge looking very ugly. This gets worse as the cut edges of the leaves soon turn brown.

RENOVATING AN OVERGROWN HEDGE

Most overgrown hedges can be brought back to a neat formal shape over a period of two or more years. Bear in mind, however, that lavender, Lawson's cypress, Leyland cypress and thuja are all reluctant to break from old wood and should therefore be scrapped and a new hedge started. Yew responds well to treatment and after a few years will have fully recovered.

In the first year cut down one side of the hedge, cutting it back to beyond the thickness required. If the hedge is to be much thinner, cut the top at the same time. Cut the other side of the hedge as normal. This will leave enough leaves to produce energy for regrowth. Once the first side has grown out to the required size and has thickened up, trim this as usual and cut back the other side as severely as you originally did with the first. When this has grown back sufficiently, start trimming it as normal. If it is a wide hedge do it in three stages – one side, the top and then the other side. Yew may take two or more years for each side to recover, but faster growing hedges may only take a year.

Restoring a hedge

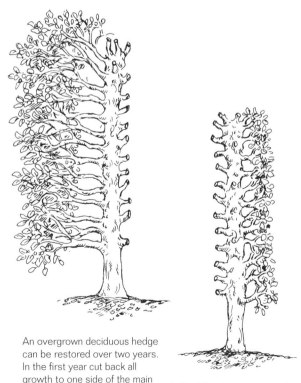

An overgrown deciduous hedge can be restored over two years. In the first year cut back all growth to one side of the main stem.

In the following year, repeat the process on the other side.

WHEN *to* CLIP HEDGES

Buxus (box): late spring and late summer

Carpinus betulus (hornbeam): mid- to late summer

Chamaecyparis lawsoniana (Lawson's cypress): late spring and late summer

Crataegus (quick-set thorn): early summer and early autumn

× *Cupressocyparis leylandii* (Leyland cypress): late spring, midsummer and early autumn

Fagus sylvatica (beech): mid- to late summer

Ilex (holly): late summer

Lavandula (lavender): spring to early autumn

Ligustrum (privet): late spring, midsummer and early autumn

Lonicera nitida (poor man's box): late spring, midsummer and early autumn

Prunus laurocerasus (laurel): mid-spring and late summer

Prunus lusitanicus (Portugal laurel): mid-spring and late summer

Taxus (yew): mid- to late summer

Thuja plicata (thuja): late spring and early autumn

GREEN TIP

Hedge clippings

Do not burn hedge trimmings, shred them. After two to three months in a compost heap they will make an ideal mulch to place along the hedge to feed it, preserve moisture and keep down the weeds.

VEGETABLES

Towards the end of this month the threat of late frosts should diminish and it should be possible to sow tender vegetables, such as beans and courgettes, in the open. If they start to appear through the soil and there is forecast of a frost, cover them with fleece or drape newspaper over the row. Remove these as soon as the frost lifts.

Also towards the end of the month, once the frosts are passed, plants of tender vegetables that have been sown under glass can be planted out. Make certain that they are hardened off before they are planted. Tender herbs, such as basil, can also be planted out at this time of year.

Continue to sow successional crops at fortnightly intervals throughout the month.

As the season warms up pests are likely to increase in numbers. Keep an eye out for them and take appropriate action. Blackfly on broad beans is one of the big problems at this time of year. One way of coping with this is to take preventative action and remove the succulent tips of the plants on which the aphids congregate. The best time for pinching out the tips is when the plant is in full flower.

TENDER VEGETABLES

Sow the following after frosts have finished or sow them under glass and plant out after threat of frost has passed: aubergines, celeriac, celery, courgettes, cucumbers, French beans, marrows, melons, peppers, pumpkins, runner beans, squashes and tomatoes.

THINNING SEEDLINGS

It is essential that seedlings and eventually plants do not become too crowded. Overcrowded plants become spindly and do not develop correctly. They are usually malnourished and are frequently more prone to disease than plants that have space around them to grow properly. Remove unwanted seedlings as soon as possible. Choose a day when the soil is moist but not ringing wet. If the soil is crumbly, the unwanted plants can be pulled out of the ground, leaving the healthiest ones undisturbed. Some gardeners prefer to break off or cut the stem of the unwanted seedling at ground level, leaving the roots behind so that the other plants are not disturbed. Others prefer not to do this as they do not like the idea of the rotting remains next to healthy plants.

Carrots are always a problem because the smell of the bruised leaves and stems travel a long way and can attract the carrot root fly to the remaining plants, where they soon make their unwelcome home. The best way to avoid this is to sow very thinly in the first place, then there is less thinning to do. Another point to remember is to carry out the thinning in muggy, windless weather when the tell-tale smell does not travel far. Bury the thinnings on the compost heap to mask the smell.

Thinning Distances

beetroot	7.5–10cm (3–4in)
broad beans	23cm (9in)
carrots	7.5cm (3in)
dwarf French beans	20cm (8in)
fennel	25cm (10in)
kohl rabi	20cm (8in)
lettuce	23cm (9in)
parsley	15cm (6in)
peas	5cm (2in)
parsnips	15–20cm (6–8in)
radishes	2.5–5cm (1–2in)
runner beans	25–30cm (10–12in)
salsify	15cm (6in)
scorzonera	15cm (6in)
spinach	15cm (6in)
spring onions	2.5cm (1in)
swedes	30cm (12in)
swiss chard	30cm (12in)
turnips	15cm (6in)

See also Planting Distances (p. 88).

DEEP BEDS

Most gardeners still grow their vegetables in rows with a narrow path between each to give access for tending and harvesting. In recent years, however, a system based on square or rectangular beds has been finding favour. It is not a new idea by any means, having been around for centuries in different parts of the world.

It has several advantages over the more conventional method. For a start, the plants are grown in blocks, with the result that less space is wasted with paths. Second, the soil is deeply dug, which encourages the plants to send down deep roots, and this has the advantage that plants are generally grown closer together, thus giving weeds less chance to germinate. Deep beds are often raised, which means that they drain quickly, while the incorporation of plenty of organic material ensures that it still retains sufficient moisture for the plants. The last advantage is that once the bed is established, little or no digging is required. The gardener does not walk on the bed and so there is no compaction of the soil.

The beds should not be too large – it must be possible to reach the vegetables without standing on the soil. A good size for each plot is about 1.2m (4ft) wide, with the length being as long as you like. It can be the width of the vegetable garden or it can be divided up into smaller plots, one for each vegetable. Double dig the bed (p. 25),

Runner beans are an easy crop to grow and produce a plentiful crop over a long period. Prepare the ground well in advance and keep it well-watered for the best results.

incorporating as much well-rotted organic material as possible. This will help to build a good structure in the soil as well as providing nutrients and improving water retention for the plants.

Once dug, the bed will be higher than the surrounding soil, partly because it is now broken up and partly because of the bulk of organic matter that has been added. As more is added over the years, so the bed becomes higher, making it even deeper and more free draining. If your garden has very poor subsoil – solid clay, for example – rather than spend years getting it into shape, you can build up the beds from the start, surrounding each with a low wall of brick or wood. Fill the beds with a mixture of good quality topsoil and garden compost.

Once dug and as long as the soil is not compacted, the top 5cm (2in) or so can be loosened with a rake or hoe before planting – rake some bonemeal into it as you do this – and cover the whole with a 5–7.5cm (2–3in) layer of well-rotted garden compost or manure at least once a year.

Sow seeds in short rows or by broadcasting over a block. Although rows can be used, there should be several of them so that the resulting plants are in a block. When thinning, the plants can be much closer than in conventional planting.

Weed regularly. Because the plants are close together, the weeds will have to be removed by hand rather than with a hoe. However, once the plants mature they should prevent any further weed seedlings appearing. Because only the very top layer of the soil is disturbed, weed seeds further down in the ground will not be brought to the surface, and after a few years there should be fewer seeds left at the surface to germinate. This, of course, depends on any garden compost or manure that is used as a top dressing, being free of weed seed.

RUNNER BEANS

The returns from growing runner beans are always high, both in quantity and in flavour, and, although they can take up quite a bit of space, they are a very popular crop. Dwarf varieties need no supports, but the more traditional climbing varieties are still the most popular. As the beans get older they tend to become more stringy, and to overcome this several 'stringless' varieties have been bred. Runner beans are attractive plants and as well as growing them in the vegetable garden they are also sometimes grown in a more prominent position, such as in a flower border. The typical plants have scarlet flowers, but some have white or pink flowers and some even have a mixture of white and red flowers.

Dig a trench in the autumn, place a layer of well-rotted manure in the bottom and then refill. Spring is the time to erect the support that the growing plants will need. This can be a row of poles (or canes), netting supported on a framework or vertical strings supported on a framework. A method using far less space is to grow them up a wigwam, made from poles or by strings. The vertical supports should be about 25–30cm (10–12in) apart.

When all threat of spring frosts has passed, plant two seeds at each support. If both seeds germinate, remove the weaker of the two, using it to fill in gaps if necessary. Seedlings can also be started by sowing seeds in individual pots in the greenhouse. Sow more seeds two or three weeks later to get a second and later crop.

Water well once the flowers appear. Mulching helps to keep in the moisture and the organic material in the soil

Supporting beans

Runner beans can be supported on a net supported between two canes.

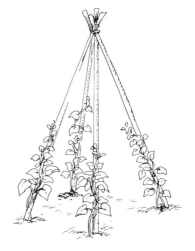

A traditional wigwam of canes is ideal for French beans, with one plant growing at the base of each cane.

Make a double row of canes, about 30cm (12in) apart, more stable by tying in a horizontal cane across the top.

will help to keep the roots moist. Slugs can be a nuisance when the seedlings first appear, and they are capable of grazing off the entire bed of shoots.

Pick the beans as soon as they are large enough. Do not let them get too big or they will be tough and stringy. The excess can be frozen. Allow some pods to grow to maturity if you want to collect your own seed. Leave them until they turn brown, hang them in a dry, airy place until they are brittle, then remove the seed.

Dwarf, bush varieties are grown in the same way except there is, obviously, no need for a supporting framework.

RECOMMENDED VARIETIES *of* RUNNER BEAN

'Achievement'
'Butler': stringless
'Crusader'
'Desiree': white flowered, stringless
'Enorma'
'Gulliver': dwarf
'Hammond's Dwarf Scarlet': dwarf
'Ivanhoe'
'Kelvedon Wonder'
'Lady Di': stringless
'Painted Lady'
'Pickwick': dwarf, stringless
'Polestar': stringless
'Red Knight': stringless
'Red Rum'
'Royal Standard': stringless
'Scarlet Emperor'
'Streamline'
'White Emergo': white flowered

BEETROOT

Beetroot is at its best when it is young and succulent, but it can be stored for winter use and makes a valuable addition to the choice of vegetables at that time of year. There are several types, many depending on colour, with golden and white varieties as well as the more standard red. There are also cylindrical beetroot, which will give more even slices when prepared. Beetroot has a habit of bolting (going to seed early), and several varieties have been bred especially to reduce this, while some growers have produced small varieties, which are very succulent.

They like a sunny site and a light, well-drained but fertile soil. Do not use freshly manured ground. Sow

where they are to grow in shallow drills. Sow thinly and once the seedlings are large enough to handle, thin to 7.5–10cm (3–4in). They are slow to germinate, but this can be speeded up by soaking the seeds in warm water for an hour before sowing.

Do not let the soil dry out, otherwise a sudden return to moist conditions is likely to split the roots. Harvest as and when they are ready and wanted. In well-drained soil they may be left in the ground during the winter and lifted as required, but in heavier conditions and where the weather is cold it is safer to lift them and store them in trays of damp sand.

RECOMMENDED VARIETIES *of* BEETROOT

'Action': miniature
'Albina Verduna': white flesh
'Boltardy'
'Burpee's Golden': gold flesh
'Cheltenham Green Top'
'Cylindrica'
'Detroit – Little Ball': miniature
'Monodet'
'Monogram'
'Monopoly'
'Motown'
'Red Ace'
'Tardel': miniature

KALE

Kale is a very valuable vegetable as a winter stop-gap. The plants are hardy and can be left to stand throughout the coldest months, providing a continuous supply of leaves, but they can also be grown for summer use.

Kale likes a sunny position and a fertile soil, preferably one that has had organic material added to it for a previous crop. The seeds can be sown in the open ground, either in seed beds and then transplanted or where they are to grow. They can also be sown in pots under glass. Sow last month or this for summer crops, and next month for autumn and winter crops. When you are transplanting, set the plants at intervals of about 60cm (24in). In colder areas it can be a good idea to grow dwarf varieties, which can be covered with cloches during the worst of the weather. These varieties should be planted about 45cm (18in) apart. All types of kale may need net protection against pigeons and pheasants.

Rhubarb is used in a wide variety of culinary dishes. It is easy to grow and can be left in the same position for several years, without the need for more attention than top dressing with well-rotted organic mulch.

Planting Distances

Plants that have been grown under glass or in nursery beds, as opposed to being sown directly in their cropping position, need to be planted at the correct distance apart to prevent overcrowding.

asparagus	30–38cm (12–15in)
aubergines	60cm (24in)
broccoli	60cm (24in)
Brussels sprouts	50–75cm (20–30in)
cabbages	30–50cm (12–20in)
calabrese	15–23cm (6–9in)
cauliflowers	50–75cm (20–30in)
celeriac	30–38cm (12–15in)
celery	23–30cm (9–12in)
courgettes	60cm (24in)
cucumbers	60cm (24in)
garlic	15cm (6in)
globe artichokes	75cm (30in)
Jerusalem artichokes	30cm (12in)
kale	45cm (18in)
leeks	15cm (6in)
marrows	60cm (24in)
onion sets	10cm (4in)
peppers	45–60cm (18–24in)
potatoes	30–38cm (12–15in)
pumpkins	90–180cm (36–72in)
rhubarb	75–90cm (30–36in)
runner beans	25–30cm (10–12in)
seakale	30cm (12in)
shallots	15–17.5cm (6–7in)
sweetcorn	30cm (12in)
tomatoes	60cm (24in)

RECOMMENDED VARIETIES *of* KALE

'Cottagers'
'Dwarf Blue Curled Scotch'
'Dwarf Green Curled'
'Fribor'
'Frosty'
'Hungry Gap'
'Pentland Brig'
'Tall Green Curled'
'Thousandhead'

Beetroot comes in various colours, including rich red, gold, white and even stripes. It should be harvested when still relatively small. These have reached their maximum useful size.

WATER FEATURES

As the water in the pond begins to warm up, so its plants come into growth. Now is a good time for planting.

When you are choosing plants for a pond, the depth of water has to be taken into account. There are three basic categories: those that like deep water, those that prefer shallow water, and those that live in the muddy margins of the pond. Check carefully on the label of the plants to see what depth is required. If a little thought went into the pond's construction, it should have ledges around the edge so that it can accommodate all three categories.

In a natural pond, the plants can, of course, be planted directly into the muddy bottom or sides, but this is obviously impossible in one that has a liner or that is made of plastic or concrete. However, it is quite a simple task to plant even these ponds – the answer is to put the plants into pots.

The pots that are used are not the conventional ones, but ones that have mesh or lattice sides to them, making them more like a basket than a pot. This allows water to pass through the compost and also allows the plant's roots to spread out into the water and the surrounding ooze.

The baskets are lined with hessian sacking or with a special liner to prevent the soil from washing out. The planting medium that is used is garden soil or special compost, which can be obtained from specialist nurseries or the larger garden centres. If the compost contains peat or a peat substitute, there is the problem that, because it is lighter than water, it will float away, leaving the plant bare-rooted. Garden soil is heavy enough to stay put. It is not generally recommended that potting compost is used because this contains not only a lot of organic material but also fertilizer, which will encourage the formation of algae, the last thing most gardeners want in their ponds. If you have to use a compost with peat or other similar material in it, cover the top of the compost, after planting, with a 2.5cm (1in) layer of grit to prevent anything from floating away.

Plant the plant in the container in the same way as you would a terrestrial plant and place it in the appropriate depth of water. While it is easy to put plants round the margins of the pool it is not so easy to site them in the middle. There is one ingenious way of doing this. Thread two long strings through either side of the basket and then

Run lengths of string under a basket so that the string can be easily removed when the plant has been positioned in the pond. If the pond is large, will be easier if two people stand at opposite sides to hold the ends of the strings.

two people, one at each end of the pair of strings, walk to opposite sides of the pond with the basket suspended between them. When the plant is in the right position the basket is lowered into the water. One person releases the strings, and the other pulls them out of the lattice sides and out of the pond.

If the water is deep and the plant young, place some heavy blocks in the water and put the basket on top, taking away one block at a time as the plant grows, until it is eventually sitting on the bottom of the pond.

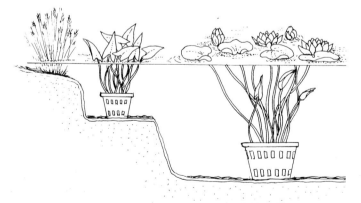

A pond with ledges will be able to accommodate all three types of water plant.

JUNE

This is one of the best months in the garden, and it is a joy to be working there. The air is warm and the is ground firm but, with luck, still full of moisture, which it is passing on to the quickly growing plants. Everywhere there are signs of life. The borders are full of early summer perennials, and everything has a fresh look about it. The colours are clear, and the foliage is at its best.

There should be no danger of frosts now, and tender plants can be moved outside. This applies both to annuals for beds and containers and to tender vegetables, such as French beans.

Although the season seems to have only just begun, the garden should already be giving its rewards. Broad beans should be ready in the vegetable garden soon, and gooseberries are heading the list of fruit that should be ripening over the next few months.

Try to keep on top of chores, such as weeding and mowing the lawn, but at the same time you should begin to think ahead for next year, so that you can start preparations in time. This is particularly important if you will need a lot of plants or if you need to prepare new beds. It is a good idea to go round the garden at least once every month just to see if there are any improvements you can make next year. Now is the time to think about these changes, not in winter when it is difficult to visualize the borders in flower.

CHECKLIST

General

- Water when necessary (p. 92)
- Keep control of weeds (p. 92)
- Watch out for pests and diseases and take appropriate action (p. 98)

Annuals and Tender Perennials

- Finish planting out tender annuals and perennials (p. 92)
- Plant up outside baskets and containers (p. 51)
- Fill gaps among perennials (p. 98)
- Move out ready-prepared baskets and containers (p. 51)
- Clear away spring annuals, such as forget-me-nots (p. 92)
- Water in dry weather (p. 92)
- Sow biennials (p. 75)

Bulbs

- Cut grass around naturalized bulbs (p. 60)
- Collect seeds from spring bulbs (p. 76)
- Remove dead foliage of late-spring bulbs (p. 52)
- Lift and either divide and replant or store spring bulbs (p. 94)
- Plant autumn-flowering bulbs (p. 154)
- Check for pests, especially lily beetle (p. 94)

Fruit

- Net all soft fruit against birds (p. 54)
- Spread straw mulch under strawberry plants (p. 76)
- Pick early gooseberries, raspberries, strawberries and white- and redcurrants (p. 95)
- Peg down strawberry runners to form new plants (p. 95)

- Tie in new blackberry, loganberry and tayberry canes (p. 95)
- Thin tree fruits if necessary (p. 95)
- Pinch out shoots and tie in wall-trained fruit (p. 95)
- Start summer pruning of trained soft fruit (p. 95)

Greenhouse

- Make sure the greenhouse is adequately shaded (p. 96) and ventilated (p. 77)
- In hot weather dampen the floor to cool and humidify the greenhouse (p. 96)
- Pinch out and tie in tomatoes, cucumbers and melons (p. 96)
- Water plants at least once a day and feed once a week (p. 96)
- Thin out bunches of grapes (p. 96)

Lawns

- Mow regularly, but not closely or too frequently if the weather is dry (p. 78)
- Water thoroughly if necessary (p. 113)
- Prepare sites for new lawns (p. 141)

Perennials

- Deadhead flowers as they go over (p. 79)
- Check that all plants that need supporting are supported (p. 80)
- Watch out for pests and diseases and take appropriate action (p. 98)
- Fill any unexpected gaps with annuals (p. 98)
- Water as necessary (p. 98)
- Pot on spring-sown perennials (p. 37)

Rock Gardens

- Collect and sow seeds as required (p. 101)
- Deadhead and cut back spring-flowering plants (p. 101)
- Shear over aubrieta and alyssum when they have finished blooming (p. 101)
- Plant container-grown plants and keep watered (p. 41)
- Remove weeds on sight (p. 63)
- Take soft cuttings (p. 101)
- Pot on seedlings (p. 101)

Trees and Shrubs

- Plant container-grown trees and shrubs and keep well watered (p. 102)
- Check that ties are not cutting into growing trees (p. 102)
- Remove suckers (p. 102)
- Deadhead spring-flowering shrubs (p. 102)
- Prune spring-flowering shrubs (p. 65)
- Cut hedges as necessary (p. 82)
- Trim topiary as necessary (p. 102)

Vegetables

- Continue successional sowing of vegetables (p. 44)
- Plant out tender vegetables if you have not already done so (p. 84)
- Sow swedes (p. 105)
- Plant outside tomatoes if you have not already done so (p. 84)
- Plant out autumn and winter brassicas (p. 103)
- Plant out leeks (p. 103)
- Earth up potatoes (p. 44)
- Lift early potatoes as required (p. 44)

ANNUALS

By now it should be quite safe to plant out tender bedding plants and to bring out any prepared containers. Before planting out, always harden off the plants thoroughly (p. 75). If you fail to do so, you will at best check the plants and at worst kill them.

As well as bringing out the new plants, the change of seasons heralds the time to remove the old. The early annuals, such as forget-me-nots, are finished now and should be removed as soon as possible. If you leave them too long they will not only seed everywhere but will also create large holes in the border when they are removed because the other plants will have grown up around them. If you remove them as soon as they have finished flowering, the emerging plants will more readily fill the gaps or, at least, soften the edges so that the gaps are not quite so obvious. The gaps themselves can be filled with new bedding plants.

Annuals tend to be in continuous growth and are constantly in flower. This means that they use copious quantities of water in their development stage. For the best displays, make sure that they do not ever dry out and water them whenever necessary. In dry soils many annuals will look very sparse and they may flower themselves to death.

Keep an eye out for weeds, especially in the first few weeks when the plants are still developing. Once the annuals are fully grown they are likely to merge, forming a living mulch that should help prevent further weeds from germinating.

If you have not already done so, there is still time to sow biennials for flowering next year. Wallflowers, sweet williams and foxgloves are examples of the type of plant that can be sown, preferably in rows, in a spare piece of ground or in the vegetable patch, ready for planting in their permanent positions in the autumn.

BEDDING SCHEMES

Bedding schemes are not as popular as they once were, possibly because mixed borders, especially those with perennials and shrubs, are now more in favour. Many gardeners, however, still like to have whole beds of annual bedding plants, which provide a colourful show over a long period. Although it is possible to use subtle colour schemes, there is a tendency for them to be bright and cheerful in a way that perennials can never be.

Petunias have always been good bedding plants, and the trailing varieties for hanging baskets have given them a new lease of life.

ANNUALS *for* BEDDING

Ageratum
Alyssum
Calendula (pot marigolds)
Callistephus (Chinese asters)
Centaurea cyanus (cornflowers)
Dahlia
Dianthus chinesis (Chinese pinks)
Heliotropium (heliotrope, cherry pie)
Impatiens (busy lizzies)
Lobelia
Nemisia
Nicotiana (tobacco plant)
Pelargonium
Petunia
Phlox drummondii
Salvia
Silene pendula
Tagetes (French and African marigolds)
Verbena
Viola × wittrockiana (pansies)
Zinnia

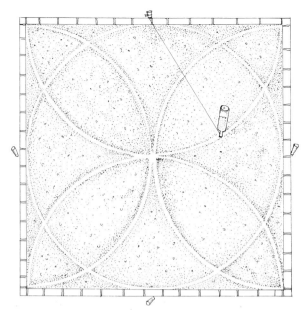

It is best to marked out complicated bedding schemes with sharp sand. Smooth curves can be achieved by attaching a length of string to a peg and tying the other end of the string to a container of sand, so that it can trickle out in an even line.

Lilies are always eye-catchers as summer-flowering bulbs. There are many types from which to choose, including this *Lilium pyrenaicum*.

Whole beds can be planted in blocks or in patterns. The patterns are best exemplified by municipal planting schemes, which at times can be quite intricate – a city's coat of arms, for example. While the average gardener would probably not want to create anything as complicated as this, using bedding plants provides an opportunity for gardeners to give their imaginations free rein.

The least complicated designs simply involve filling a bed with just one subject – red salvias, for example. A slightly more interesting bed can be created by using two different plants – red and blue salvias, for example – laid out in blocks or intermixed. Mixing colours creates a 'busy' scene that, while exciting, is not very restful on the eye. Blocks of vibrant colours are still exciting but not as distracting to look at. An alternative to several blocks is to use a main block of one colour, outlined with another. The combinations are endless. For something really eye-catching, a pattern can be created using several different colours and heights of bedding plant. One former favourite, which is not as frequently seen these days, is the floral clock.

Planning for bedding schemes, either simple or complicated, should be undertaken in the drab days of winter. It can be fun to sit down with some graph paper and work out your scheme using coloured pencils. Next, match the colours with appropriate plants and order the relevant seed. When you are planning, do not forget to think in three dimensions as well as in colour. The eventual height of the plants is important.

Raise plenty of plants, preferably more than you will need, as you are likely to need a few spares to fill in gaps where the odd plant dies or is the wrong colour. Any left-over plants can always be given away. Prepare the bed in the autumn and give it a quick fork over in spring. Some complicated designs are easier to appreciate if the bed is made on a slope, with the back higher than the front.

When it gets to planting time, outline your plan on the bed using silver sand (p. 50). Fill a plastic bottle with the sand and let it trickle out onto the bed as if you were drawing the outlines with a pencil. Finally, plant up your scheme, watering as you go.

ANNUALS *for* BEES

It is always worth encouraging honey bees to visit the garden, even if you are not a bee-keeper, anxious to provide the maximum amount of food for your charges. Bees help to pollinate the flowers that produce fruit and vegetables and seeds on ornamental plants. Besides, this there is nothing more evocative of a peaceful summer's day in a garden than the hum of busy bees.

> *Asperula*
> *Bartonia aurea*
> *Borago officinalis* (borage)
> *Centaurea cyanus* (cornflower); *C. moschata* (sweet sultan)
> *Cerinthe major*
> *Clarkia*
> *Collinsia bicolor*
> *Cynoglossum*
> *Dracocephalum moldavica*
> *Echium*
> *Iberis* (candytuft)
> *Linaria* (toad flax)
> *Lobularia maritima* (sweet alyssum)
> *Nigella damascena* (love-in-a-mist)
> *Phacelia*
> *Rudbeckia*
> *Salvia hormium*
> *Scabiosa*

BULBS

The leaves of most naturalized bulbs will have died back by now, and it is time to cut the grass in which they are growing. Leave it any longer and the grass will grow rank and difficult to cut. However, if you want to collect any seed, remember to do so before you cut the plants back.

Lift spring bulbs such as daffodils and tulips if they are in the way. Clean off any soil, dry them off, remove any dead scales and then store them in a cool, dry place away from mice or squirrels. If they are not a nuisance where they are, leave them.

One of the worst scourges that bulbs face is the lily beetle. Fortunately, it is restricted to lilies and fritillaria, but it can devastate these beautiful plants. Keep an eye out for the beetles and destroy them as soon as you see them. They are bright red and show up very well. It is the grubs, which are like bird droppings, that do the damage, however. It is possible to spray against the insects, but the slimy coating of the grubs protects them. Picking them off by hand is the most effective line of attack.

BULBS IN THE BORDER

In the earlier part of the year, bulbs form the most conspicuous part of the garden, shining with all their brilliance against the other emerging plants. By the time the summer has arrived, herbaceous plants and trees and shrubs are taking over the main role, while bulbs are slipping into second place. They still have an important role to play, but as part of a team rather than as stars in their own right. They give great delight as they emerge between and blend with other plants. This month, for example, the yellow Pyrenean lilies (*Lilium pyrenaicum*), shine out beautifully among the green leaves of adjacent shrubs, while later in the season the large hybrids will add breath-taking beauty to the borders. Never think that bulbs are restricted to spring – always plan to have at least a few in your summer and autumn borders.

Bulbs used in borders can be a nuisance, because once the leaves have died back there is little indication that they are there. It is very easy to dig them up or damage them by accident. The first line of defence is to label them very clearly. Another method is to plant them in the plastic baskets that are sold for water plants. This may seem an odd thing to do, but it has several advantages. The border fork is more likely to strike the basket before it hits the bulbs and so you are warned that there is something to look out for. Another advantage is that it keeps all the bulbs together. The latticed sides of the pots allow the roots of the bulbs through to feed and to pick up moisture, but they do not let the bulbs themselves pass through, not even the small bulbils. This means that if you want to lift the bulbs, either to split them up or to move them somewhere else, you always dig up the lot in one go when you lift the basket. This method also allows different flower colours to be kept separate. It is, for example, impossible to tell from simply looking at the bulbs which will produce red flowers and which yellow, but each basket can be clearly labelled so that when the bulbs are lifted they can be replanted in the correct positions.

Part fill a basket with potting compost, put in the bulbs and fill up the basket to the rim. Dig a hole in the border and bury the basket so that its rim is below the surface of the soil, out of sight. If you want a large patch of bulbs, use several baskets. If you want to keep track of what is in each basket a label can be attached to the lattice sides with a piece of wire and buried along with the basket.

BULBS *and* TUBERS *for* EARLY SUMMER

Allium
Anemone coronaria
Arisaema candidissima; *A. consanguineum*
Camassia leichtlinii
Dracunculus vulgaris
Iris (English, Spanish and Dutch irises)
Ixia
Lilium
Moraea
Nectaroscordum
Ornithogalum (star of Bethlehem)
Rhodohypoxis
Scilla peruviana
Triteleia laxa (syn. *Brodiaea laxa*)

 FRUIT

Early summer sees the beginning of the fruit-picking season. By the end of this month early strawberries, raspberries, gooseberries and white- and redcurrants will all be ready to pick. The worst pests at this time of year are birds, which are attracted to the ripening fruit. Fortunately, it is possible to control the problem without being unduly aggressive to the birds. Plastic netting is inexpensive, and it should be draped over the plants, preferably over a framework of some sort. For best results make certain that there are no ways in for the birds, many of which find even the smallest hole through which to get at the fruit (p. 53).

Keep picking the fruit as it ripens. If you cannot consume it all, most can be frozen or preserved in some other way for winter use. Frozen strawberries and raspberries are never as good as fresh ones and are inclined to go mushy, but they are perfectly acceptable in dishes that do not require whole fruit. Gooseberries freeze well, as do white- and redcurrants. They can all also be bottled or turned into preserves.

Most of the berries – blackberries, loganberries, tayberries and so on – produce new canes throughout the summer. As these grow, they should be tied into the retaining wires. If they are left free they are likely to thrash around in the wind, not only damaging themselves but also the neighbouring fruiting canes.

Tree fruits will be swelling. In prolific years, apples, plums and pears may need thinning. Normally nature will take a hand and many of the excess fruits will fall off during the 'June drop'. Nevertheless, it may still be necessary to remove excess fruit by hand. Thin the fruit so that no two will be touching when they are fully developed by snipping off the unwanted fruit with a pair of secateurs. If they are not thinned the fruit will not develop fully and will be small in size and of substandard flavour. Another problem is that overburdened branches are likely to break, damaging the tree.

Start the summer pruning of trained soft fruit and wall-trained fruit. The new side shoots of established cordon and fan-trained white- and redcurrants and gooseberries should be pruned back to about five leaves.

STRAWBERRIES

Strawberries are one of the most delicious of fruits and one that few gardeners like to be without. They are not particularly difficult to grow and can even be grown in containers if you have a patio garden or a balcony (p. 138).

When the strawberries have finished fruiting, remove all the foliage and stems and burn them. Remove any new plants that have rooted at the end of the runners and use these to start a new row. Strawberries are best replaced every three years, preferably in fresh soil. In order to make certain that there is no break in the supply of fruit it is a good idea to have three beds or rows, one of which is replaced each year.

There are few people who do not consider strawberries to be one of the finest of fruits. As long as the birds and slugs can be kept at bay, they are not too difficult to grow. By making the right choice of varieties, the gardener can provide fruit over a long season from late spring through to the autumn.

◆ THE GREENHOUSE

Probably the most important thing to watch in the greenhouse at this time of year is the temperature. The strong sunlight can soon push up the level of heat beyond the endurance of many plants. Ventilation (p. 77) is of prime importance, followed closely by shading (see below) to prevent the heat getting in in the first place.

The atmosphere can become very dry, so increase the humidity by pouring water over the floor. The evaporation helps to keep the greenhouse cool as well as increasing the amount of water in the atmosphere. Moisture in the air helps to reduce the transpiration rate of the plants and therefore the amount of water that they need, particularly because in hot weather the plants need more moisture than their roots can take up and they will then begin to wilt. Another advantage of a moist atmosphere is that it reduces the chances of attack from red spider mite.

Keep an eye on tomatoes, cucumbers and melons, which will all be growing fast. Remove all the unwanted side shoots and tie in the main shoots as they grow. You should water them at least once a day and feed once a week with a liquid feed.

Grapes (p. 157) should be developing. To increase the final size of the fruit, thin out the bunches with a fine-pointed pair of scissors.

SHADING

There are various forms of shading that can be used to help keep the greenhouse cool. Unfortunately the best are the most expensive, but there are inexpensive alternatives that are more than adequate for general use.

The ideal is to prevent the sun's rays from entering the greenhouse. This means that the protection should be put on the *outside* of the house. If the shading is put on the inside the sun has already got in by the time it is blocked, and although it might not shine directly onto the plants, it means that the house will still heat up appreciably.

The best method is to have blinds, of plastic mesh or wooden slats, that can be draped over the outside of the glass. Traditionally, these blinds are wound onto large rollers along the ridge of the house so that they can be rolled up in dull weather and opened out when the sun shines. This is the ideal, and if your greenhouse is not large it is possible to make light wooden frames over which plastic netting is stretched and that can be clipped over the roof in sections.

A much simpler solution, although not as satisfactory because it cannot be easily removed and replaced as the weather changes, is to spray the outside of the glass with a white reflective material. This is easy to apply and can easily be cleaned off at the end of the season, but it is a nuisance to do it every time the sky clouds over and the greenhouse can be dark in dull weather. There are some types that turn transparent when it is raining and thus let in more light, but they still create too much shade in dull, dry weather.

Simple shade-netting can be fixed to the inside of the house using special clips that fix into the aluminium channels. This is an inexpensive and relatively simple operation, but it is not as effective as fixing the netting to the outside of the house.

 LAWNS

By now you should have established a regular mowing regime so that your lawns are kept under control. The grass is growing fast at this time of year, and it may be difficult to bring the lawn back to a green, even appearance if you miss a few cuts.

Sun and wind can rapidly dry out the ground, so water if necessary, making certain that the whole area receives a good soak and not just a small, useless dribble of water.

Although it may seem early, now is a good time to prepare the ground for a new lawn to be sown in the autumn.

MOWING

As long as weather allows, try and mow all lawns and grass paths at least once a week. For a high quality appearance it should be cut twice a week, or even three times when the grass is growing at its fastest. Lawns grow at their fastest in warm, moist weather, which mainly means in the early and late summer, although any wet period in the summer is likely to increase the growth rate. Cutting the grass when the weather is wet or the lawn is soaked will do more harm than good, however, and in periods of drought the growth rate slows right down and less frequent cuts are required.

Before mowing, sweep over the lawn with a birch broom (besom). This will remove any stones, twigs or any

other rubbish as well as breaking up any worm casts. It will also lift the blades of grass so that a better cut is achieved. Towards the end of the year, when the lawn is slow to dry out, brushing it with a broom, or even sweeping a large cane over it, will knock droplets of water from the blades of grass. This will allow the lawn to dry out more quickly so that it can be safely cut.

Do not cut the grass too short in dry periods. Areas that are regularly used for walking or for play should not be cut too short or the grass is likely to be damaged by the activity – 1–2.5cm (½–1in) is a good length for this type of lawn. For fine lawns that are more for looking at than for heavy activity, the height can be reduced to 5mm (¼in). Cut the lawn regularly. A sudden bout of activity to reduce the grass from say 5cm (2in) to 5mm (¼in) will cause sudden shock to the grass from which it may not be able to recover. Reduce gradually, over several mowings, the height of the grass to that required.

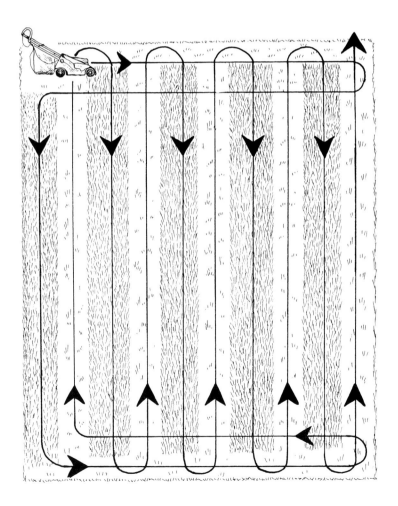

If you want a neatly striped lawn mow in parallel lines, remembering to finish the ends with horizontal cuts.

When the lawn is cut at frequent intervals the mowings should be short enough to be left on the lawn for the earthworms to incorporate in the top layer of soil. This allows the clippings to break down, feeding and improving the structure of the soil. However, do not allow cuttings, particularly longer cuttings, to accumulate on the lawn or they will smother the growing grass, causing yellow or brown patches.

A striped effect can be achieved by using a mower with a roller. Cut strips in alternate directions, up and down the lawn, each slightly overlapping the other. When you have finished, cut across the ends of the lawn to tidy the area where you turned. For an irregularly shaped lawn the same technique is used, except you start and finish with a run round the perimeter of the lawn so that the end of each strip is neatened. A rotary mower without a roller will not give the same striped effect, but it is still necessary to follow the above pattern, to make certain that all the lawn is cut evenly.

PERENNIALS

This is one of the best of all the months in the flower garden. Not only has the rich summer flowering begun in all its glory, but it still retains the freshness of spring. Later, although there is even more opulence, the sparkling newness of everything is somewhat diminished. The leaves will not be as fresh and green again, nor will the colours be so bright.

Keep the display fresh by removing dead flowers as they go over. This encourages the plant to produce more flowers as well as preventing large quantities of energy being used up on producing seed. It also keeps the borders tidy. Plants with dead or half-dead flowers look scruffy and the simple process of removing the heads can make all the difference between an attractive garden and a passable one. Remember to leave on a few heads if you want to collect seed, either to use yourself or to give to others.

Any plants that need support should have already been staked (p. 80), but check to make certain that all that require it have been dealt with. Sudden swirling summer winds can cause havoc, and remedial action may sometimes be needed, even for plants that are normally strong enough. Sticks around the plant with string threaded around and through it are usually sufficient, but you should avoid tying the plant in too tightly or it will never look natural.

Watch out for any pests and diseases and take appropriate action. Aphids are likely to be the biggest problem at this time of year. A mixed border with plenty of variety of flowering plants tends to attract beneficial insects, which help to control the pests, and a perennial border full of different plants is usually much less prone to either pests or diseases than one that is devoted to one type of plant, such as roses. However, should there be an outbreak of any sort, the earlier it is spotted and dealt with the less trouble it will be. If you use chemicals follow the directions on the packet and spray only the plants that need it.

Gaps often appear in a perennial border. These may be caused by plants finishing flowering – oriental poppies do not last very long, for example, and they are cut to the ground when they are finished, leaving a big gap. Gaps also occur because a plant fails for some reason or other and dies. It is always a good idea to keep a few annuals growing on in pots to fill these gaps. Loosen and water the soil, removing any weeds. Plant the annuals and keep them well watered until they are established. Annuals frequently come in mixed colours, but when they are used in a perennial border it is often a good idea to select just one colour strain because a single colour is likely to be more sympathetic to the overall design. Mixed colours in one bed may well be too vivid and eye-catching and clash with the existing plants.

DESIGNING WITH PERENNIALS

When you are designing the layout for a perennial border there are several things that must be taken into consideration. The first is the growing conditions that the plants will have to face. It is no good trying to grow plants that will not tolerate the conditions in your garden. If you live on chalk, you will have to grow only those plants that will grow in that type of soil. Similarly, if you live near the coast, choose plants that can survive the constant buffeting of salty winds. Moisture-loving plants, such as primulas and meconopsis (blue poppy), are best grown in moist, cool atmospheres; they will not do at all well in dry, hot conditions. There is little chance of growing Mediterranean-type plants if you live an area that has cold, damp winters. A little research into your local conditions and the types of plant that will suit those conditions will limit your palette, but it will save a lot of disappointment later on. That said, it is surprising how many plants are suitable for most areas and a variety of climates.

SHAPE AND FORM

Many people tend to think of the colour of the plants' flowers as being the only factor to consider when they are laying out a border, but there are several other important aspects to think about. Among the most important of these are height and structure. A flat bed is very boring – variations in the heights of the plants will make it much more interesting and alive. Most gardeners would accept the general guideline that you put tall plants at the back of a border and shorter ones at the front. Apart from any aesthetic value this principle gives to the border, it makes sense simply because you would not be able to see the shorter plants if they were hidden at the back.

However, plants ranked like the members of a choir in their stalls can be a bit boring, and variations in height help considerably. If the arrangement is a formal one, clumps of tall plants spaced at regular intervals give the border a symmetry and a sense of rhythm, while clumps at irregular intervals create a sense of informality. Bringing the occasional tall clump forwards also helps an informal design, particularly if its position blocks the sight line so that you cannot see what lies further along the border until you get there. Some tall plants, such as *Verbena bonariensis*, are thin and wiry, allowing the viewer to look right through them. These are excellent plants for creating variation in the border and yet not blocking the view.

Another important factor in designing the border is the shape of the plants. Some are tall and thin, taking the eye upwards, while others are short and squat, firmly anchoring the eye to the ground. Yet others have arching leaves, which create a fountain effect. These shapes not only contrast with each other to create an interesting overall image, but they also blend together to create areas of calm and tranquillity.

FOLIAGE COLOUR

The texture and colour of the foliage are also important. Shiny leaves can brighten dull spots and are especially valuable in shady areas. Dull, velvety leaves enhance rich colours, particularly purple foliage. Thin, spiky leaves, such as those of many grasses, give a different feeling altogether, almost that of a thin veil, and they often invite the viewer to run their fingers through them.

Foliage can be found in an almost infinite variety of shades of green, and it is possible to create an interesting border by exploiting those shades alone. As well as shades of green, however, foliage can be purple, golden or silver.

Silver foliage, for example, goes particularly well with pastel colours and can help to create a soft, romantic atmosphere. Variegated foliage, where more than one colour is present, adds a great deal of interest to a border, but you must be careful not to overdo it or the result will look too 'busy', with nowhere for the eye to rest. Several variegated plants of the same type planted among green-leaved plants will stand out, but if you mix the same plants with other variegated plants, their impact will be lost and they will go unnoticed.

FLOWER COLOUR

To many people the colour of flowers is the most important aspect of garden design. Even though, as noted above, there are several other factors that must be taken into consideration, flower colour is, nevertheless, of prime importance. It is a very difficult art to master first time round, and most gardeners must expect to have to move a few plants each season and add a few new ones until they have the border to their satisfaction. Very few of us would expect to take up painting and create a masterpiece with the first effort, so do not be disappointed if the effect of your first attempt is not what you expected. Half the fun of gardening is moving the plants around to try new ideas and effects.

Unless you want to make a special feature of it for some reason, avoid mixing colours in a haphazard way. This tends to make a restless, 'busy' scene in which there is nowhere for the eye to stop and will make the viewer feel, albeit subconsciously, uncomfortable and ill at ease. On the other hand, a single colour or a mixture of harmonious colours are more restful and help to create a peaceful, tranquil environment in which it is easy to relax. Harmonious colours are those that sit next to each other on an artist's colour wheel and it useful to look at one of these when you are devising colour schemes.

Soft colours tend to create a very peaceful, restful atmosphere. They are useful when creating a romantic setting. Cool, soft colours need to be viewed close to if they are to be fully appreciated, and when a border containing such colours is seen in the distance, it loses its focus and the border look longer than it is, just as the horizon seems further away in a soft, misty light than it does in a bright, harsh light when bolder colours stand out. Bright, hot colours, on the other hand, tend to create an exciting splash that immediately draws the eye. If such colours are planted in the distance, beyond a pond, for example, the eye seems to pass over

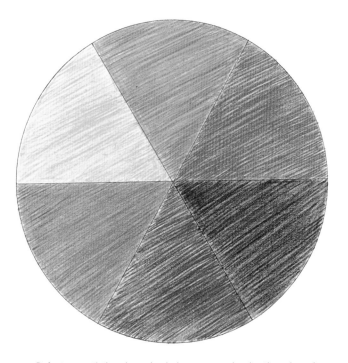

Refer to an artist's colour wheel when you are planning the colours in a border.

everything in the foreground and be drawn straight to the bright colours.

In addition to making distances seem shorter, hot colours help to create excitement. They are party colours, but, like parties, too many can be too much of a good thing and soon become boring, so use them with discretion. Bright reds and oranges are useful for arresting or drawing the eye – if you put a plant with red flowers in the middle of some softer colours your attention will be immediately caught by it.

If you look at an artist's colour wheel you will notice that colours on the opposite side of the wheel tend to contrast with each other – red and green or blue and orange, for example. Put these colours together and sparks begin to fly. Be aware, though, that too much contrast will quickly become boring and can upset the tranquil nature of a garden. However, if you use the technique with discretion, you can add a tension and excitement that is the art of good garden design.

Red flowers, such as those of *Dahlia* 'Bishop of Llandaff' and *D.* 'Blaisdon Red', will have the effect of bringing a border forwards.

An effective use of colour is to create a border, or even a whole garden, using a single colour – white gardens are probably the best known form of this. These tend to be very peaceful, serene places in which to relax. In fact, when you begin to look closely, you find that there is usually more than one colour present. In most white gardens. for example, as well as different shades of white, there are usually green, grey and silver foliage plants. These blend perfectly and create a much better picture than one that is totally pure white. The same applies to a red or yellow border. A more sophisticated design can be created by the use two colours, either sympathetic or contrasting. Yellow and blue, for example, make an excellent colour combination, although it does not have the tranquillity of, say, a border containing pastel colours.

The best way to learn about colour is to look at as many gardens as possible and to try to work out why they do or do not work. Looking at illustrations in gardening books in the winter can be equally inspiring. But remember that you can always move plants, so experiment and have fun.

ROCK GARDENS

By now many of the plants that flowered in spring will have produced seeds, which you can collect to give to friends or to increase your own stock of plants. Many plants can be grown for free (see below).

If you are not collecting seeds, continue to deadhead plants as they finish flowering. Some of the larger sprawling plants, such as aubrieta and alyssum, can be trimmed with a pair of shears to help keep them compact and free flowering. The new growth that they produce makes ideal cutting material if you want to increase your own stocks or produce plants to give away.

As long as they are watered it is not too late to plant out container-grown plants. However, avoid doing so in hot, drying weather.

Now is the time for taking soft cuttings of many alpines. They are taken and struck in the same way as basal cuttings (p. 61).

COLLECTING SEED

Many gardeners are used to buying seeds from seed merchants or garden centres, but it is always worth collecting seeds from your own plants, either for your own use or to give to others. Many of the plants that alpine gardeners grow are not available through conventional seed sources, such as garden centres. Plants are swapped between enthusiasts or they are bought from specialist nurseries. By saving the seeds of such plants they are made much more generally available. It is also a good way of conserving plants, because the more people who grow them, the less chance there is of their disappearing from cultivation.

Many gardening societies run seed exchanges, which often offer seeds that are not available from other sources. The seeds are collected by members from either their own plants or the wild and are then offered free or at a price that just covers the administration costs of the scheme. In this way, enthusiasts are able to build up interesting collections of plants. Alpines societies, such as the Alpine Garden Society or the American Rock Garden Club, can offer thousands of different species to their members, and if you are a member of one of the societies that specialize in alpines, it is worth collecting seeds to contribute to the schemes. Even if you feel you are less high powered, it is still worth collecting seeds and offering them to your local gardening club. This applies to all sorts of seed, of course, not just those of alpine plants.

Seed collecting is not a complicated task. The most difficult part is to get the timing right. With some plants this does not matter – tulips, for example, hold their seeds in a flask-like container, and as long as there is not a strong wind, it will wait there for you to collect it. Some plants – geraniums, for example – depend on an explosive mechanism for distributing seed, and as soon as the seeds are ripe they are flung some distance from the parent plant. Collecting the seeds from this type of plant needs careful timing.

With experience you will soon be able to tell when the seeds is ripe. With many of the buttercup family, for example, the seeds is ready as soon as it comes away freely when it is rubbed with the fingers. The time to collect the seeds of those plants with explosive mechanisms – the pea and geranium families, for example – is just before they explode. Again, experience will tell you when this is, but a foolproof method is to place a muslin or paper bag over the seedheads to prevent the seeds from being spread far and wide.

Go round the garden as frequently as you can, cutting off seedheads and putting them into paper bags. Label each bag as you put the seeds into it. If you leave it to later you will be bound to forget what seed is in which bag. Unless the seedheads are explosive, in which case you should close the bags, leave the bags open so that the air can circulate around the seeds and allow them to dry off. Remove all the pieces of seed capsule, dust and other detritus from the seeds. Some of the larger seeds can be picked out by hand, but smaller seeds can be put though different size sieves. A fine sieve will allow the dust through but retain the seeds and larger detritus; a sieve with a larger mesh will allow the seeds through but keep back everything else. Another method is to put it all in a dish and lightly blow over it. The lighter pieces of detritus, such as the seed capsules and old petals, will be blown away, leaving the heavier seeds behind.

Once the seeds has been separated from the chaff, place the seeds in a paper envelop and store them in a dry, cool place. Do not forget to label the packet.

🍃 TREES AND SHRUBS

Although bare-rooted trees and shrubs cannot be planted at this time of year, it is possible to plant those that have been raised in containers. Add plenty of well-rotted organic material to the soil before planting and make certain that the ground is thoroughly soaked. Avoid planting in really hot or drying weather.

Trees and shrubs are now in full growth and it is necessary to check that none of the ties is so tight that it is cutting into the stems or trunks. Ease ties that seem tight off slightly, but do not allow them to become too loose or the whole purpose of the support will be lost.

Suckers are beginning to appear around many trees and shrubs, either shooting up from below ground of from around the base of the trunk. Remove these as they appear so that the strength of the plant is not diminished and its shape is not spoilt. Suckers may not be the same variety as the main tree or shrub if it has been grafted, and you should trace the sucker back to its origin and cut it off close to the root or trunk.

If spring-flowering shrubs that have finished their display need pruning, now is the time to do it (p. 65). This will allow the shrub to put on fresh growth and develop flower buds for next year. If you leave it until later in the year the wood will not mature, and the shrub will produce a poor show next spring.

Hedges need to be regularly clipped to keep them neat (p. 84). Regular cutting will not only keep the hedge compact but will also make it easier to cut. Once a hedge has become overgrown and straggly, it might be difficult to restore. If you find it difficult to cut hedges regularly, an informal hedge may be the answer (see below).

Topiary as well as hedges will be growing fast now, and unless they are regularly trimmed they can begin to look a bit tatty. Regular clipping not only keeps them neat but keeps the piece dense and makes it easier to retain the shape.

INFORMAL HEDGES

Hedges used to be little more than a stock-proof barrier between the garden and the outside world. Now, however, they are more likely to be decorative features of the garden, and this visual function brings with it the need to keep them clipped and tidy. Some of the functions of a hedge, in particular providing screens and internal division, can be taken over by informal hedges, which are, in effect, little more than rows of bushes that merge to form a decorative barrier.

Most informal hedges retain the shaggy, unrestrained look of the original bushes and are not clipped tight, as a formal hedge is clipped. Because they are left unchecked, this type of hedge will often produce flowering and fruiting stems. A good example of this are the wonderful rugosa rose hedges with their dark green foliage setting off red, pink or white flowers over a long season.

There is no reason that informal hedges should not provide just as secure a barrier as a denser, more formal one. Thorny berberis or rose, for example, grown in a close row, will be just as much a deterrent as a clipped hawthorn hedge, but they have the advantage of looking more attractive and do away with the necessity of constant clipping.

Although it will not need clipping as often as a formal hedge, an informal hedge will still need some attention if it is to thrive. Basically, the same procedures should be adopted as if you were cultivating individual bushes, and they should be cut at the same time of year as if it were a simple bush. Cut out any wayward stems, especially those that are likely to thrash around it in the wind, and any dead wood, and remove some of the older growth to encourage the production of new wood. The time to cut most informal hedges is soon after they have finished flowering, unless you are growing them for their fruit, in which case cut them immediately after fruiting.

SHRUBS *for* INFORMAL HEDGES

Berberis	*Corylus*
Buddleja	*Cotoneaster*
Chaenomeles	*Escallonia*
Cornus	*Forsythia*

Fuchsia
Hebe
Hippophae
Hydrangea
Hypericum
Lavandula
Mahonia
Osmanthus
Pittosporum
Potentilla

Pyracantha
Rhododendron
Ribes
Rosa
Salix
Spiraea
Symphoricarpos
Syringa
Tamarix

FEDGES

This unusual form of boundary is a combination of a fence and a hedge – hence its name. Basically it is a fence over which is grown a climbing plant. This can be something like a clematis or a passion fruit, but one of the best types of fedge is framework simply covered with ivy. This makes a dense, evergreen hedge. It can be kept formal by cutting once a year in late winter or it can be left to ramble in a more informal way, when only those stems that get too long or wayward should be cut back.

The fence can be made of any type of material, and this method is a good way of disguising an ugly constructions such as wire or chain-link fences.

VEGETABLES

If you have not already done so, it is time, now that the threat of frost has passed, to plant out or sow any tender vegetables (p. 66). There is still time to sow successional crops, such as lettuce, to give a constant supply of produce right through to the late autumn. Even the tender crops can be sown successionally – runner beans, for example, that are sown two or three weeks after the initial sowing will produce a new crop of tender beans just as the first sowing is running out of steam. Similar sowings of French beans will also supply a continuous crop.

Although swedes are a hardy crop they are not normally sown until this month. They should be sown where they are to grow and thinned once they are big enough to handle (p. 105).

Leeks and autumn and winter brassicas that have been grown in a seed bed can now be planted out into their growing positions.

Early potatoes will be ready to eat. Lift as required. Continue to earth up later varieties (p. 44).

CARING FOR VEGETABLES

To obtain a good crop it is essential to spend time each week caring for the vegetable beds. As each crop germinates, thin out the seedlings as soon as they are big enough to handle (p. 84). This avoids overcrowding so that each vegetable develops to its full flavour and size and does not become drawn.

Regularly hoe or weed by hand. When you are hoeing take care that you do not to get too close to the vegetables and damage them. This is particularly important with crops such as carrots, because the smell from bruising or a cut will attract carrot root fly. It is best to hoe between the rows but to hand weed between individual plants. If the beds have been prepared properly the only weeds should be annual ones, which means that if the top is hoed off they will not reappear. However, if there are any perennial weeds, such as couch grass, in the bed, hoeing will not kill them because the underground roots store enough energy to reappear. A war of attrition, involving the removal of the top growth as soon as it appears, may reduce them but the best way is to clear the ground and dig them out or, if necessary, kill them with a herbicide.

One way to keep the weeds down and to help retain moisture in the soil is to mulch. Many gardeners like to spread grass clippings between the rows. This should not be too deep – no more than 5cm (2in) – or the heat generated by their decomposing could adversely effect the plants. Black polythene mulch is another possibility. This can be laid between the rows or it can be use to cover the complete bed. If you choose black polythene, lay it in

A mulch spread under a plant will help to keep down weeds and reduce moisture loss. If you use lawn clippings, the mulch should be no deeper than about 5cm (2in) or it will generate too much heat.

position and cut slots through which the vegetables are planted. It must be porous so that rain soaks through.

Close planting is another method of mulching. This is best achieved by using the deep-bed method (p. 85), in which plants are set in blocks rather than in rows.

Watering is essential in dry periods. Some plants – peas, for example – do not require watering until the flowers are set and the peas begin to swell, while others – celery, for example – do not like to dry out at all. Always water thoroughly: a trickle or light sprinkle is useless.

FRENCH BEANS

French beans are one of the staple vegetables of the late summer. They have a different taste and texture from runner beans and have the advantage that many varieties are stringless. As well as green-podded varieties, there are also purple and yellow forms. The purple colour is, unfortunately, lost in the cooking, but the yellow is retained. Most varieties have round pods, but some have flat pods, and these can become stringy. Another variation is that there are both dwarf varieties, which grow in unsupported rows, and climbing varieties, which grow and are treated in the same way as runner beans (p. 86). A further variety is known as haricot beans, and these are grown for their seeds rather than the pods.

All varieties like a sunny situation and a well-drained soil that has had plenty of well-rotted organic material added to it. The soil must be allowed to warm up before sowing or the seeds will not germinate. Last month or this is about the right time. They can be sown directly into drill, with the seeds placed about 7.5–10cm (3–4in) apart. Once germinated, they can be thinned to about 15–20cm (6–8in) apart. Watch out for slugs, particularly at the early stages of growth. Seeds can also be sown inside and the resulting plants planted out in early summer. Keep well watered during dry spells. Mulching will help keep in the moisture as well as keep the weeds down. Climbing varieties should be treated in th same way as runner beans (p. 86).

Pick the beans as they are ready and remove all pods before they get too old. French beans can be frozen. Haricot beans are left on the plants until the pods have turned yellow. Dig up the whole plants and hang them in bunches in a dry, airy place. Collect the seeds once the pods have become brittle.

A vegetable garden can be decorative as well as productive, although if you intend to eat the produce, you must be prepared to put up with gaps in the design from time to time.

Florence fennel is an excellent vegetable that should be more frequently grown.

RECOMMENDED VARIETIES of FRENCH BEAN

Dwarf varieties
'Atlanta'
'Capitole'
'Daisy'
'Delinel'
'Golddukat': yellow podded
'Masai'
'Mont d'Or': yellow podded
'Primel'
'The Prince'
'Purple Queen': purple podded
'Purple Teepee': purple podded
'Radar'
'Royalty': purple podded
'Vilbel'

Climbing varieties
'Blue Lake'
'Hunter'
'Kentucky Blue'
'Largo'
'Musica'
'Romano'

Haricot varieties
'Chevrier Vert'
'Comtessa de Chambord'
'Limelight'

SWEDES

Swedes are yet another member of the cabbage family and are prone to most of the same problems. Never grow swedes on the same ground for two years running. They do best in a light, fertile, moisture-retentive soil. Sow in shallow drills set 45cm (18in) apart and thin the resulting seedlings to about 30cm (12in) apart. Water in dry weather and keep weeded. Harvest as required and leave in the ground in winter. In warmer areas, lift and store in early winter to prevent the swedes from becoming too woody. Store in just-moist sand.

RECOMMENDED VARIETIES of SWEDE

'Best of All'
'Devon Champion'
'Marian'
'Ruby'
'Western Perfection'

FLORENCE FENNEL

Florence fennel is not one of the main-stream vegetables, but it is gaining in popularity. It is the fleshy, anise-flavoured bulb at the base of the stems that is eaten, although the feathery foliage can also be used as a flavouring or garnish. It needs a light, well-drained but fertile soil in a sunny but sheltered position. Prepare the beds in the autumn and sow the seeds in shallow drills, 45cm (18in) apart, during this month or next. Sowing earlier can result in the plants' bolting, as can any check in their growth, especially if it becomes too dry. Thin to 25cm (10in).

Weed regularly and water during dry weather. As the bulbs swell, earth them up. To harvest remove the earthed-up soil and cut just above the base. The latter can be dug out or left in to develop new foliage for flavouring and garnishing.

RECOMMENDED VARIETIES of FLORENCE FENNEL

'Cantino'
'Herald'
'Perfection'
'Sirio'
'Sweet Florence' ('Di Firenze')
'Zefa Fino'

JULY

The weather will be at its warmest now, and there may be times when gardeners feel like hanging up their boots. There is little point in slaving over a garden if you leave little time to enjoy it. One advantage of getting on top of the work in winter and spring is that there is more time left now to enjoy the fruits of that labour.

Another reward that the gardener can take delight in at this time of year is the sudden rush of ripening vegetables and fruit and the wealth of colourful flowers. Although there may be too much produce for your own use, try to keep picking it to encourage a succession as well as to prevent fruit from rotting on the plants. If you have too much, freeze the excess or give it away to friends and neighbours – such gifts are always welcome.

As the middle of the year passes, a gardener's thoughts will turn from birth to death. Many flowering plants are finished and will need to be cut back, while others have dead flowers that need removing. At this time of year one of the criteria of a successful garden is to keep it looking good by removing the dead and the dying. This not only removes the distractions of brown or tatty vegetation, but also makes those plants that are still in flower more visible.

CHECKLIST ✓

General

- Water when necessary (p. 92)
- Keep control of weeds (p. 92)
- Watch out for pests and diseases and take appropriate action (p. 98)

Annuals and Tender Perennials

- Use late-sown annuals to fill gaps in borders (p. 98)
- Water hanging baskets and containers daily (p. 110)
- Water beds and borders when necessary (p. 108)
- Feed hanging baskets and containers once a week (p. 120)
- Deadhead regularly and cut back straggly plants (p. 108)

Bulbs

- Plant autumn-flowering bulbs (p. 154)
- Check for pests, especially lily beetle (p. 94)
- Collect ripe seeds (p. 76)
- Order next year's bulbs (p. 110)

Fruit

- Pick soft fruit as it ripens (p. 111)
- Pick cherries and some other early stone fruit (p. 112)
- Continue thinning tree fruit (p. 95)
- Remove raspberry canes that have finished fruiting (p. 156)
- Tie in new raspberry canes (p. 156)
- Cut off leaves and remove mulch from strawberries that have finished fruiting (p. 138)
- Summer prune soft fruit (p. 95)
- Bud fruit trees (p. 111)

Greenhouse

- Make sure that the greenhouse is adequately shaded (p. 96) and ventilated (p. 77)
- In hot weather dampen the floor to cool and humidify the greenhouse (p. 96)
- Pinch out and tie in tomatoes, cucumbers and melons (p. 96)
- Pick early tomatoes and cucumbers (p. 113)
- Water at least once a day and feed once a week (p. 96)
- If the greenhouse is not used for tomatoes and other crops, thoroughly clean and disinfect it (p. 113)

Lawns

- Mow regularly, but not closely or too frequently if the weather is dry (p. 78)
- Water thoroughly if necessary (p. 113)
- If the weather is suitable give a light application of fertilizer (p. 60)
- Prepare sites for new lawns (p. 141)

Perennials

- Deadhead flowers as they go over (p. 79)
- Watch out for pests and diseases and take appropriate action (p. 98)
- Fill any unexpected gaps with annuals (p. 98)
- Water as necessary (p. 98)
- Take cuttings of pinks and wallflowers (p. 114)
- Cut plants such as oriental poppies to the ground after flowering (p. 114)
- Collect seeds if required (p. 98)
- Take stem cuttings (p. 114)
- Keep beds weed free (p. 92)

Rock Gardens

- Collect and sow seeds as required (p. 101)
- Deadhead flowers as they go over unless seeds are required (p. 101)
- Shear over dwarf phlox (p. 101)
- Remove weeds on sight (p. 63)
- Continue to water new plants and other areas as necessary (p. 63)
- Take semi-ripe cuttings (p. 101)
- Re-pot bulbs (p. 101)
- Pot up rooted cuttings (p. 101)

Trees and shrubs

- Plant container-grown trees and shrubs and keep well watered (p. 102)
- Check that ties are not cutting into growing trees (p. 102)
- Remove suckers (p. 102)
- Deadhead early-summer-flowering shrubs (p. 102)
- After flowering, prune shrubs that flower on old wood (p. 128)
- Cut hedges as necessary (p. 82)
- Trim topiary as necessary (p. 102)

Vegetables

- Make last successional sowings (p. 44)
- Harvest vegetables as they are ready (p. 117)
- Lift and dry shallots (p. 185)
- Earth up potatoes (p. 44)
- Continue lifting early potatoes (p. 44)
- Keep vegetables weed free (p. 103)
- Water when necessary (p. 104)

ANNUALS

The most important garden task this month is to make sure that the plants do not dry out. This is not so much a problem in beds, but plants in containers will need watering at least once a day and sometimes even more frequently. The constant watering means that nutrients are rapidly washed out, so add a liquid feed to one watering a week.

Keep plants tidy by removing dead flowers and by cutting back any straggly growths. Although this is primarily to keep the displays looking tidy, it also helps to prolong flowering because, by removing old flowers, less energy is wasted by the plant in producing seed.

Remove any plants that have died or are looking sick and replace them with late-sown annuals. They can also be used to fill unexpected gaps in perennial borders.

It is surprising how many flowers can be dried. There are some that are easy and are generally accepted as being grown for use as dried flowers – 'everlastings', for example – but many other plants can be dried and it is worth trying anything that you feel will make an attractive display.

The 'everlastings' – *Helichrysum*, *Helipterum* and *Limonium* (statice), for example – can be grown away from the normal flower borders. It may be a special plot reserved for flowers to be cut for the house or it may be part of the vegetable garden. Another option is to use the back of borders, but remember that most dried flowers prefer a sunny position. Having a separate place for growing plants for dried flowers allows you to cut what you want without depleting the flower-power of your normal beds and borders.

As well as flowers you can also dry leaves and seedpods. Several annuals produce good pods – love-in-a-mist (*Nigella*) and poppies, for example – and honesty

DRYING FLOWERS

At this time of year annuals are at their best, and it is time to consider drying some of them for indoor displays to provide all-year round interest from plants that may only have a fleeting flowering season. A dried-flower arrangement will also provide colour later in the year when there are few flowers to pick. The crucial thing to remember about dried-flower displays is that they should be thrown away when they begin to get dusty and old. There is nothing sadder than a collection of tatty, tired-looking dried flowers that have become so familiar to their owners that they no longer see them. Plan to grow and dry a new batch of flowers each year so that you can keep your displays fresh.

Nigella damascena, love-in-a-mist, as well as being decorative in flower also produces wonderful seed pods, which not only look good in the garden but can also be dried.

(*Lunaria*), a biennial, has the most superb silvery pods. Another biennial, the teasel, is also especially worth growing just for its dried heads.

Of course, you are not restricted to annuals for dried-flower arrangements. There are plenty of perennials that can also be used, too, to add variety, especially in terms of text and size, to the materials available for making a display. The techniques required for both types of material are broadly the same.

To get the longest growing season, sow annuals under glass in early spring and plant out in rows in the late spring (p. 20). Alternatively, sow them in mid-spring directly in the rows in which they are to grow. Other flowers can be cut from plants that are used as bedding plants in the borders, although you will generally want to limit the number that you cut or you will reduce the impact in the border. Plants such as French marigolds and larkspur can be sown and grown in the conventional way and selected stems picked for drying. The wider the range of plants you grow the greater the scope you will have for making interesting displays.

The best time to pick flowers for drying is when they are about half open. Choose a dry day to pick the flowers and cut plenty of stem – it can always be trimmed back when you make the arrangement.

The simplest way to dry flowers is to tie them into small bunches and hang them upside down in a warm, airy place. Avoid damp places or places in direct sunlight. Remove the leaves from the base of the stems. Keep the bundles small and tie them together at the base of the stems so that the heads are not crushed together. Tie with soft string or use elastic bands, which will contract as the stems shrink.

SUITABLE PLANTS *for* DRYING

Annuals

Agastache
Amaranthus (love-lies-bleeding)
Ammobium (winged everlasting)
Celosia (cockscomb)
Centaurea cyanus (cornflower)
Craspedia globosa (drumstick)
Delphinium consolida (larkspur)
Gomphrena globosa (globe amaranth)
Helichrysum bracteatum (straw flower)
Limonium sinuatum (statice)
Molucella (bells of Ireland)

Nigella (love-in-a-mist)
Origanum dictamnus (sweet marjoram)
Salvia horminum (clary)
Tagetes erecta (French marigold)
Xeranthemum annuum (immortelle)

Perennials

Acanthus (bear's breeches)
Achillea (yarrow)
Anaphalis (pearl everlasting)
Astrantia (masterwort)
Cynara (cardoon, globe artichoke)
Delphinium
Echinops (globe flower)
Eryngium (sea holly)
Gypsophila (baby's breath)
Liatris (gayfeather)
Limonium latifolium (sea lavender)
Paeonia (peony)
Sedum spectabile (ice plant)
Solidago canadense (golden rod)
Tanacetum vulgare (tansy)

Foliage shrubs

Cotinus (smoke tree)
Erica (heather)
Hydrangea
Helichrysum italicum (curry plant)
Lavandula (lavender)
Phlomis fruticosa (Jerusalem sage)
Rosa (roses)
Rosmarinus officinalis (rosemary)
Salvia officinalis (sage)
Santolina (cotton lavender)
Senecio

Seedheads

Allium (decorative onions)
Aquilegia (columbines)
Carlina acaulis (carline thistle)
Dipsacus fullonum (teasel)
Iris foetidissima (stinking iris)
Lunaria annua (honesty)
Nicandra physaloides (shoo-fly plant)
Nigella (love-in-a-mist)
Phlomis russeliana
Papaver somnifera (opium poppy)
Physalis franchetii (Chinese lantern)
Typha (reedmace, bulrush)

Grasses

> *Avena* (oats)
> *Briza* (quaking grass)
> *Bromus* (rye brome grass)
> *Cortaderia selloana* (pampas grass)
> *Dactylis* (cocksfoot grass)
> *Deschampsia* (hair grass)
> *Festuca* (fescue grass)
> *Hordeum* (barley)
> *Lagurus ovatus* (hair's tail grass)
> *Miscanthus* (miscanthus)
> *Pennisetum* (feathertop grass)
> *Phalaris canariensis* (canary grass)
> *Stipa* (feather grass)

WATERING CONTAINERS

It is very important to keep containers watered through the summer months. The plants are usually tightly packed in containers, and there is a mass of roots, all searching for moisture. At the same time, the heat and, possibly, drying winds not only cause the plants to increase their rates of transpiration and therefore use up more water but also dry out the compost in the pots. This is particularly true of containers made of terracotta, which lose moisture through the sides.

The simplest method of coping is to water every day, more than once if the plants look thirsty. This may not always be possible, however, and one way of overcoming this is to add water-retaining crystals to the compost. These crystals hold a lot of water, which is slowly released to the plants. Follow the instructions on the packet. Another solution is to equip all the containers with a drip feed, although this has the disadvantage that it is rather dependent on all the pots being in the same place as it is impracticable to have unsightly hosepipes draped over the whole garden. Another method that can be used if the pots are all in one place is to stand them on capillary matting, which is supplied with water from a reservoir.

If you are going to be away, possibly the best way of coping with watering is to ask a friend or neighbour to do it for you – agreeing to a reciprocal arrangement for their absence may help persuade them. It may be worth inserting coloured labels into every pot so that it obvious to a stranger if one plant needs a different watering regime from another – succulents, for example, need far less water than herbaceous plants.

Do not overwater during overcast or wet periods. Plants need moist but not flooded compost, and this also means that you should avoid standing containers permanently in trays of water.

With constant watering, minerals and nutrients are quickly flushed out of the compost by the water passing through. It is necessary to replace these by adding a liquid feed to one watering a week.

Watering for ground-level containers is best carried out with a watering can. Hosepipes can be used, but they should be used with care because the force of the jet of water can do damage. Hanging baskets or containers sitting on a wall can be a problem if a stepladder is needed before you can use a watering can. It is possible to buy special waterers which have a long rod and curved spout. These work with a pump action and can easily deliver water to hanging baskets while the gardener stands firmly on the ground.

BULBS

Midsummer is not a period that is generally associated with bulbs and yet is still an important time. If nothing else it is time to look at catalogues and order bulbs to be planted in the autumn for flowering next year. If you order just a few new varieties each year, the garden will soon contain enough to put on a very colourful and interesting display that will be the envy of all visitors.

BULBS *and* CORMS *for* MIDSUMMER

> *Allium*
> *Anemone coronaria*
> *Cardiocrinum giganteum*
> *Cypella herbertii*
> *Dierama*
> *Eucomis*
> *Galtonia*
> *Gladiolus*
> *Iris*
> *Ixia*
> *Lilium*
> *Nomocharis*
> *Triteleia laxa* (syn. *Brodiaea laxa*)
> *Zantedeschia*

For those who specialize in 'alpine' bulbs, which generally means dwarf bulbs because most do not come from alpine regions, it is time to re-pot all the bulbs that you have in containers or special beds. Knock out the compost and riddle through it very carefully so that you find all the bulbs, including the very tiny offspring. If the bulbs have increased they can all be put in a larger pot, split into two pots or re-potted in the same size pot with the excess bulbs being given away or swapped. Use new compost, preferably one that is free-draining – that is, one with extra grit in it. Once the bulbs have been re-potted, top dress them with a layer of grit or fine stones. Do not water until it is time for the bulbs to start into growth.

FRUIT

This is a delightful month as there should be plenty of delicious fruit to pick and eat. Strawberries, gooseberries, red-, white- and blackcurrants, raspberries, cherries and several others should all be ripening. Keep picking the fruit as it ripens, and remove any rotting or damaged fruit at the same time.

Apples, pears and plums should all be swelling by now. It may be necessary to make a second thinning if the fruit are still tightly packed on the branches. The first and main thinning should have been last month, but it is worth checking over the trees again.

Some of the early varieties of strawberry will have finished fruiting this month. Cut off the old leaves (being careful not to damage the newly emerging ones) and remove the straw mulch from around the plants. Burn both of these to destroy any diseases that may be lingering. Hoe along the rows, removing any weeds and any runners that are not required.

If you want to propagate your own fruit trees now is the time to make bud-grafts onto new rootstock.

GRAFTING

Bud-grafting or budding and shield-budding or T-budding are forms of grafting that are particularly useful for increasing your stocks of roses and fruit trees. On roses it is carried out at ground level on seedling rootstock, but on fruit trees the budding is undertaken at about 30cm (12in) above the soil on one of the standard rootstocks.

Shield- or T-budding involves making two slits to form a T-shape in the bark. Both the resulting flaps are opened up, and into these is inserted a slice of stem containing a bud of the type of rose or fruit tree you want to graft. The flaps are closed and the bud is bound into place with special budding tape, which is bound around the stem so that the bud is left exposed.

T-budding onto a rootstock

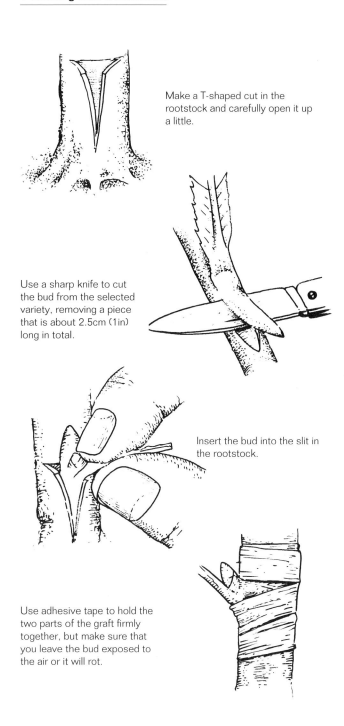

Make a T-shaped cut in the rootstock and carefully open it up a little.

Use a sharp knife to cut the bud from the selected variety, removing a piece that is about 2.5cm (1in) long in total.

Insert the bud into the slit in the rootstock.

Use adhesive tape to hold the two parts of the graft firmly together, but make sure that you leave the bud exposed to the air or it will rot.

In the process known as chip-budding a slice of the rootstock is removed and a similarly sized slice, including a bud, from the tree you want to propagate is bound into its place. Once either form of budding has taken, the tape is removed and any of the original rootstock above the new growth is removed.

Cherries are enjoyed by both people and birds. Any gardener who wants even a few cherries must net trees to protect the fruit from birds.

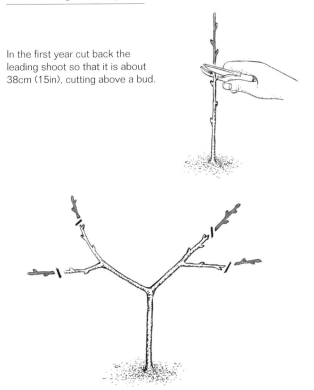

In the first year cut back the leading shoot so that it is about 38cm (15in), cutting above a bud.

In the following spring cut back the new stems by about half.

In the autumn of the fourth year, and in subsequent years, cut back all branches that have borne fruit to one bud.

CHERRIES

Until recently cherries have not been widely grown in gardens, partly because the trees were so large and partly because cherries were self-sterile – that is, two different varieties were needed for pollination. Cherry trees are now grown on 'Colt' rootstock, which produces much smaller trees. The importance of this is not only that they should fit into most gardens but also that they are small enough to be netted. Any un-netted tree will be stripped of its fruit by birds long before the gardener has a look in.

There are two main types of cherry: sweet, which are good for eating and cooking, and acid, which are really suitable only for cooking. Acid cherries grow on smaller trees and have had a longer garden history than sweet varieties. Both can be grown on 'Colt' stock as small trees or as fan-trained plants against wires or a wall.

They need a fertile soil and a sunny position. Fan-trained cherries require wires or a wall to about 2.5m (8ft). The fruit buds on cherries appear on wood that is at least two years old, so pruning is mainly confined, on both trees and fans, to pinching back the new growth to six or so leaves before fruiting and then again, after fruiting, to about three leaves. More formative pruning is carried out in the winter.

Cherries are best eaten fresh, although they can be frozen or bottled. The best known acid cherry is 'Morello' and, like most acid cherries, it is self-fertile so one tree can be grown by itself. There is a larger range of sweet cherries, but most are better suited to orchards than the garden. One variety, 'Stella', is suitable for the garden because it is one of the few self-fertile sweet cherries and it can be grown on 'Colt' stock.

THE GREENHOUSE

The most important thing at this time of year is to ensure that the greenhouse is shaded and well ventilated. Keep the atmosphere moist by damping down the floor with water. Regularly water all plants that need it. One or two day's neglect could spell disaster. However, those plants that are dormant in summer, such as some bulbs, should not be watered until growth restarts.

Continue to pinch out and tie in melons and tomatoes (p 38). Early tomatoes and cucumbers (p. 37) will be ripening and these should be picked.

Those gardeners who do not grow tomatoes or cucumbers in the greenhouse but tend to use it only for raising seeds in spring and overwintering pot plants find that this is a good time of year in which to clean out the greenhouse and thoroughly wash and disinfect it. Move any pot plants outside while doing this. A good way of disinfecting the greenhouse, as it kills off all unwanted bugs and fungal spore is to close it right up and burn a sterilizing smoke bomb in it. These can be obtained from a garden centre. It is important to follow the instruction on the packet.

LAWNS

Keep mowing all grass regularly. If the weather is very dry increase the height of the cut slightly so that the grass is a bit longer and will thus be better able to survive use during the drought.

Although it is not necessary to water lawns unless there is the real threat that the grass may die without water, many gardeners like to keep them looking green, which does require moisture. If you water, do so thoroughly, supplying at least 2.5cm (1in) at a time. A light sprinkle is useless.

Think well ahead if you are planning a new lawn and start to prepare the ground now. Leaving it fallow until sowing or turf-laying time in the autumn will give you plenty of time to make certain that all perennial weeds have been removed.

HOLIDAYS

This is the time when many people take their holidays, and it is also a time when lawns can suffer by the owner's absence. Unkempt lawns can be an eyesore to many owners and may also, if they are visible from the road, be an indication to burglars that there is no one at home.

Many people might be tempted to cut the lawn a bit tighter before they go away, but this can do more harm than good, especially if it is already quite tightly cut. Give it its normal trim, as close as you can to the day you go away. If you can, arrange for a neighbour or friend to cut it for you while you are away. During hot dry weather the lawn is unlikely to grow to much anyway, but there may be a problem if the lawn contains several different types of grass as well as different weeds, all of which are bound to grow at varying rates, giving the lawn a ragged look.

If you have to let it grow while you are away, no harm will happen to it. After its initial spurt of growth since the last cut, the growth rate will slow down. If it does grow excessively, treat the longer grass as you would in spring – that is, do not try to cut it straight back to its summer length, but take it at stages, the number of cuts depending on how long the grass has grown.

A delightful mixture of wild flowers in a meadow garden. Such gardens are a joy, but for success they must be treated as any other type of flower garden – which means that they require plenty of work.

WILDFLOWER MEADOWS

Wildflower gardening has become increasing popular in recent years as many gardeners see not only the beauty in wildflowers but also the necessity of creating refuges to ensure their continuance. Some people create special wild gardens, while others prefer to create a wild meadow. This may be a lawn that is allowed to grow or, if the gardener is lucky, a small field or plot next to the garden.

The essential point about a wildflower meadow is that the grasses must not be allowed to swamp the flowers. If it is just left to its own devices this is what will happen in a true meadow. Coarser grasses will move in, eventually shrubs and trees will seed and, finally, the meadow will change to woodland. With good management, however, it will remain a pleasant, flowery meadow.

If you already have a field, cut the grass at regular intervals for a couple of years. This will reduce the coarser grasses and create a more lawn-type appearance. Once you have reached this stage, wildflowers can be planted in the grass. If you can, it is preferable to raise the plants from seeds in pots and plant them out in a random pattern. Meadows are more easily established in this way than simply scattering the seed. However, once the plants have become established and start flowering they will soon start self-sowing. Another option is to plough the field and sow it with a mixture of soft grasses and wildflower seed.

On a smaller scale it is possible to turn a lawn or part of a lawn into a meadow garden. Again, plant a few wildflower plants into the lawn and let the grass grow long.

In both cases, the grass must be cut in the early summer, once most of the flowers have finished seeding. Remove the cuttings if they are long, or they will smother both the grass and flowering plants. Cut at least twice more during the year or allow animals to graze on it after the first cut.

PERENNIALS

The perennials season is now at its height. This is the best time to wander around the garden and enjoy the fruits of your labour. As you look around, take time to assess what you see. Make notes of plants that are becoming old and need replacing and of plants that are in the wrong place and should be moved in the autumn or spring. They may be too tall for their current position, the colour of their flowers may clash with that of a neighbouring plant, or they may just look better against something else.

Try and be objective and look at everything with a critical eye. Very few gardeners get it right the first time and one of the arts of achieving the flowering gardening is the ability to see what you have done and how you could move things to improve the scene. A static garden tends to be a boring one. A notebook is essential – you are almost certain to forget what you decided once all the plants have died back for the winter and it comes to the appropriate time to move plants.

Although this time of year may be the quietest time from the point of work there is still a lot to be done if you want to keep your garden in prime condition. Regularly walk round the beds and deadhead. This will not only make things neater but also provide extra energy for the plants to produce more flowers. As you go round, keep an eye out for pests and diseases and take appropriate action.

Some plants, such as the oriental poppy (*Papaver orientalis*) or lady's mantle (*Alchemilla mollis*), should be cut right to the ground and they will make a fresh set of leaves and act as foliage plants. If they are left they will look tatty and dog-eared and contribute little to the appearance of the border.

This month is a good time to take cuttings of short-lived perennials, such as pinks and wallflowers. Take a dozen 7.5cm (3in) cuttings from non-flowering stems and place them around the edge of a 9cm (3½in) pot of cutting compost. Water and place them in a propagator or a polythene bag out of direct sunlight. Pot up when roots have formed, and plant out in the autumn.

ROCK GARDENS

Unless you have a wide selection of plants, midsummer in the rock garden can be one of the least colourful times of year. Most true alpines have finished flowering by now, and some may even have retired back below ground. However, small plants from more Mediterranean-type climates are still flowering and can make a good display. A few mat-forming annuals, such as *Silene pendula*, are also excellent.

Although there is not much new to do in the rock garden at this time of year it is important to stay on top of routine jobs. Collect and clean seeds as they ripen. Remove dead flowerheads from plants as they finish flowering (unless you want the seeds) and tidy up the plants. Remove weeds as they appear. Never allow them to get a hold otherwise it may be necessary to dismantle the whole rock garden to remove them.

MAKING SINKS AND TROUGHS

Troughs are a marvellous way of creating small landscapes in which delicate plants can be seen at their best as well as providing a situation in which they can be easily tended. They make very attractive additions to an area around a rock garden or to a patio. For those with only a small garden, they are useful gardens within gardens and can be used to increase the number of plants that can be grown.

Old sandstone troughs that were once used on farms and stables are the ideal, but they are now getting very rare and are very expensive even if you can find one. Increasingly, garden centres are selling troughs especially made for rock gardens but these are also relatively expensive, although once purchased they will last many lifetimes.

A much cheaper alternative is to make your own. There are two ways of doing this – using a old sink as a former or creating a trough from scratch – and both methods involve a material known as hypertufa, which is simply a cement/sand mixture with peat added to it. The peat not only softens the colour and creates a sandstone-like texture but also gives a surface that is sympathetic to weathering, just like real stone. The mixture is one part cement, two parts sharp sand and one or two parts sieved peat (all parts by volume), mixed together (the proportions need not be exact and can be varied to personal preference). Water is added until it has a consistency of thick cream.

Although they are becoming more difficult to find, many old glazed sinks were thrown out of kitchens when they were replaced with those made with more modern materials such as stainless steel. These make ideal troughs. Thoroughly clean the sink and dry it, then cover it with an adhesive. Apply a layer of hypertufa over the surface. Use a stiffish mixture and apply it so that it creates a 2cm (æin) layer over the whole of the outside of the sink (not the bottom) and over the top rim and down inside for about 7.5cm (3in). There is no need to cover all the inside, only the part that will show at the top, because it will be full of compost when the trough is planted. Cover the sink with a damp sank or piece of cloth. After 36 hours it will be cured enough for you to carry out any finishing work. You can rough up the surface of the hypertufa or make it look even more like hewn rock by carving the surface with an old chisel or file. Once this is complete leave it to dry completely before filling.

The other method is to make your own trough. The simplest way is to find two cardboard boxes that fit inside each other with a 5cm (2in) gap between them. Support the outside box with bricks or pieces of wood so that it does not collapse, and fill the base with 5cm (2in) of hypertufa. Place the inner box in position and fill the gap between it an the outer box with hypertufa. So that the inner box does not distort or collapse completely, fill it with earth or sand at the same time. Ram the hypertufa well down to ensure that there are no air gaps. Again, cover with a damp sack and leave for 36 hours. Remove the sack and tear off the cardboard before finishing off the surface with an old chisel or file. Before the trough dries any further, it is essential to bore or cut some drainage holes through the base.

If you anticipate making several troughs, you could make some wooden formers so that you do not have to use cardboard boxes. These can be used again and again.

Move the trough into its final position before filling it with compost, because a full trough is very heavy and moving one could easily damage your back. Putting it on a brick base to raise it above the ground not only improves the drainage but also makes it look better.

Place a layer of drainage material in the bottom – old clay pots or small stones will do – and then fill it with a compost that is made up of one part loam, one part peat or peat substitute (leaf-mould is ideal) and two parts grit. Fill the trough to the top. A few small rocks can be let into the surface, and these will not only improve the appearance but will also provide the plants with a cool root-run. Plant the plants and then top dress with grit or small stones. Troughs containing more delicate plants can be protected from the worse excesses of winter rain and cold by covering them with a temporary shelter of glass or clear polythene.

PLANTS for SINKS and TROUGHS

Anchusa caespitosa	*Hypericum*
Androsace	*anagalloides*
Aquilegia (dwarf forms)	*Juniperus communis*
Asperula suberosa	'Compressa'
Campanula (dwarf forms)	*Oxalis adenophylla*
Chamaecyparis obtusa	*Paraquilegia*
'Nana Minima'	*Phlox subulata*
Daphne petraea	*Phyteuma*
Dianthus (dwarf forms)	*Polygala chamaebuxus*
Draba	*Primula*
Erigeron aureus	*Saxifraga*
Gentiana saxosa; G. verna	*Sedum* (dwarf forms)
Geranium farreri; G.	*Soldanella*
subcaulescens	*Thymus*

While alpine plants are interesting in themselves, they become even more so if they are displayed well. This trough provides the perfect home for a collection of such plants. It has been landscaped with tufa, which, together with the inclusion of shrubs, gives it a three-dimensional feel often lacking in troughs. The sempervivum in terracotta pots add even more interest to the scene.

TREES AND SHRUBS

Even at this time of year it is possible to plant trees and shrubs that have been purchased in containers. However, it is very important that they should not be allowed to dry out. If hot, dry weather follows planting it may help the struggling plant if it is sprayed with water or given some form of shading. Both will help to reduce the transpiration rate and the amount of water the roots need to take up.

Continue to carry out other routine jobs such as checking that the growing trees are not being cut into by their ties, removing suckers and pruning shrubs that flower on old wood immediately after flowering.

TOPIARY

Topiary, or the art of shaping trees and shrubs, is almost as old as gardens themselves. It is a wonderful way of creating permanent, all-year-round interest in the garden. The shapes vary considerably, from simple geometric shapes such as balls and cones and more complex ones such as spirals, to intricate 'carvings' such as birds or even whole tableaux – there is a famous one of a fox-hunting scene. The choice of subject is infinite and limited only by the imagination of the gardener. It may be that you want to use formal shapes to give the garden dignity or perhaps something lighter, such as a tea-pot, to introduce a touch of levity.

Topiary is best made from slow-growing, compact evergreens. Yew (*Taxus baccata*) and box (*Buxus sempervirens*) are two of the very best. Other, looser shrubs – privet (*Ligustrum*), for example – can be grown but, although they will grow more quickly into the shape you want, they will need more frequent trimming.

The best way of creating topiary is to start with a new plant, it is more difficult to 'carve' an existing one into shape. Plants can be bought in containers from a garden centre or nursery or they can be grown from cuttings or seeds.

Simple shapes, such as cones, can be cut by hand, but more complicated ones need some type of former against which the growing stems can be trained. In some cases, once the topiary has reached its final shape the former can be removed, but it often a good plan to leave it there permanently as a guide to the shape. With time, shapes can vary considerably unless there is some form of guidance.

Temporary formers can be made of wood and wire netting, but permanent ones are best made up from steel by a blacksmith. Even though it might look out of place, insert the framework at an early stage. As well as using the framework as an initial guide to clipping the topiary, use it to tie in branches to cover gaps. It will also be essential when creating shapes such as tails of peacocks, where it is important to train branches in one particular direction.

Once the final shape has been achieved, the topiary must be clipped regularly while it is growing to keep it in shape. Nothing looks sadder than an overgrown topiary, especially as it might be difficult to restore its shape. Use secateurs or shears rather than electric trimmers because they will give you better control and are less likely accidentally to cut off a tail or some other important part. Do not clip bushes after the beginning of autumn because any new shoots will be unlikely to harden sufficiently to withstand the winter. As well as following the outline of the underlying former, it may be necessary or desirable to make a template, even a simple one of canes, so that the shape is regularly cut. A cone, for example, is easier to cut if you use a template of three or four canes tied at the top. Similarly, the profile of a ball can be cut in board and kept to be used each year. (Make the profile of half the ball.)

A quick way to achieve topiary shapes is to use ivy (*Hedera*). Create the shape you require with wire netting and then let the ivy grow up and over it. Once it is the desired shape, trim the ivy regularly. Using two layers of wire netting with moss sandwiched between them gives the ivy a better base on which to grow.

Another way to create something different is to grow plants so close together that they appear to be one bush. A

possibility might be a plain green one and a golden or variegated one. Cut each to form a different part of the shape. Thus the top half of a ball might be golden while the bottom half is green. A more complicated shape would be a green bird with golden wings.

SHRUBS SUITABLE *for* TOPIARY

Buxus sempervirens (box)
Hedera (ivy)
Ilex (holly)
Laurus nobilis (bay)
Ligustrum ovalifolium (privet)
Lonicera nitida
Taxus baccata (yew)

VEGETABLES

In the early part of the month make the last successional sowings. If you leave it later than this there will not be time for the vegetables to mature before the weather becomes too cold. The season can, of course, be extended by the use of cloches.

The vegetable garden is at its most prolific from now on. Keep picking vegetables as they ripen, freezing them or otherwise storing them if there are too many for immediate consumption. If you go on holiday ask neighbours or friends to continue picking for you, perhaps as repayment for watering or mowing the lawn. This is more than just a philanthropic gesture, because the output of many plants suffer if they are not regularly harvested. Courgettes, for example, will grow into marrows and no new courgettes will be formed if they are not picked regularly; regular cropping, however, will make sure that there is a constant supply of new blooms and fruit. Runner beans are similarly affected.

Most vegetables, once they have started swelling, appreciate a constant supply of moisture, so water during dry spells. It is best to be consistent with this rather than doing it in fits and starts. Tomatoes, for example, are likely to crack if they are allowed to dry out and are then watered.

A lot of patience (or money) is required to obtain such attractive plants as these. Given time, it is perfectly possible to train box, *Buxus sempervirens*, starting from cuttings.

AUGUST

The garden takes on a sleepy quality this month. The colours are a little more subdued and the air is full of buzzing bees and lazily fluttering butterflies. This is certainly the month when gardeners can afford to relax a little and not only enjoy their own gardens but also those of others. When you are visiting, always remember to carry a notebook with you so that you can jot down any ideas that appeal to you. You may see individual plants or a particularly good grouping that you would like to copy. If you do not make a note of them now, you will, like most gardeners, forget them before you get back to your own garden.

This is also a time when many gardeners are away on holiday. If possible, ask a neighbour or friend to keep an eye on your garden while you are away. Offer them payment in the form of the fruit and vegetables that ripen during your absence. This will not only be fair recompense for their time but will encourage the plants to produce more.

Greenhouse

- Continue to make sure that the greenhouse is adequately shaded (p. 96) and ventilated (p. 77)
- In hot weather dampen the floor to cool and humidify the greenhouse (p. 96)
- Pick tomatoes and cucumbers, melons, aubergines and peppers (p. 113)
- Water at least once a day and feed once a week (p. 96)
- If the greenhouse is not used for tomatoes and other crops, thoroughly clean and disinfect it (p. 113)
- Sow hardy annuals for early flowering next year (p. 50)
- Take pelargonium and fuchsia cuttings for next year (p. 122)

Lawns

- Mow regularly, but not closely or too frequently if weather dry (p. 78)
- Water thoroughly if necessary (p. 113)
- Feed lawns (p. 60)
- Apply weedkillers (p. 79)

Perennials

- Deadhead flowers as they go over (p. 79)
- Watch out for pests and diseases and take appropriate action (p. 98)
- Continue to weed when necessary (p. 92)
- Fill any gaps with late annuals (p. 98)
- Water as necessary (p. 98)
- Collect seeds if required (p. 98)
- Take stem cuttings (p. 114)
- Move or divide irises (p. 124)
- Layer carnations (p. 125)

Rock Gardens

- Collect seeds if required (p. 101)
- Deadhead flowers as they go over unless seeds required (p. 101)
- Remove weeds on sight (p. 63)
- Take semi-ripe cuttings (p. 101)
- Finish re-potting and potting-on (p. 101)
- Shear over helianthemums (p. 101)

Trees and Shrubs

- Take cuttings (p. 139)
- Make chip-buddings if required (p. 111)
- Cut hedges as necessary (p. 82)
- Trim topiary as necessary (p. 102)
- Prune pleached trees (p. 129)

Vegetables

- Sow spring cabbage (p. 130)
- Sow last crops of lettuce (p. 130)
- Plant out spring cabbage if ready (p. 130)
- Harvest vegetables as they are ready (p. 130)
- Lift and dry onions (p. 46)
- Keep vegetables weed free (p. 103)
- Water when necessary (p. 104)

ANNUALS

It is already time to start thinking about next year! If hardy annuals, antirrhinums or marigolds (*Calendula*), for example, are sown now they will flower much earlier than if they are sown in spring. This will help to fill the gap early in the year before the majority of annuals come on stream. They can be sown where they are to flower or sown in pots, pricked out and planted out in late autumn. If the ground is not ready they can be overwintered under glass before planting out in early spring.

Annuals are getting past their best at this time of year and may be beginning to look a bit tired. Check them regularly, removing any dead flowers and any straggly stems as well as generally tidying them up. This will prolong their useful life.

If the ground is ready and available you can transplant biennials such as wallflowers into their flowering positions, although this can be delayed until next month if the beds are still full of plants.

MAINTAINING CONTAINERS

Containers should have been flowering now for several months and they may be beginning to show the strain. However, with careful attention they can still have plenty to offer. Regular watering is still the main priority. Unless it rains, most containers will require watering at least once a day, possibly more during hot weather. It is possible to add water-retaining crystals to the compost when you make up the container, and it is claimed that the crystals will reduce the need to water by up to a third. The crystals mean that the pots will need regular watering but that they do have a bit in reserve during really hot weather. During dull, overcast days, particularly if the weather is damp, watering can be reduced to once every two days. Always check the condition of the soil before watering. If it is already wet, do not water because although plants need plenty of moisture, very few like being waterlogged.

Hanging baskets also dry out rapidly and will need daily watering. If they cannot be watered from above, buy a special pump-action waterer, which has a long pipe and spout so that baskets above head-height can be reached easily from the ground.

As well as watering, containers will need feeding. This can be achieved by mixing a slow-release, granular fertilizer in the compost when you make up the container or by inserting a fertilizer stick into the top of the compost. The stick can be renewed when necessary. Most gardeners, however, still rely on adding a liquid fertilizer to one watering every week.

To prolong the life of a container and to keep it looking neat, remove any dead flowers as soon as they begin to fade. Most can be easily removed by hand but you may need to use secateurs or scissors for others to make a neat job of it. At the same time, snip off any wayward or straggly stems. This is partly to keep the plant tidy, but also to prevent some plants overpowering others, and upsetting the appearance of the container.

If a plant finishes flowering and does not have sufficient merits as a foliage plant for it to be kept in the container, dig it out and replace it with a spare plant. It is always a good idea to keep a few in reserve for just such a purpose.

Check that containers raised off the ground on bricks or short legs, do not have an accumulation of leaves and detritus under them. Compost may have washed through the drainage holes, adding to the rubbish under the pot. As well as possibly impairing the container's drainage, this is the perfect home for slugs. If the pot is too heavy to move, carefully rake out anything that has found its way underneath with a stick or piece of bent wire.

SELF-SOWING ANNUALS

Some annuals and biennials self-sow and will come up each year with little effort from the gardener except to thin out the plants if necessary. Make the initial sowing in an area that you want the plants to colonize. Do not remove the plants immediately after flowering but allow the plants to set and shed their seeds before you tidy them away. When they germinate, thin out the seedlings to the appropriate distances.

GREEN TIP
Collecting rainwater

Always collect as much rainwater as you can, not only from greenhouse roofs but also from the roofs of sheds and garages as well as the house. If you have space, create an underground cistern to hold it all and you should not be short of natural water.

RECOMMENDED SELF-SOWING ANNUALS

Alcea rosea (hollyhock)
Angelica archangelica (angelica)
Antirrhinum majus (antirrhinums)
Argemone (prickly poppy)
Atriplex hortensis (orach)
Borago officinalis (borage)
Calendula officinalis (pot marigolds)
Chrysanthemum segetum (corn marigolds)
Collomia grandiflora
Digitalis purpurea (foxgloves)
Eryngium giganteum (Miss Willmott's ghost)
Eschscholzia californica (Californian poppy)
Euphorbia lathyris (caper spurge)
Hesperis matronalis (sweet rocket)
Isatis tinctoria (dyer's woad)
Limnanthes douglasii (poached-egg flower)
Lunaria annua (honesty)
Malcomia (malcolm stock)
Myosotis (forget-me-not)
Nicotiana (tobacco plant)
Nigella (love-in-a-mist)
Oenothera biennis (evening primrose)
Omphalodes linifolia
Onopordum (giant thistle)
Papaver somniferum (opium poppy)
Silybum marianum (milk thistle)
Tanecetum parthenium (feverfew)
Tropaeolum majus (nasturtium)
Verbascum (mullein)
Viola (pansy, viola, violet)

The Californian poppy, *Eschscholzia californica*, readily self-sows, but generally reverts to the orange species.

 FRUIT

This is the main time of year for picking fruit. The late varieties of many of the early fruits, such as strawberries and raspberries, are still cropping, blackberries and their relatives are in full swing, while early plums and apples are beginning to ripen. Try to keep on top of the picking, removing any over-ripe or damaged fruit as you go. If you are taking a holiday, get a neighbour or friend to remove ripe fruit – and tell them to keep it for their trouble. Any excess of most fruits can be frozen, but most early apples do not store well and should be eaten before the skins begin to wrinkle. Unfortunately, they do not freeze fresh, but they can be stored in a freezer if they are cooked and puréed.

Continue to summer prune trained trees and soft fruit. Cordon and fan-trained fruit can really romp away unless it is cut back, and in doing so it will use up valuable energy as well as becoming overgrown.

Once blackberries and other briar fruit have finished fruiting, remove the old canes from the base. Tie in new ones to prevent them whipping about in the wind as well as keeping them tidy. Old raspberry canes should also be removed and new ones continue to be tied in to the wire work (p. 156).

Strawberry runners should have developed into substantial plants. Pot them up for future use or transplant them to new beds. Keep them well watered if the weather is hot and dry. In hotter areas it may be better to wait until next month.

THE GREENHOUSE

Throughout the summer the main routine in the greenhouse is to ensure that it is shaded, well ventilated and that all the plants have adequate water. Continue to keep the atmosphere moist to deter red spider mite by pouring water on the floor and allowing it to evaporate.

Pick the fruit of tomatoes, aubergines, peppers and melons as they ripen. Store or give away any you cannot use rather than leaving them on the plants. Most will not keep for long, but some can be frozen, although you may have to cook them first.

If the greenhouse is empty at the moment, take the opportunity to clean it out (p. 113).

It is time to be thinking of next year. Hardy annual seeds can be sown now (p. 50), and you can also take cuttings of pelargoniums and fuchsias now, so that they have rooted before winter sets in and will provide good sized plants for next year.

WATERING

One of the main tasks in the greenhouse at any time of the year is watering. Because of the warm atmosphere and the fact that most plants are grown in pots in a relatively small amount of compost, they require far more attention than plants in the open garden.

The simplest way is use a watering can, preferably filled from a water tub or barrel. Water used directly from the tap may have harmful chemicals – chlorine, for example – which evaporate if the water is left in a barrel before it is used. This may be of little consequence to relatively tough plants, such as tomatoes, but it is far more crucial when you are dealing with delicate plants such as alpines. Rain water collected from the roof of the greenhouse is the ideal. Another advantage of using water from a barrel is that it is at the ambient temperature, whereas tap water may be very cold. Some sophisticated greenhouses have a cistern or reservoir build into the ground under the bench with an input pipe direct from the roof's gutter. Such cisterns must be well protected if there is the chance that children may fall into them.

The best time for watering is in the evening or morning, many gardeners preferring the latter. If plants are watered during the day droplets of water may act as lenses, allowing rays of the sun to scorch the leaves. However, if the greenhouse is properly shaded (p. 96) this should not be a problem. The important thing is to make certain that if a plant needs water it gets it, irrespective of the time of day.

Plants should be watered only when they need it. This is particularly important in winter, when they use up far less. If the compost in a pot is already wet, do not water. Few plants will tolerate waterlogged conditions, and it is often the case that more plants die from overwatering than die from lack of moisture. Experience will tell you when a pot needs water. Pick it up and if there is no ring of dampness below it then it needs watering. The weight of a pot is often a clear indication, too. Terracotta pots will 'ring' when you strike them if they are too dry. If you prefer to trust technology, there are various devices that will tell you when compost needs watering (although not necessarily when a plant needs water). Plants rarely need watering when they are dormant, so you should not, for example, water dormant cyclamen corms.

It is possible to set up an automatic watering system. This can be as simple as a dribbling hose that has outlets in each pot or it can be capillary matting, which supplies constant moisture to the bottom of the pots from a reservoir. Equipment and instructions for both methods are widely available from garden centres and suppliers. If you go away on holiday, do not forget to arrange for a friend or neighbour to do your watering.

LAWNS

Continue to mow at regular intervals, but ease back a bit on frequency and cut slightly higher if the weather is particularly dry and hot. If you are having a party on the lawn or lots of visitors allow the grass to grow slightly longer so that it is better able to cope with the additional wear and tear.

TEXTURED LAWNS

Many gardeners like to mow their lawns regularly, keeping it well cut so that it looks like a striped billiard table. The cut never varies, and the grass always has a short, manicured look about it, which extends over the whole area. Any variation is usually caused by weeds, which are speedily dealt with.

Some gardeners, however, regard slight variations in a lawn as attractive features, however. It is, for example, possible to mow so that the grass is shorter in some areas than in others. The idea works best on a large expanse, where there is room to work out a bold design. The simplest designs to execute are those involving straight lines – a chequer-board effect, for example – but there is no reason why curved lines or even an intricate pattern cannot be introduced. One of the possible effects is that of a knot garden. Children, on the other hand, will find a maze fun, the shorter grass being the path and the higher grass the 'hedges'. They will spend hours running around trying to find the way in and the way out. It is much quicker to establish and easier to maintain than a conventional hedge maze, and there is the advantage that you can enjoy its shape simply by looking at it.

A simpler version of this is to cut pathways through longer grass. This works well in meadows or orchards where the grass is left to grow as they contain wildflowers. Even when there are no plants in flower, it is still a pleasant experience to be drawn along these paths by the short grass. See also Wildflower Meadows (p. 114).

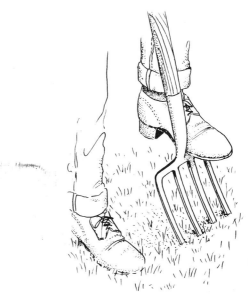

An ordinary garden fork is a good way of aerating a fairly small lawn. Insert the fork straight down, then lean it back slightly to enlarge the hole.

AERATION

During the course of the summer, lawns and paths in constant use get trodden down and the underlying soil compacted. Grass roots need air to grow properly and they also need water, which tends to run off the tightly packed soil. One way to improve their condition is to aerate the ground.

This involves making holes in the lawn so that both air and water can enter. The simplest way of achieving this is to push the tines of a garden fork into the lawn and pull back on it slightly so that a series of holes is formed. This is continued over the whole lawn, a tedious task but a valuable one. Quicker and less laborious methods are to be had by using machines. These are not worth buying as the amount of use would not justify their cost, unless you had a lot of lawn. Fortunately, they can usually be hired. One of these machines has a series of sharp 'cogs' on the back, which dig into the lawn and make a series of short slits. Another machine inserts tubes into the lawn and digs out a row of cores. It is possible to buy a simple tool, a bit like a hollow-tined fork so that this can be carried out by hand.

When a corer is used the resulting holes are bigger than those made by the other methods and they need to be filled with a soil mixture, consisting of sharp sand, peat (or peat substitute) and sieved soil. It is also a good idea to brush some of this mixture into smaller holes as it helps to keep them open, but you will not need anywhere near so

The perfect lawn with a surface like a billiard table. The chequered pattern can be created by mowing up and down and across at right angles. A fine, moss-free lawn will add character and beauty to your garden.

much. The top dressing can be spread by a mechanical spreader or, over smaller areas, by hand. Alternatively, it can be worked in using a birch broom (besom) or a lute, a special tool consisting of bars that brush the ground.

BEARDED IRISES

This is the time of year when it is best to lift and divide bearded irises. They can be transplanted at any time between now and spring, but now is the best time if you want to get them re-established quickly. Lift them with a fork and shake the soil from the roots. Use a sharp knife to cut the rhizomes into individual pieces and discard the older material. Cut the leaves back to a fan about 15cm (6in) long before replanting in rejuvenated soil or in a new position. Plant them 15–20cm (6–8in) apart with the roots well spread out and the rhizomes covered with soil only about half way up their sides; the top should be completely clear of soil. Water and readjust the soil level if necessary.

PERENNIALS

The most important thing to do with the perennial borders at this time of year is to enjoy them. They still have plenty of flower-power left, but they will soon begin to go beyond their best and preparations for winter will begin. It is still warm, and wandering through the borders can be a pleasant way to spend an afternoon. Early morning and evening strolls show the colours and textures in different lights, and, as you walk round, remember to make a note of any ideas you may have for improving the colour scheme or ideas you have about what should be replaced or removed. If you do not record your thoughts you are likely to have forgotten them by the time you come to carry them out.

While you are walking around your garden, keep an eye out for any pests and diseases and take appropriate action. If you have a bit more energy, take the secateurs with you and remove dead flowers and any stems of plants that are going over.

LAYERING

Layering is a useful way of increasing your stock of carnations and many woody plants. It is a particularly useful way of propagating plants that are difficult to root. The simplest way is to bend down a steam and partially bury it in the soil. This can be done on many shrubs and will provide the odd new plant whenever you should need to add to your stocks.

A more systematic method can be used for serious propagation. Remove the leaves from the length of the stem where you want rooting to occur. Make a slanting cut partially through the stem on its underside. Dig a hole or small trench and place the stem so that the cut part lies in the hole or trench. Peg down the stem with a piece of bent wire and replace the soil. Water well. Once the layer has rooted – and this may take a considerable time with some plants – cut the stem to the parent plant. Dig up the new plant and transplant it to a pot or to its new home.

If the soil is poor, dig a deeper hole and partly fill it with compost before inserting the stem, and then cover it with more compost.

An alternative method is to place a pot in the hole and to arrange the stem so that, when the stem from the parent plant is eventually severed, the new plant can be lifted straight from the ground, already potted up.

HERBS

Herbs are doubly useful in the garden. First, they are useful in themselves – for cooking, for example – and second, they are decorative. They can be grown in any number of ways. You could create a herb garden – with a whole area devoted just to herbs – or you can mix them into the borders with other plants, or you can grow them in containers.

The advantage of the herb garden is that all the herbs are grown in one place. It can be a wonderfully fragrant

Layering

Dig a hole or small trench by the side of the main plant, preparing the soil with some additional grit or peat.

Make a slanting cut in a stem and bend it, so that the cut faces downwards, into the trench. Use a metal hoop to hold the stem firmly in place until the new roots have formed.

Bearded irises come in a wonderful mixture of colours.

place, constantly filled with the sound of bees in summer. Herb gardens can be of any shape or size, but it is usually a good idea if the beds are not too large so that all the plants can be reached from the path. Herb gardens should be sited in an warm, sunny position, away from overhanging trees. If you use herbs a lot in cooking, it should also not be too far from the back door. If possible, include a bench or seat so that you can enjoy the heady summer scents. When you are designing a herb garden, remember that many of the plants, although small to begin with, will eventually grow quite large and you should allow plenty of space for them.

If you do not have the space for a herb garden or only want to grow a few different kinds, there is no reason they should not be incorporated into other borders. Chives or parsley, for example, can be used to edge a bed, or rosemary and sage can be used in place of other shrubs. Lavender will fit in almost anywhere. If you need to harvest them regularly, make certain that they are not too far into the border and that preferably they can be reached from the path.

Many gardeners who grow only a few basic herbs put them in spare ground in the vegetable garden. This is a particularly useful way of coping with annual herbs, such as basil. If you like your vegetable plot to be decorative or grow it as a potager, herbs are very useful for lining the edges of individual plots.

If space is limited, growing herbs in containers is a very good idea. They can be grown in individual pots or in special herb planters, which will accommodate several different herbs, often in holes in the side of the pot. One big advantage of this method of growing herbs is that the pot can be placed close to the kitchen door or even on a windowsill.

Herbs need to be watered regularly, and when plants are in full growth they should be fed with a liquid feed added to the water once a week. Do not overcrowd the pots, and large subjects, such as bay, are best given their own container. Once roots start coming out of the bottom of the pot it is time to re-pot into a larger container or to start again with smaller plants. Use fresh compost every time you re-pot.

Herbs need well-drained soil, but it must have plenty of organic matter in it so that it is reasonably moisture retentive. Plant perennials in autumn or spring, and annuals in late spring or early summer when the threat of frost has passed. Deadhead regularly unless you are growing the herb for its seed. Some of the shrubby plants, such as lavender and thyme, need to be lightly sheered over after flowering and then again more tightly in spring to prevent them from becoming too straggly.

Annual herbs such as basil and tarragon, need to be sown each year from seed. This can be done in a greenhouse or propagating frame at the same time as you sow your half-hardy annuals. Alternatively, they can be purchased as young plants from a garden centre or nursery.

Some herbs – mint is a good example – can be invasive and if they are put unprotected into a herb garden or ordinary border the questing roots may romp away through every other plant and become a nuisance. One way of coping with this is to plant it in a large pot or bucket with drainage holes in the bottom, and then sink the container into the ground so that the rim is level with the surface. As the plant cannot travel in search of new territory it will soon exhaust the soil in its container and it will need replacing from time to time. Other plants, such as lemon balm, self-seed invasively and need cutting back before the seeds are ripe.

Many herbs can be stored for winter use by drying. Collect the herbs on a dry day. Most are at their best before they have flowered and certainly before the leaves become old and tough looking. They can be hung upside down in bunches, in a warm place out of direct sunlight. Another way is to freeze them fresh in individual portions in ice cubes, using the ice making tray in a freezer. A third way is to use them to flavour oils or vinegars.

CULINARY HERBS

Anise: seed, leaves; annual
Angelica: stem, seed, leaves; annual
Basil: leaves; annual
Bay: leaves; shrub
Bergamot: leaves; perennial
Borage: leaves; annual
Caraway: seed; annual/biennial
Camomile: leaves; perennial
Chervil: leaves; annual
Chives: leaves; perennial
Coriander: seed, leaves; biennial
Dill: leaves, seed; annual
Fennel: leaves, stems; perennial
Horseradish: root; perennial
Hyssop: leaves; perennial
Lemon balm: leaves; perennial
Lovage: seed, leaves; perennial
Mint: leaves; perennial

Mustard: seed; annual
Oregano/marjoram: leaves; annual/perennial
Parsley: leaves; annual/perennial
Pot marigold: flowers, leaves; annual
Rosemary: leaves; shrub
Sage: leaves; shrub
Summer savory: leaves; annual
Sweet cicely: leaves, seed; perennial
Tarragon: leaves; annual/perennial
Thyme: leaves; shrub

🍃 ROCK GARDENS

Apart from keeping the beds tidy there is not a great deal to do in the rock garden in the late summer. However, it is a good time for preparing new rock beds, ready for planting in spring. This gives the bed time to settle down and to allow any weeds to show up and be removed.

BUILDING A ROCK GARDEN

The key to building a successful rock garden is to get it right the first time. If things go wrong – if, for example, perennial weeds are left in the soil – it may be necessary to take out all the plants, dismantle at least some, often all, of the rock work and start again. This may seem a rather arduous thing to do, but it is by far the most satisfactory thing in the long run. However, with thought and careful preparation, you should get it right the first time.

The first thing is to work out what you want. A keen enthusiast will need a garden that provides a series of habitats suitable for growing alpine plants. Many gardeners have far less elaborate needs and require only a rock structure down which they can grow colourful aubrieta and rock roses. Although, if done properly, they are basically both the same, the former is obviously going to be more sophisticated.

The choice of site is important. It should be in an open, sunny position, where there is plenty of fresh air but not a constant draught – avoid site between two buildings for this reason. It should be well drained, but the underlying soil is not too important because the rock garden is usually built above it.

The best rock to use is a local one. This is partly because it will fit in with the landscape and the general feeling of the area and garden, but also because local stone will be much cheaper than material brought from further afield. Use a strong stone that does not shatter in

Building a rock garden

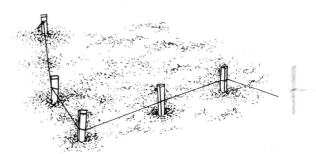

Clear the site of any perennial weed roots and other rubbish before you add a layer of gritty compost. It can be useful to mark the position of the main rocks with string before you actually move anything.

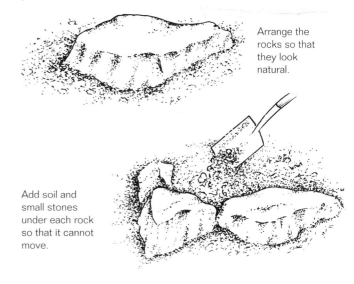

Dig a small depression for each large rock so that it is as stable as possible.

Arrange the rocks so that they look natural.

Add soil and small stones under each rock so that it cannot move.

The aim is to provide a range of planting areas to give scope for a variety of plants.

the frosts – sandstone and limestone are the two favourites – but avoid lumps of concrete, which rarely look other than what they are – concrete. Do not choose pieces of stone that are too big, because, although they may look impressive, they are very difficult to move and unless you have access to machinery, they can cause back problems.

The soil should be a free-draining mixture of a good loam, peat (or a peat substitute such as leaf-mould) and grit. The proportions will vary depending on how free-draining the soil is, but a mixture of two, loam and one each of the others, is about right. Add more grit if the soil is not free draining.

Start by clearing the site of any weeds and rubbish. It is important that there are no perennial weeds left because these are bound to cause serious problems later on. Build up the layers of soil, adding the rocks so that they look like a natural outcrop. Arrange the stone in layers so that it resembles the natural strata, and take care that if there are geological lines in the rocks, that they are horizontal to the ground. Avoid piling all the soil into a heap and then dotting the stones all over it. Each rock should be bedded into the soil, with at least a third below the surface. This may seem a waste of stone but it is important that the rock is firmly bedded because you will often have to walk on them when you are tending the plants and because many plants tend to curl their roots under the rocks, both for moisture and protection.

Build the bed up layer by layer. You may find that you need to create a temporary earth ramp up which you can roll the stone. At all costs, avoid lifting stones – roll them, push them on barrows or rollers, or lever them. When you place two pieces together, watch out for trapped fingers, it is easy to do and very painful.

Make the rock bed look as natural as possible – look at plenty of examples and pictures. Leave vertical crevices between rocks for planting as well as pockets of soil on the ledges, and vary the type of soil to make it suitable for different plants. You could, for example, use a peatier soil on the shady side of a rock so that you can plant primulas there. Allow the

bed to sink and then top up with more soil before planting. Once planted (p. 41), top dress the whole of the soil surface with grit or small stones.

🍃 TREES AND SHRUBS

This is the last month for cutting topiary or hedges. After this any new growth that is put on is unlikely to harden and will therefore be liable to being burnt off by frosts. This is not fatal but may leave the hedge or topiary looking a bit of a mess, especially if it is evergreen.

PRUNING RAMBLER ROSES

The best time to prune ramblers is in the late summer after they have finished flowering. Ramblers can be quite prolific in their production of suckers and after a few years can produce a thicket that can take an age to sort out. If possible, try to prune each year. The first thing to do is to cut out any dead or damaged material. After this, if you can release the stems from their support and spread them out on the ground so that you can get at them more easily. Cut out any weak stems and remove up to a third of the older material. This will open up the bush and allow in more air and light as well as promoting a continuing supply of young and healthy shoots, which will keep the rose healthy.

From the remaining stems, reduce the length of the side shoots and cut back the main stems, removing any unripe

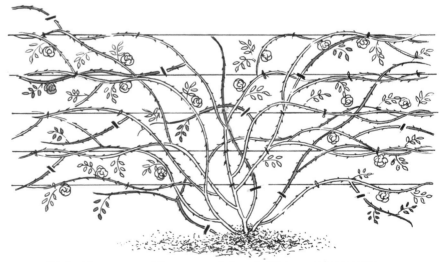

It is best to prune a rambling rose regularly so that it does not become too overgrown. As well as removing dead and damaged stems, cut stems that have flowered hard back and tie in new growth to the supports.

wood. Tie the stems back against the framework or wires, gently arching each stem if possible so that the branches spread out horizontally. This will help to increase the number of flowers in the following season, a point worth remembering for most roses. As you tie in the stems, remove any that cross over existing ones or that lie awkwardly.

PRUNING WISTERIA

If it is to flower well, wisteria needs regular pruning. In late summer or early autumn cut back the long new growth to about 15cm (6cm). In winter reduce these shoots even further, cutting them back to about 7.5cm (3in).

PLEACHING

Pleached trees used to seen only in large gardens where they were used to create avenues. They were also used as screens and sometimes branches were trained across between two rows of trees to form a 'roof' so that a complete box or room was created. Nowadays the technique is also being used on a smaller scale in many gardens, where it is used mainly as a screen, either between the garden and the outside world or as an internal division.

Pleaching is not a difficult technique but it needs patience because it is several years before the final result is visible. The basic idea is to reduce the number of branches on a tree and train those that remain onto a horizontal framework until they intertwine, forming a 'hedge in the sky' or a 'hedge on stilts'. The two best types of tree for this are the hornbeam or lime, but others can also be used.

A tumbling waterfall of blue and white wisteria will create a spectacular sight in spring. Regular pruning is needed to keep the climber at its best.

Wisteria needs pruning twice a year if it is to flower well. In summer cut back long, leafy shoots to about 15cm (6in). In winter cut back the same shoots again to 10cm (4in)

GREEN TIP
Natural aeration
Earthworms make one of the best natural aerators. Do not try to discourage them with chemicals.

It is best to start from scratch rather than trying to convert existing trees or hedge. You will need a framework to begin with, but once the trees are established this can be dispensed with. Set the 3m (10ft) posts about 2.5–2.75m (8–9ft) apart along the desire line. These will be in place for several years, so make sure that they are strong enough, that they are buried in the ground to a sufficient depth that they will not move and that they have been treated with preservative (but not creosote). Between these fix horizontal battens or wires. The lowest should be about 1.8m (6ft) from the ground, with additional ones at 60cm (2ft) intervals.

Pleaching

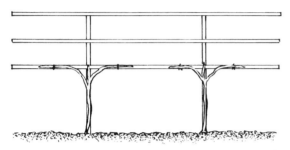

Erect a framework of uprights and horizontals and plant a tree at the base of each upright. The uprights should be about 2.4m (8ft) apart. Tie in laterals that are height of the first row of horizontal supports and remove any lower side shoots.

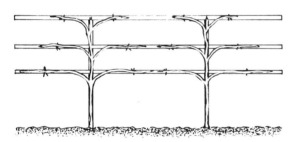

The following year cut back the laterals to encourage new side shoots. Tie in new laterals to the next horizontal support. When the leader reaches the desired height, tie it to the top horizontal support.

Plant a tree in front of each upright. Remove any laterals below the bottom batten and tie in side shoot on either side of those that are at the right height. If the tree is tall enough to have laterals at the level of the second batten, tie these in too, removing any others. Remove any side shoots from the laterals. As the tree grows, continue to tie in until there is one lateral on every batten on each side of the tree. Remove any addition laterals and cut back any side shoots to two buds. Once the leader has reached the top batten, cut out the tip. If you want to create a 'roof' bend the leader over and train it horizontally along a wire

or batten going across to the opposite row of trees. Allow further laterals to fill in the space of the 'roof' in the same way the lower laterals filled the 'walls'.

As the laterals lengthen cut them back to a strong bud to stimulate new growth and tie in the resulting branches, intertwining them with those of the next tree as they get long enough. Once the branches are intermeshed the framework can be removed. Keep removing any new laterals on the main stem and prune back any excessive growth of both laterals and side shoots. so that the pleached effect is maintained.

TREES *for* PLEACHING

> *Carpinus* (hornbeam)
> *Salix* (willow)
> *Sorbus* (whitebeam)
> *Tilia* (lime)

🍃 VEGETABLES

There is not much sowing to do at this time of year. Spring cabbage (see below), the last sowing of lettuce and sowing for winter of parsley are the main things. If spring cabbage was sown last month and is big enough, it can be planted out now.

The main job in the vegetable garden is to continue harvesting the crops as they ripen. Lift onions, dry them off in the sun and store them. Continue to pick all beans, courgettes and tomatoes as they ripen to encourage further cropping.

CABBAGE

Gardeners seem to more fond of cabbage than non-gardeners, perhaps because they grow more tasty varieties and know that they should not over-cook them. There are cabbages for virtually every month of the year and a careful choice of cultivars can provide a constant supply for the kitchen.

Spring cabbages are sown at the end of summer and are overwintered in the ground. Early summer varieties are sown in late winter or early spring under glass. Summer varieties are sown slightly later but in the open garden. Both autumn and winter cabbages are sown in late spring.

All cabbages need a fertile soil that was manured for a previous crop. They also appreciate a firm soil and having the soil firmed in well around them when they are planted.

CABBAGE PROBLEMS

One of the worst problems from which cabbages of all kinds suffer is clubroot. The incidence of this can be reduced by using different ground for brassicas each year, by improving the drainage and by liming the ground to reduce its acidity. Another problem that occurs at root level is with cabbage root fly. These can be deterred if you put felt collars around the seedlings to prevent the female fly from laying eggs.

Alternatively, dust with the appropriate chemical available at your garden centre. Leaves are often damaged caterpillars, and this can be prevented by covering the plants with a fine net or fleece to stop the butterflies laying eggs. If caterpillars appear they can be picked off by hand or the plants can be sprayed or dusted with one of the safe vegetable chemicals available from the garden centre. At the seedling stage flea beetles can be a menace. They make so many holes in the leaves that the plant is eventually killed. Dust the seedlings with derris or one of the other recommended chemicals, following the instructions of the packet. Keep the slug population under control and cover the plants with netting if birds are a problem.

Water when you plant and keep watered until they are established. Keep weeds down. Autumn and winter varieties tend to stand well once they have matured, but some of the spring and summer varieties bolt, so use them as they become ready.

When it is properly prepared cabbage can be a superb vegetable. Fortunately, most gardeners realize this, and it is still popular as a garden vegetable, although its sales in the greengrocer have declined. One of the main problems is keeping the butterflies from laying eggs, which in turn produce the caterpillars that turn every leaf to lace. Picking the caterpillars off by hand or spraying them with chemicals are two ways, but covering the plants with a light fleece keeps the butterflies off in the first place.

RECOMMENDED VARIETIES *of* SPRING CABBAGE

'April'
'Durham Early'
'Greensleeves'
'January King
'Offenham 1 – Myatt's Offenham Compacta'
'Pixie'
'Spring Hero'

RECOMMENDED VARIETIES *of* SUMMER CABBAGE

'Castello'
'Derby Day'
'Hispi'
'Minicole'
'Primo'
'Quickstep'

RECOMMENDED VARIETIES *of* AUTUMN CABBAGE

'Autoro'
'Bingo'
'Castello'
'Minnicole'
'Rapier'
'Winnigstadt'

RECOMMENDED VARIETIES *of* WINTER CABBAGE

'Capraccio'
'Christmas Drumhead'
'Duncan'
'Hidena'
'Novusa'
'Ormskirk 1 – Ormskirk Late'
'Tundra'
'Wivoy'

RECOMMENDED VARIETIES *of* RED CABBAGE

'Kissendrup'
'Metro'
'Red Drumhead'
'Red Dutch'
'Ruby Ball'
'Vesta'

SEPTEMBER

Autumn is a mellow time – colours change and the pace of garden annual cycle slows down. It is also a season of flavours – wonderful juicy blackberries come into season, and apples and pears are coming into their own.

The lazy time is nearly over, however, and it is time to start gardening again. The gardener must always be thinking ahead and planning. There is no such thing as 'instant gardening' – forethought and preparation are needed if you want to have a productive and attractive garden next year.

Now, as autumn approaches, is the time to start tidying and getting the garden ready for winter. It is also time to start preparing the ground for the following year. This not only gives the soil time to weather but also allows any organic material to finish rotting down. Many plants, vegetables in particular, prefer to be planted into soil that was manured some months earlier rather than into ground that has only recently been treated.

CHECKLIST

General

- Start the autumn tidy up, especially on heavy soils (p. 143)
- Shred and compost all dead herbaceous and woody material (p. 23)
- Start autumn digging and ground preparation on heavy soils (p. 143)
- Plan next year's flowers (p. 124) and vegetables (p. 26)

Annuals and Tender Perennials

- Make final sowing of hardy annuals in open ground (p. 134)
- Sow hardy annuals under glass (p. 50)
- Remove faded annuals from containers and baskets (p. 120)
- Tidy up those still flowering (p. 120)
- Replant containers with winter-flowering annuals (p. 134)
- Lift and store tender perennials in cold areas (p. 134)

Bulbs

- Plant spring-flowering bulbs, except tulips (p. 135)
- Collect and sow lily bulbils (p. 135)
- Pot up bulbs for forcing (p. 135)
- Lift and store gladioli as foliage dies back (p. 53)
- Lift and store dahlias after first frosts (p. 153)
- Sow bulb seeds (p. 76)

Fruit

- Pick apples and pears as they ripen (p. 122)
- Store keeping varieties of apples and pears (p. 168)
- Finish planting strawberries (p. 138)
- Order plants for replacements and new fruit projects (p. 137)
- Prune Morello cherries (p. 112)
- Pick autumn raspberries (p. 156)
- Finish budding fruit trees (p. 111)

Greenhouse

- Sow hardy annuals (p. 50)
- Reduce watering as growth slows for the winter (p. 122)
- Stop feeding (p. 139)
- Service heaters before the frosts begin (p. 158)
- Bring in chrysanthemums and fuchsias for overwintering (p. 134)

Lawns

- Reduce amount of mowing (p. 140)
- Do not cut grass too short (p. 140)
- Rake to remove thatch (p. 59)
- Spike to alleviate summer compaction (p. 123)
- Top dress with mixture of fine organic material, sand and loam (p. 141)
- Feed if necessary (p. 60)
- Apply moss-killer if necessary (p. 79)
- Prepare ground for laying lawns in spring (p. 141)
- Sow new lawns on previously prepared ground (p. 141)

Perennials

- Remove dead and dying herbaceous material (p. 134)
- Deadhead as flowers go over (p. 79)
- Collect seeds (p. 98)
- Remove weeds on sight (p. 92)
- Start preparing new beds and borders (p. 143)
- Plant out spring-raised plants (p. 142)
- Pot on rooted cuttings and late seedlings (p. 142)
- Lift and divide clump-forming plants (p. 40)

Rock Gardens

- Prepare new beds and rock gardens (p. 127)
- Plant or replant beds (p. 63)
- Sow seeds in pots (p. 41)
- Remove weeds (p. 63)
- Reduce watering for alpines in pots (p. 144)
- Remove shading from frames and alpine houses (p. 144)

Trees and Shrubs

- Cut back wisteria (p. 129)
- Prune rambling and climbing roses (p. 128)
- Take semi-ripe cuttings (p. 139)
- Take cuttings of marginally hardy shrubs and overwinter inside (p. 139)
- Mulch trees and shrubs (p. 103)
- Trim hedges when necessary (p. 82)

Vegetables

- Lift and store potatoes and other tender root crops (p. 147)
- Remove and compost finished crops (p. 147)
- Start autumn digging (p. 25)

ANNUALS AND TENDER PERENNIALS

There is still time to make final sowings of hardy annuals in the open ground. Later than this and they will not be large enough to flower in early summer, so you might prefer to wait and sow in spring. You can, however, continue to sow hardy annuals under glass, overwintering the resulting seedlings in pots or deep trays.

Many of this year's annuals will be in decline. Remove them as they go over and lightly fork through the ground, removing any weeds as you work. Continue to tidy up those annuals that are still flowering.

In cold areas it may be necessary to lift and store tender perennials, such as chrysanthemums (see below), pelargoniums and fuchsias. Bring in pots of pelargoniums and fuchsias and keep them in a cool, frost-free place in the light. Keep them just moist. Do not forget to label all the stored plants. This activity will, of course, depend on the weather. Even if you live in a comparatively warm area, an unexpectedly early frost can do serious damage. Most tender perennials will take a light frost, as long as it does not penetrate the soil.

CHRYSANTHEMUMS

Tender chrysanthemums must be lifted before the first serious frosts. Cut back the stems to just above ground level and dig up the plants, shake or wash off most of the soil and place them in boxes of peat or peat substitute and store them in a cool but frost-free place – under a greenhouse bench, for instance. Keep them just moist. In January the boxes of chrysanthemum stools should be brought into the light in a warm greenhouse or conservatory. Water them to stimulate them into growth, and once the shoots are 5cm (2in) tall, remove them and treat them as basal cuttings (p. 61) to produce plants for the following season.

WINTER CONTAINERS

Many summer containers are now coming to the end of their life, and it is time to clean them out and replant for the winter. Any containers can be used as long as they are frost-proof. Hanging baskets may freeze solid in very cold spells, but even they can be used successfully in winter, especially with plants such as winter pansies. Although there are a few annuals that can be used, many of the plants used in winter containers are either perennials or shrubs, but, because they are left in the container for only one season, they may be regarded as annuals.

Remove the summer's plants from the container, tip out the compost and thoroughly clean the pot, both inside and out. Discard the old compost. It is a false economy to reuse it in a container, although it can be used on the garden. Put in a drainage layer of broken clay pots or small stones and refill the container with new potting compost. Since growth rates are much slower in the winter there is no need to add extra fertilizer or to mix water-retaining crystals with the compost.

Add the plants of your choice, firm down the compost around the plants and level it off so that its surface is about 2.5cm (1in) below the rim of the container. Water thoroughly. Large containers should be filled and planted where they are to flower, but smaller ones can be kept to one side until the plants have filled the container or are beginning to put on a display.

Keep watered during the warmer weather but once it becomes cool be careful not to overwater. Unless the display is kept under shelter, there will probably be sufficient moisture from rainfall. Add extra drainage material, such as grit, into the compost if you garden in an area of high winter rainfall, because the plants will dislike becoming waterlogged.

PLANTS *for* WINTER *and* EARLY SPRING

Aucuba japonica 'Variegata' (spotted laurel): shrub
Bergenia: perennials
Conifers: shrubs, dwarf trees
Crocus: bulbs
Cyclamen: bulbs
Erica (heathers): shrubs
Galanthus (snowdrops): bulbs
Hedera (ivy): shrubs
Helleborus (hellebores): perennials
Hyacinthus: bulbs
Iris reticulata (winter irises): bulbs
Narcissus (daffodils): bulbs
Muscari (grape hyacinths): bulbs
Ophiopogon planiscapus 'Nigrescens': grass
Primula (primroses, polyanthus): perennial
Ranunculus ficaria (lesser celandine): perennials
Rhododendron: shrub
Sarcococca (Christmas box)
Skimmia japonica 'Rubella': shrubs
Viola × wittrokiana (pansies): annuals

BULBS

If you have ordered bulbs by mail order they should be arriving this month. It is also the time to make your selections from the local garden centres or nurseries. Having got them it is time to plant them (see below).

Some lilies produce bulbils. These are little bulb-like objects that appear in the axils of the leaves (where the leaves join the stalk). These can be removed and 'sown' as if they were seed. This can either be in nursery beds in the open garden or in trays in a coldframe. After a few seasons they will have grown into full-sized flowering bulbs, identical to their parent. It is a good, easy and reliable way of increasing your lily stock.

In colder areas it is time to lift gladioli (p. 53) and dahlias (p. 153). In milder areas or in mild years dahlias may continue to flower for another two months or even more, but keep an eye on weather forecasts and bring them in before deep penetrating frosts begin.

PLANTING BULBS

Bulbs are planted at different times of the year, depending on whey they flower. Autumn-flowering bulbs are planted in spring; spring-flowering bulbs are planted in autumn. The planting technique for both types is the same.

When you are choosing bulbs buy plump, healthy-looking specimens. Most of the bulbs that are sold at this time of year are dried, but there are some that should always be bought 'in the green'. Snowdrops (*Galanthus*) for example, should either be bought in pots or as plants that have just been dug up (p. 21). Cyclamen should always be bought in pots (p. 22). Only buy bulbs that have been raised by nurseries; never buy bulbs that have been harvested from the wild, where they are in danger of becoming extinct.

Mixed bulbs are usually much cheaper than single coloured, but on the whole, a patch of a single colour is more pleasing to the eye than a mixed clump. Most bulbs can be planted this month with the exception of tulips, which should be planted next month. If you delay planting bulbs such as daffodils, they will be late starting into growth and they may not be as prolific as they would have been.

Most bulbs come from hot Mediterranean areas, and they prefer a free-draining, sunny position in the garden. There are, however, some woodlanders, which need a more humus-rich soil and shadier conditions. This group includes *Trillium*, *Erythronium* (dog-toothed violet),

Planting bulbs

Roll back a small area of turf and plant small bulbs in the ground before covering them with the turf.

Use a garden fork to make holes in the lawn into which small bulbs can be planted for naturalizing.

Scatter bulbs on the ground and plant them where they fall for a natural effect.

Use a special bulb planter for inserting larger bulbs into lawns.

There are not a great number of summer bulbs, but the large range of lilies makes up for this. As long as lily beetle can be kept under control, they are reasonably easy to grow.

Arisaema, Anemone nemorosa and it allies (wood anemones), and many of the *Galanthus* (snowdrops).

In bedding schemes bulbs may be laid out in serried ranks, but in most schemes they are usually planted in clumps or seemingly at random, and even within clumps, the plants are not ordered. If you are naturalizing bulbs or planting large areas it is important not to set them in rows or they will look rather odd. It is surprising difficult to plant bulbs so that they look natural. One often-suggested method is to throw a handful of bulbs gently onto the ground and to plant them where they fall.

Dig a hole about three times the height of the bulb, so that when it is planted the top of the bulb is twice its own height below the surface. In prepared soil a wide, shallow hole can be dug and all the bulbs put in place before it is refilled. In unprepared ground, such as in lawns, the bulbs should be planted singly. A trowel can be used but if you have a lot of bulbs, a special bulb planter is useful. This removes a plug of soil, which can be replaced over the bulb after it has been inserted into the hole. For small patches of smaller bulbs, a strip of turf can be rolled back and then replaced over the bulbs.

BULBS *for* LATE SUMMER *and* EARLY AUTUMN

Cardiocrinum giganteum
Crinum × powellii
Crocosmia
Dierama
Eucomis
Galtonia
Gladiolus
Lilium
Nomocharis
Tigridia
Watsonia
Zantedeschia

LILIES

Among the most popular of the summer-flowering bulbs is the lily. While they are not grown for exhibition in the same way that many other bulbs are, they are addictive enough to get many gardeners hooked on growing as many varieties as they can. Although some have a delightful simplicity, others are truly exotic and are, perhaps, some of the most exotic plants to be grown in the open garden in temperate climates.

There are so many species and hybrids to choose from it is often difficult for the gardener to know where to begin. Possibly the best way is to get a catalogue from a bulb merchant specializing in lilies and look through for those you like best. Some, as you would expect, are more difficult to grow than others, but it is usually the more obscure species that are the most difficult, with most of the hybrids presenting no real problems.

Lilies can be grown in a wide range of position, but possibly look best when they are grown in a border among other plants. They associate well with shrubs and those

GREEN TIP
Buying bulbs

Always buy bulbs that are certified as being horticulturally propagated and not plants removed from the wild. Areas, such as Turkey, are being denuded of native bulbs as millions are indiscriminately grubbed up and sold to the western world without thought to the resulting extinction or near extinction in the wild.

that like a shady position are particularly suitable for this. Lilies need not be grown with other plants – they also make magnificent container plants.

The range of lilies is such that there are some for every type of soil, and it is worth checking with a catalogue that the ones you are buying are suitable for your conditions. Basically they all like to have a deep, well-fertilized but well-drained position. With the exception of *Lilium candidum*, which needs to be planted just below the surface, all lilies should be planted at a depth of about 2½ times the height of the bulb. Plant bulbs in autumn, although *L. candidum* is planted in late summer.

If they are well protected by shrubs, lilies may not need staking, but when they are in a more open position they may well need support (p. 80). One of the worst problems for lilies is the lily beetle (p. 94), the grubs of which can quickly eat the whole plant. They also suffer from viruses, for which there is no cure, so be careful to buy virus-free stock and to burn any infected plants.

🍂 FRUIT

Fruit continues to ripen and there should be plenty of apples, pears and plums to pick this month. Apples and pears can be stored and plums frozen or bottled.

There is still time to finish planting new strawberry beds, either from your own runners or from new certified stock (p. 138). Never use plants that are obviously diseased or of doubtful origin.

From next month it will be time to plant new fruit trees and bushes, so this month it is worth spending a bit of time choosing what varieties you want and ordering them. If you have not already done so, prepare the ground for these new plants.

Blackberries are one of the easiest fruits to grow. The worst of the problems is their vicious thorns, but even this can be overcome by using a thornless variety such as 'Loch Ness'. They can be grown on wires in the main part of the garden, or they can be trained against a fence so that they take very little space in the garden.

BLACKBERRIES

Many country gardeners still rely on wild blackberries for their pies, but where these are not commonly available cultivated blackberries are widely grown. Their fruit is plumper and sweeter than the wild forms, and even where the latter are available the cultivated forms are preferred, especially as they are not difficult to grow.

A good framework of posts and wires is required to support the blackberries, although they can be grown against a fence. Rid the soil of any perennial weeds because the blackberries are likely to stay in the same place for many years, and cleaning around the roots is not easy. Dig in plenty of well-rotted organic material. Plant bare-rooted specimens between autumn and mid-spring at intervals of 3.7m (12ft). The stems can be either all trained to one side along the wires or spread out to form a fan. If you adopt the former approach, tie the new canes into the other side as they appear, to make it easier to remove the old canes once fruiting has finished. With the fan-like arrangement, the new canes are tied provisionally in the centre and then tied on either side for their fruiting year, leaving a gap in the centre for the next year's new canes.

To increase stock, peg down the tip of a new shoot into the soil. This will be firmly rooted by spring, when it can be cut free from the parent and potted up or planted out.

Pick all fruit as soon as it ripens. Excess can be frozen.

HYBRID BERRIES

Several hybrid berries have been raised, mainly created by crossing the blackberry and raspberry. Among these are loganberry, tayberry, dewberry, marionberry, boysenberry, sunberry, tummelberry and Japanese wineberry. They are grown in a similar way to blackberries.

RECOMMENDED VARIETIES *of* BLACKBERRY

'Ashton Cross': late
'Bedford Giant': early
'Himalayan Giant': early
'John Innes': late
'Merton Thornless': early
'Oregon Thornless': late
'Smoothstem': late

STRAWBERRIES

Strawberry plants need a warm sunny site, preferably in a light, well-drained soils. The best soils are slightly acidic, a pH of 6–6.5 being the ideal. To prepare the beds, dig them deeply and incorporate plenty of well-rotted organic material. Always choose disease-free stock from a reputable source. If they are supplied bare-rooted, soak the roots before planting. Do not leave them packed up until you can deal with them – heel them into a spare piece of ground or into a bucket of compost if you are not able to plant them straight away.

The best time for planting is in late summer or autumn. This gives the plants time to establish themselves, and they should fruit next summer. The plants also establish well if planted in spring but they will not fruit until the following year. Rake a general fertilizer into the soil at a rate of 70–105g per sq m (2–3oz per sq yd) depending on how deficient the soil is of nutrients. Plant them at intervals of about 40cm (15in), in rows that are 75cm (30in) apart.

Keep the strawberries free from weeds and mulch the plants before they come into fruit by placing fresh straw or plastic sheeting under the leaves and trusses of flowers. This prevents the soil from splashing up onto the fruit when it rains or when the plants are watered. Both the straw and plastic make ideal sheltering places for slugs and snails, which have a particular liking for strawberries, so take whatever precautions you normally make to reduce their numbers. It is usually safe to use slug pellets because the netting will keep both birds and pets away. As an added precaution the pellets can be placed well down in the straw or under the plastic.

There are five main types of strawberry. The first three categories are straightforward early, mid- or late season. The fourth group is perpetual strawberries, which fruit briefly at the beginning of the season and then again later in the year. They are best in areas where there are long, warm autumns. The fifth category is of alpine strawberries. These produce miniature fruit, which appear for a long season throughout the summer.

RECOMMENDED VARIETIES *of* STRAWBERRY

Early season

'Cambridge Early Pine': medium-sized fruit; good for wet areas

'Cambridge Prizewinner': moderate cropping with juicy fruit of good flavour

'Cambridge Rival': heavy cropping; very early; good under cloches

'Cambridge Vigour': heavy cropping; good flavour; good for freezing; best as maiden crop

'Gorella': heavy cropping but suffers from mildew

'Pantagruella': very early but not very heavy cropping; good under cloches

Mid-season

'Cambridge Favourite': heavy cropping; very popular variety

'Cambridge Sentry': fruits in late summer; good for wet areas

'Elista': medium sized fruit; heavy cropping; good for wet areas

'Grandee': largest fruit with very good flavour

'Hapil': heavy cropping; large fruit with good flavour

'Jamil': good cropper with large fruit

'Red Gauntlet': large fruit, will crop again in autumn

'Royal Sovereign': an old cultivar with good flavour, but suffers from disease

'Souvenir de Charles Machiroux': very heavy cropping; large fruit with very good flavour

'Tamella': good cropper with large fruit over a long season

'Tantallon' very heavy cropper; well-flavoured fruit

'Tenira': heavy cropper; very good flavour; freezes well

'Totem': very good for freezing, holds its firmness

Late season

'Cambridge Late Pine': large fruits with distinct flavour; frost resistant

'Domanil': large fruit; frost and drought resistant; freezes well

'Fenland Wonder': large fruits over a long season

'Hampshire Maid': continuous late summer and autumn crop; flavoursome fruit; freezes well

'Le Sans Rivale': very heavy cropping variety, from autumn to Christmas with protection

'Litessa': heavy cropper; good flavour

'Merton Dawn': heavy cropper over long season; freezes very well

'Montrose': heavy cropper; frost resistant

'Saladin': heavy cropper; good flavour; resistant to botrytis

'Talisman': heavy cropper; long season and good flavour; frost resistant

'Tyee': heavy cropper; flavoursome fruit; good for freezing

Perpetual (remontant) varieties

'Aromel': heavy autumn crop; fine flavour; best as maiden crop

'Gento': crops well throughout summer and autumn; small fruit; freezes well

'Ostara': heavy cropper but suffers from mildew

'Rabunda': heavy autumn crop; fruits until December with protection

'Red Rich': heavy autumn crop; large fruit

'St Claude': heavy cropper of good flavour

Alpine varieties

'Alexandria': good flavour; does not produce runners

'Baron Solemacher': long, conical fruit; one of the best varieties

'Delicious': good flavour; no runners

'Multiplex': small fruit; double flowers

'Yellow Wonder': heavy cropper; yellow fruit; no runners

🍃 THE GREENHOUSE

Hardy annuals can be sown in pots or trays and kept in the greenhouse over the winter months, ready for planting out in the early spring. Cuttings can also be taken for overwintering (see below).

The growth rates of many plants slow down at this time of year, and it is important to reduce the amount of watering and feeding, too. Do not water pots unless they are drying out; plants should not be waterlogged. Most plants will not need feeding for the next few months until they come into active growth again.

It will not be long before the greenhouse will need heating, so this is the time to make certain that all heaters are working and to get them serviced if necessary.

CUTTINGS

Semi-hard cuttings of perennials and shrubs can be taken at any time between early summer and early autumn, depending on when the new growth begins to harden. At this time of year it is particularly important to take cuttings of perennials that are marginally hardy and may be killed by frosts. Having a few cuttings in the greenhouse is good insurance against their loss. Penstemons are a good example of this, but there are also other tender perennials that are treated like annuals, such as pelargoniums, from which cuttings taken at this time of year are used to produce next year's plants.

For most plants tip cuttings are best. Cut a non-flowering shoot, 7.5–10cm (3–4in) long, cutting it just below a node (where a leaf joins the stem). Remove the lower leaves cleanly so that only the top two pairs remain. Dip the cut end of the cutting into a rooting compound and place it at the edge of a pot of cutting compost. The rooting powder helps the cutting to develop roots, and although it is not necessary for those plants that root readily, it has got the advantage that it contains a fungicide, which will protect the base of the cutting.

Place the cuttings in a propagator, which need not be set high – just a few degrees above freezing will be sufficient. If it is too high the cuttings will romp away and be ready

Taking semi-hard cuttings

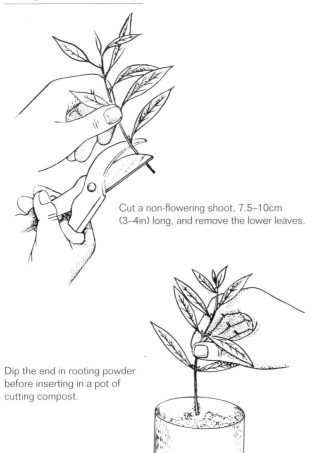

Cut a non-flowering shoot, 7.5–10cm (3–4in) long, and remove the lower leaves.

Dip the end in rooting powder before inserting in a pot of cutting compost.

Pelargoniums can readily be increased from cuttings taken in autumn, which saves the expense of buying new plants every year.

far too early. It is better to keep them in the pot until next spring when they can be potted up individually. If the greenhouse is kept heated they can be raised more quickly and potted up during the winter. Even so, those plantlets that are potted up during the winter should not be put outside until warmer weather comes and they have become established.

PLANTS *from* EARLY AUTUMN SEMI-HARD CUTTINGS

Argyranthemum	*Melianthus major*
Artemisia	*Muelenbeckia*
Ballota	*Pelargonium*
Calluna	*Penstemon*
Fuchsia	*Petunia*
Hebe	*Pieris*
Helichrysum petiolare	*Rosmarinus*
Hibiscus	*Santolina*
Iberis	*Senecio*
Indigofera	*Viburnum*
Kolkwitzia	

LAWNS

As summer turns to autumn, the frequency of mowing should be reduced, and you should cut only when it is necessary. The height of each cut should also be increased as the growth rate of the grass slows down. Avoid cutting during wet weather or when the lawn is too moist from dew or fog. Dew can be removed from the grass by brushing with a birch broom (besom) or by stroking it with a long cane. Leave for an hour or so after de-dewing to allow it to dry further. Continue to mow throughout the autumn and winter whenever the weather and soil conditions allow. Avoid cutting in frosty weather, but if the weather is fine and the grass is continuing to grow well in warm conditions, it is worth giving the lawn a trim, so that it is not too long when you come to cut it in spring.

Give the lawn a good rake to remove any thatch and if you have not already done so, spike the lawn to aerate it (p. 123). Top dress the lawn with a mixture of sifted organic material, such as leaf-mould or peat, sand and loam, brushing it into the spiked holes as well as working it down among the roots of the grass.

Apply weed- or moss-killer if necessary. Do not automatically do it if your grass does not require it.

Prepare the ground for laying grass or seeding, and sow new lawns (see below).

SOWING LAWNS

Lawns are best sown when the soil is warm and moist, and the best time is in early autumn, with spring being the second best time.

The ground should be prepared some time before you actually sow the grass seed. This gives it time to settle down and an opportunity for any perennial weeds to appear. A successful lawn must be completely free from perennial weeds. Dig and break down the soil to a fine tilth, removing any weeds and stones. The best way to ensure clear ground is to spray the weeds with a proprietary weedkiller before digging; follow the instructions on the packet. Roll and rake the soil until it is level or, if it is on a slope, until it follows the line you want.

Just before sowing rake over the soil and remove any further weeds that have appeared – you may have to dig deeply to remove pieces of persistent weed. Fill in any hollows that have appeared.

Grass seed can be sown by hand, but it is easier to hire machine to cover larger areas. Sow half the seeds travelling in one direction and the other half travelling at right angles to this so that you can be sure that the seeds will be spread evenly over the whole area. Use the wheel tracks as a guide to where you have been.

Sowing or broadcasting by hand is a bit more difficult. Divide the area into 1m (3ft) squares with string. Work out how much seed is required for each square (see the packet) and divide this in half. Spread one half by hand in

Sowing a new lawn

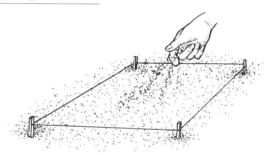

If you are sowing seed by hand, use string to divide the area into squares so that you can apply the appropriate amount of seed accurately and evenly.

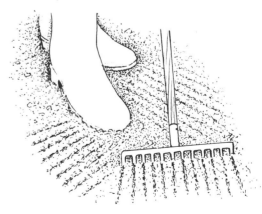

After sowing, rake the surface lightly, taking care that you do not rake the seed into piles.

GREEN TIP

Spraying

If you have to use sprays of any kind, try to use them in the evening, when beneficial insects, such as bees, and butterflies are no longer flying.

one direction and the other at right angles, and then move on to the next square. Be careful to cover the whole square, there may be a tendency to be uneven around the edges, leaving a sparse areas of grass between adjacent squares.

After sowing, rake gently over the area, being careful not to drag the top of the soil and the seeds into heaps. To keep birds and pets off put a net over the sown area or suspend cottons between sticks. If the weather is dry, spray and, if necessary, continue to do so at regular intervals until it rains. When the seeds have germinated put a light roller over the lawn; if you do not have a roller, the one on the mower will do as long as the blades are not rotating. Do not cut the grass until it has reached about 5cm (2in), and from an autumn sowing, this may well not be until next spring, although if conditions are favourable it may be in late autumn. Do not cut it shorter than 2.5cm (1in) at the first few cuts, but then you can gradually lower the height of the blades to cut at your preferred length. Try not to overuse the lawn during its first year and remember to keep it watered in dry weather.

If you have the space sow some seeds on a spare plot so that you have a few turves of the same grass to repair any damage during its first year.

LAWN GRASSES

Fine lawns include the following, singly or in mixtures:

> *Agrostis castellana* (highland bent): cool climates;
>   *A. tenuis* (browntop bent): cool climates
> *Cynodon dactylon* (Bermuda grass): warm climates
> *Festuca rubra* var. *commutata* (Chewing's fescue):
>   cool climates; *F. r.* var. *rubra* (red fescue): cool
>   climates
> *Stenotaphrum secundatum* (St Augustine grass):
>   warm climates
> *Zoysia* (Japanese lawn grass): warm climates

Hard-wearing lawns include the following, singly or in mixtures:

> *Axonopus* (carpet grass): warm climates
> *Eremochloa ophiuroides* (centipede grass): warm
>   climates
> *Lolium perenne* (perennial ryegrass): cool climates
> *Paspalum notatum* (bahia grass): warm climates
> *Poa pratensis* (Kentucky blue grass): cool climates

PERENNIALS

There should still be a lot of colour left in the herbaceous borders, but it may be masked or diluted by the number of plants that are beginning to turn brown. Cut down all spent vegetation and continue to deadhead on a regular basis so that those plants that are still flowering look their best and can be seen.

Before you cut down everything, however, consider whether you want seeds of any of the plants; if you do, leave at least some for the seeds to mature. Remember, too, that if you are a flower arranger many of the perennials make very good dried stems and seedpods. Again, leave a few if you think they are worth while saving.

Early autumn is the time to start preparing new beds for planting next spring (see below). Perennials that were sown in spring, that were propagated by cuttings or that were increased by division should be ready to plant out into borders. If you garden on heavy soil in an area that is prone to cold, wet winters, it may be better to delay planting them out until spring, but in most areas if they are planted now they will be established enough to withstand the winter weather.

PLANTS TO ATTRACT BUTTERFLIES

One of the joys of any garden is the wildlife it contains. The plants provide food, protection and living quarters for a wide range of animals. Flowering plants are particularly attractive to bees and butterflies. While not everybody is keen on bees, perhaps fearing that they might get stung, very few people dislike butterflies. These decorative insects are attracted to a wide range of plants, and they can be seen fluttering around the garden at any time between spring and autumn. The largest concentration seems to be towards the end of summer and the beginning of autumn. In good years clouds of them will erupt from plants as you walk by.

They are attracted to the plants for their nectar and therefore it is this type of plant that must be grown in order to lure them into the garden. Many of the modern hybrids seem to lack nectar and are sterile from the point of view of both butterflies and bees. Many of the old-fashioned cottage garden plants are much congenial to insects, and these are the ones to plant in the garden. Many herbs attract butterflies, and a herb garden will often be full of them.

Day-flying moths are attracted to much the same plants as butterflies, and there are times when you cannot see catmint (*Nepeta*) for fluttering wings. Many of the white, plants that are fragrant in the evening are attractive to moths – indeed, they are both white and scented to attract the moths as pollinators. Plants that will attract butterflies, bees and moths are grown in the same way as any other plants, except that they all do especially well in a sheltered position where there is not too much wind.

BUTTERFLY PLANTS

Ageratum (annual)	*Lavandula* (shrub)
Aster	*Mentha*
Buddleja (shrub)	*Nepeta*
Centranthus	*Origanum*
Coreopsis	*Rubus* (shrub)
Echinacea purpurea	*Scabiosa*
Eryngium	*Sedum*
Erysimum	*Solidago*
Hesperis (biennial)	*Stokesia laevis*
Hyssopus	

PREPARING PERENNIAL BORDERS

One of the best ways to ensure a good perennial border is to make certain that it is carefully prepared in the first place. Unless it is completely cleared of weeds there will be constant problems, but if the ground is well dug and plenty of manure is incorporated into it, the plants are much more likely to thrive and have a much better chance of withstanding drought.

As with any bed, it is important to clear a perennial border as thoroughly as possible. If it is an existing bed, remove as many plants as you possibly can. Many herbaceous plants can be transplanted, but established trees and shrubs cannot, of course, be moved simply to enable you to refurbish a bed and so you must work around them. Some herbaceous plants, particularly those with tap roots or large roots – peonies, for example – are not happy about being moved and may take several years to come back into flower. Many are very difficult to move at all and are likely to die if you do attempt to transplant them. Unless the border is in a very bad state it is better to try to work around them. The real problem comes if the questing roots of weeds such as couch grass are tangled up with the roots of a plant you want to keep. It is sometimes possible to extract them, but if you cannot, you may have to decide to remove the plant because leaving weeds of this type in the border is asking for trouble.

When you have transplanted to another part of the garden those plants you want to keep the next task is to remove all the weeds. The most satisfactory method of doing this is with a weedkiller. Like all garden chemicals, weedkillers should not be used unless they are absolutely necessary and then only with care. If used properly, a proprietary weedkiller will quickly kill off the weeds and will not be needed again. Repeated use is not recommended. If your soil is friable it is usually possible to sift through it, removing weeds by hand. If you can leave the border for a couple of months before planting, any weeds that have escaped will begin to show themselves again and can be removed. If you begin planting before the ground is thoroughly cleared, life will be a constant battle against the weeds. Thorough preparation is one of the keys to an easy life in the garden.

Clearing a border

Remove the roots of large weeds with a garden fork.

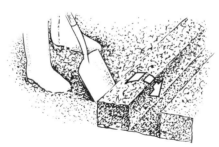

Double dig, incorporating organic matter into both the upper and lower spits.

Fork over the ground to aerate it and break up the soil.

Hoe regularly to remove annual weeds as they germinate.

Left: *Centranthus ruber*, red valerian, is one of those good perennial plants that comes up without fail each year and yet needs very little attention, other than tidying it up at the end of the year. It has a very long season and attracts butterflies. It has the additional advantage that it will grow in dry, stony soil.

Opposite: For the keen gardener a peat bed is a must. It provides a perfect habitat for a wide range of beautiful plants, many of them woodland plants, which are difficult to grow in the ordinary garden.

Once you are satisfied that the ground is clear, dig over the bed. Although it is more effort, it pays to double dig a border (p. 25). Incorporate well-rotted organic matter, such as manure or garden compost, into both the lower and upper spits. This helps to improve the structure of the soil, provides nutrients for the plants and also helps to retain moisture around the plants' roots.

After digging, leave the bed for several weeks, preferably for two months, so that any remaining perennial weeds can be removed. Annual weed seeds will also have germinated, and these can be forked or hoed off. The soil will continue to hold annual weeds seed for several years, but as long as all the weed is removed before seed is set, you will eventually get the better of them and their numbers will gradually fall. If, during the period that the bed is lying fallow, you hoe through it once a week, you are likely to kill off several generations of weeds, because each time you hoe you not only kill those that have just germinated but also bring more seeds to the top, where they will germinate. Repeating this simple action can save a lot of effort in the long run.

Once the bed has been planted, it should be mulched with organic matter of some kind. This will help keep weeds down and moisture in, but will add to the organic material in the soil. Top this up at least once a year with a top dressing of weed-free compost or manure.

ROCK GARDENS

There is still time to prepare new beds and rock gardens before the winter weather sets in (p. 127). You should be able to continue into the winter but avoid working once the soil become too wet or it will become compacted under your weight and this is last thing you want in a rock garden.

If you have already prepared the beds, now is the time to start planting. If you live in areas where the soil lies wet and cold during the winter, it may be a good idea to put off planting until the spring, but if container-grown plants are planted at the beginning of this month there should still be enough warmth left in the soil for them to establish themselves before winter sets in.

If you have alpines in pots in a glasshouse or coldframe, it is time to reduce the watering and to remove shading from the glass. Most alpines need water only when they are in active growth and, as this slows down, so must the watering be reduced.

PEAT BEDS

Although rock gardens are generally thought of in terms of rock and quick-draining screes, many alpine gardeners

also create beds that will accommodate those plants that need a moister environment. Many of the plants that can be grown in such beds are woodland plants, which enjoy deep leaf-mould in their natural environment. Although they are generally shade-loving plants, many, if kept moist at the root, will tolerate quite a bit of sun.

Peat beds are so called because they are traditionally built with peat, although in these more environmentally conscious times they are often made with some form of peat substitute. Even before peat was widely used, leaf-mould was considered to be one of the best soil conditioners. Do not raid the woods for supplies of leaf-mould, however, because this does even more damage than extracting peat.

A peat bed is best sited where it will receive some sun but not its main force. Light dappled shade is ideal. Avoid siting it near trees with hungry, surface-feeding roots, such as birch, because the bed will soon be filled with the trees' roots, making it very difficult to keep moist.

As with all beds, thoroughly clean the ground of weeds before you start, using a herbicide on the tougher perennial weeds if necessary. Work out the outlines of your bed and its various levels. Use peat blocks, which should be soaked in water for several hours before you start work, to build up low retaining walls. Overlap the blocks in much in the same way as if you were using ordinary house bricks and push the blocks tightly against one another. Build the wall so that it slopes inwards slightly and secure it by pushing sticks at intervals through the blocks into the soil below. As an alternative and for additional security, every so often turn a block sideways so that it lies overhanging into the bed and acts as an anchor. Once the bed has been planted for a while roots will grow through the blocks and bind the wall together.

Fill in the area behind the wall with a mixture of two parts loam, two parts peat or peat substitute and one part grit (all measurements by volume). Once this mixture has been firmed down, build another wall and fill in behind this until, you have completed the number of terraces that you need or want. Make sure that the soil under the walls is well firmed down so that it does not sink. It is a good idea to incorporate some form of path into the bed so that you do not have to walk on it when you are tending the plants. This will prevent soil compaction. It need not be a complete path – stepping stones of stone or wood are sufficient. Wooden planks or cross-sections of tree trunks are ideal as they look more natural than stone in this type of setting, but they can be very slippery. Cover them with wire netting to help you retain your grip.

If peat blocks are not available the walls can be built with stone or wood. Stone will last longer, of course, but wood often looks better. Planks or railway sleepers are suitable, or you could use tree trunks or thick branches laid on their side.

Leave the bed for a few weeks before planting so that it has time to settle and to allow any weeds in the loam to manifest themselves. Do not allow the bed to dry out; in dry weather it will require regular watering. The infill will be bound to sink, too, so top it up before planting

Peat beds are, by their nature, acid, and they provide the ideal environment for growing acid-loving plants, such as dwarf rhododendrons. If the underlying soil is chalk, you will have problems because it will upset the acidity/alkalinity balance of the soil. One way of overcoming this is to cover the area with a thick polythene or butyl rubber liner, so that the chalk cannot get through to the peat. If you do this, however, it is essential that the base of the peat bed is raised a little, or water will run off the surface of the native chalky soil into the bed, killing many of the plants. The best way of dealing with the problem is to create a raised bed (p. 144) so that the peat is lifted well away from the influence of the chalk.

The best time to plant the bed is this month or in spring. When the plants are in position, top dress with composted or chipped bark. Once it is planted the main task is to keep it free of weeds and moist. Do not allow the peat to dry out because it is likely to be difficult to re-wet. Top up the bark mulch once or twice a year.

PLANTS *for a* PEAT BED

Adonis	*Hacquetia epipactis*
Anemone nemorosa	*Hepatica*
Anemonella thalictroides	*Hylomecon*
Arisaema	*Iris cristata*
Calceolaria	*Jeffersonia*
Cardamine	*Kalmia*
Cassiope	*Meconopsis*
Cyclamen	*Paris*
Daphne	*Phyllodoce*
Disporum	*Primula*
Dodecatheon	*Rhododendron*
Erica	*Sanguinaria canadensis*
Epimedium	*Saxifraga*
Erythronium	*Shortia*
Ferns	*Stylophorum diphyllum*
Gentiana	*Trillium*
Glaucidium palmatum	*Vaccinium*

VEGETABLES

Before winter weather sets in it is time to lift and store tender vegetables. Potatoes should be lifted, left in the sun for a couple of hours to dry and for their skin to harden and then stored in hessian or paper sacks, in a cool but frost-free place. Carrots and beetroot should be stored between layers of sand, in boxes. Turnips and swedes can be stored in the same way, but in milder areas all four can be left in the ground. Parsnips are hardy enough to be left in the ground in most areas.

Remove the traces of finished crops. Compost most of it, but burn any that are diseased. Clear up any weeds that have grown in the crops.

It is time to start the autumn or winter digging for all but the lightest of soils. Digging now will open the ground to the weather, allowing the frost to break it down to a beautiful tilth. Add in manure or well-rotted compost as you dig or cover the dug soil with a layer of compost and allow the worms to break it down further and to drag it down into the top layers of the soil.

FORCING CHICORY

Chicory can be forced by digging a root in autumn. Remove any loose soil and then cut the leaves and the base of the root. Plant it in a pot of compost, with the top showing just above the surface. Keep it moist and put it in a dark place. Alternatively, leave it in a warm greenhouse and cover it with a bucket or box to exclude the light. It can be cut after three or four weeks.

Seakale and rhubarb can be lifted and the roots placed in boxes of moist peat or potting compost. These should be placed in a dark place or covered to exclude the light. Cut as required. The roots should be discarded after use.

WATER GARDENS

The reflections of still water and the sounds of running water do much to enhance the qualities of a garden, and now is the time of year to consider building water features and preparing their beds ready for planting in the spring.

If you already have a pond, this is the time of year when you must take action to prevent falling leaves getting into a pond. Although it is not particularly attractive, one of the most effective ways of keeping leaves out of a pond is to cover it with a net, secured around the edge.

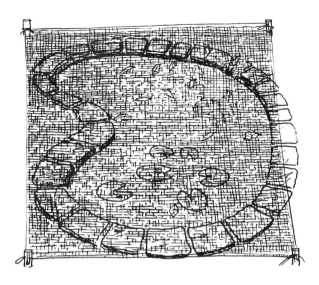

Cover the pond with a net to prevent leaves from falling into the water in autumn.

TYPES OF WATER FEATURE

Water features are an important element in the design of a garden. Not only does water offer another range of habitats for plants, but it also provides an important niche for wildlife.

There are several different types of feature. The most obvious is the pond, which range in size from a small lake to a bowl of water let into a patio. Each has its place. Ponds at different heights can be linked by streams or cascades of running water, and fountains and spouts are a good way of introducing sounds and a fresh atmosphere into a garden. Finally, there is the bog garden, which, although it has no visible water, is a wet area in which a wide variety of colourful plants can be grown.

PONDS AND POOLS

Ponds can vary widely, both in their shape and size and in their construction. They can be formal, with straight sides or regular curves, or they can be of irregular shape. The style you select will depend largely on the overall style of your garden and on where it is located. If you have a patio or paved area, for example, a formal pond generally looks better than an irregularly shaped one, but in the freely designed areas of the planted garden, a more informal pond is likely to look more appropriate. The size will be determined by the scale of the surrounding area. Larger ponds are generally best if they are a fairly natural, informal shape.

Grasses overhanging water can look very beautiful and add ornamentation to a garden. This one is *Carex oshimensis*.

Internally, the shape of ponds also varies. Larger ponds are often nothing more than a basin with steepish sides, except perhaps in one place, where the bank has a gentle slope to let wildlife get in and out of the water easily. If you are constructing a smaller pond, it is better to control the shape rather more closely so that there are several different depths. This allows a much greater diversity of planting (p. 89).

The ways in which ponds are constructed shows even greater diversity. The natural pond has much to recommend it (except in a formal garden), with its graceful curves and a lining of clay into which plants can be planted directly. Before the days of plastics, concrete was the favourite material for artificial ponds. It has been superseded by modern materials for most ponds, but it is still very useful for formally shaped pools. The construction is laborious and must be done correctly if it is not to crack and let out water. It involves the use of shuttering and reinforcing bars and mesh, but a very attractive and long-lasting pond can be created,

although you may need to seek professional assistance.

The development of plastics has brought a greater flexibility in possible shapes. Modern butyl and other liners can be laid into any shaped pond. A hole is dug, lined with sand to prevent stones from puncturing the plastic and then the liner is laid across the hole and filled with water so that it gradually assumes the shape of the hole. The other popular form of plastic pond is the preformed pond, which takes the form of a rigid shell. Whereas you can create any size pond with butyl, rigid ponds are limited in size and available in only a few different styles, but they are, nevertheless, very suitable for small gardens. They usually have preformed ledges round the margins on which plants can be stood. A hole, the same shape as the pond, is excavated, lined with sand and the pond put into position – a relatively quick job compared with other methods.

The surroundings of the pond are a matter of choice. Lawns or beds can go right up to the edge of natural ponds, but artificial ponds need to have some form of edging, otherwise the concrete or plastic will be visible. One solution is place a row of paving slabs or stones around the perimeter, positioning them so that they overhang the edge and disguise the liner. Concrete or rigid plastic ponds can be raised and a wooden or stone surround can be used to form a sitting area.

Safety must always be uppermost in the mind of the gardener, especially if young children are likely to be playing in the garden.

FOUNTAINS

Fountains and water spouts add movement to the water, disturbing reflections, and creating restful sounds. They can be placed in the pond or outside it, perhaps on an adjacent wall. Pumps providing a wide variety of spray shapes can easily be purchased, as can many different types of sculptured water spout outlet. Unless you are lucky enough to have a fountain fed by a mountain stream, you will need electricity to work the pump. This should be installed by a professional electrician because water and electricity do not mix.

STREAMS

Very few people are lucky enough to have a natural stream running through their gardens, but it is not to difficult to make one. Moving water is always a joy and there are plenty of plants that like to grow in the moist conditions of a stream's margins.

Artificial streams can be created from concrete or from plastic liners. Concrete is often more successful in that it

tends to blend in more easily with the surroundings and take on the appearance of stone, while butyl often remains visible unless it is well covered with stones. It is also possible to buy preformed modules that fit together to create a stream of whatever length you want. You will need to have a pump installed to circulate the water, which can simply emerge at the top end of the stream or can supply a pond, which in turn overspills into the stream down to a lower pond. Pumps are available in a wide range of styles and strengths, so you can create quite a swiftly flowing stream if you wish.

BOG GARDENS

Bog gardens need a considerable amount of thought in their construction and a considerable amount of maintenance. What is required is a bed that will hold a certain amount of water, so that the plants never dry out, and although it can occasionally be flooded, it should not be constantly under water. One way to achieve this is to dig out a shallow basin and to line it with a plastic liner. A few drainage holes should be made with a fork so that excess water drains out. Fill the basin with a humus-rich mixture of loam and leaf-mould, along with any other well-rotted organic material you have. Farmyard manure might make the soil too rich, so it would be better to use compost made from rotted vegetation. If there is not sufficient rainfall to keep the area wet, flood it occasionally from a nearby pond or use a hosepipe. Water draining from an adjacent roof will also help. A wide range of water-loving plants can be grown. Unfortunately, weeds also like these conditions, and the bed will have to be weeded regularly to prevent them from taking over.

GREEN TIP

Removing algae

One of the curses of ponds and pools is green algae. These can be removed by chemicals but try immersing a sack filled with barley straw to prevent algae forming. First, however, you must remove all existing algae. This is a laborious task but can be achieved using a spring-tined rake as a sieve or by twisting the algae around a stick or pole.

PLANTS *for* BOG GARDENS

Aruncus	*Lobelia cardinalis*
Astilbe	*Lythrum*
Cardamine	*Osmunda regalis*
Cimicifuga	*Peltiphyllum peltatum*
Eupatorium	*Persicaria*
Filipendula	*Phragmites*
Gunnera	*Primula*
Hemerocallis	*Rheum*
Hosta	*Rodgersia*
Iris ensata; I. sibirica	*Trollius*
Ligularia	

OCTOBER

By now autumn is beginning to make itself felt. In mild autumns, the frosts may have not yet started, but it is likely that there will have been a few, even if only light ones. This is your last opportunity to check that all plants that can be affected by frost have been lifted and stored or given some other form of protection.

You should, of course, always look after tools, but at this time of year, as the autumn rains start, they may get muddier than usual. Because you may put them away and not use them again this year, it is worth making doubly sure that they are clean and oiled to protect them from rusting. Do not just clean the metal parts; wipe down the handles as well. The same applies to any machines that you have been using.

In the fruit and vegetable gardens there is more produce to be harvested and stored. Storage can be a problem if you have not got a suitable outbuilding, built of brick or stone. Garages and wooden sheds are reasonable substitutes, but they may get to cold, with the temperature dropping below freezing in midwinter. If you can, line them with polystyrene or use a thermostatically controlled heater to keep the temperature just above freezing. Another possibility is to use a defunct chest freezer. This will keep the frost out when the lid is closed, but it should be closed only when the weather turns really cold. At other times it should be left open because air should be allowed to circulate freely around all stored produce.

CHECKLIST

General

- Start collecting fallen leaves for composting to leaf-mould (p. 174)
- Shred and compost all dead herbaceous or woody material (p. 23)
- Plan next year's ornamental display (p. 124) and crops (p. 26)
- Order seeds (p. 120)

Annuals and Tender Perennials

- Sow hardy annuals under glass (p. 50)
- Remove the remains of this year's bedding plants (p. 134)
- Replant containers with winter-flowering annuals (p. 134)
- Plant out hardy biennials such as wallflowers and sweet williams (p. 75)
- Sow sweetpeas under glass (p. 180)
- Prepare beds for next year's displays (p. 143)
- Lift and store tender perennials (p. 134)

Bulbs

- Plant tulip bulbs (p. 153)
- Plant lilies (p. 136)
- Lift and store dahlia tubers after first frost (p. 153)
- Sow bulb seeds (p. 76)

Fruit

- Pick apples and pears as they ripen (p. 122)
- Store keeping varieties of apples and pears (p. 168)
- Remove fruiting canes of blackberries and other briar fruit (p. 138)

- Tie in new canes of blackberries and other briar fruit (p. 138)
- Finish ordering new and replacement plants (p. 137)
- Take hardwood cuttings of gooseberries and currants (p. 154)
- Prepare beds for new fruit trees and bushes (p. 143)
- Remove netting when fruiting finished to allow birds to clear pests (p. 54)
- Put sticky grease bands round apple and cherry trees (p. 154)

Greenhouse

- Sow hardy annuals (p. 50)
- Sow sweetpeas (p. 180)
- If you have not already done so, clean out and disinfect the greenhouse (p. 113)
- Protect plants from frost if necessary (p. 158)
- Reduce watering (p. 122)
- Remove all shading and wash down the glass (p. 158)
- Fit insulation or secondary glazing (p. 158)

Lawns

- Reduce amount of mowing (p. 140)
- Do not cut grass too short (p. 140)
- Rake to remove thatch (p. 59)
- Spike to alleviate summer compaction (p. 123)
- Top dress with mixture of fine organic material, sand and loam (p. 141)
- Prepare ground for laying lawns in spring (p. 141)
- Turf new lawns on previously prepared ground (p. 182)

Perennials

- Collect late seeds (p. 98)
- Remove and shred dead and dying herbaceous material (p. 23)
- Clean and tidy borders (p. 173)
- Remove, clean and store re-usable plant supports (p. 80)
- Sow seeds in pots (p. 20)
- Plant prepared borders (p. 152)
- Renew and renovate borders (p. 143)
- Prepare new beds and borders for spring planting (p. 143)
- Lift and divide clump-forming plants (p. 40)

Rock Gardens

- Prepare new beds and rock gardens (p. 127)
- Plant or replant beds (p. 63)
- Sow seeds in pots (p. 41)
- Reduce watering for alpines in pots (p. 144)
- Clear away leaves and debris (p. 41)
- Top dress beds with gravel or small stones (p. 41)

Trees and Shrubs

- Check and renew if necessary all stakes and ties (p. 163)
- Check that all climbers are tied in (p. 162)
- Clean under hedges (p. 175)
- Take hardwood cuttings (p. 154)

Vegetables

- Plant out spring cabbage (p. 130)
- Carry on autumn digging (p. 165)
- Sow broad beans (p. 16)
- Plant garlic (p. 165)

ANNUALS

This month sees the end of the annual year. Unless it has been an exceptionally warm year, most annuals are now over and should be removed from the beds.

In addition, all the old summer plantings should be removed from containers. The compost can be thrown out and the container thoroughly cleaned, and then either stored or replanted with winter and spring displays (p. 134).

Continue to sow hardy annuals under glass. Any that were sown earlier in the autumn and are large enough can be planted out at the beginning of the month, but it may soon become too cold for them to establish themselves, in which case leave them until spring. Sweetpeas can be sown now so that they will be ready for planting out in spring. This will get them off to a flying start, ensuring an early crop for cutting.

Once beds have been cleared, they can be prepared for next year's display (see below).

If chrysanthemums (p. 134) and dahlias (p. 153) are still in the ground, lift them before the frosts start, and store them in a cool, but frost-free place.

PLANTING BIENNIALS

If you have grown biennials from seed during the year you should be planting them out this month if you did not do so in September. Some may have been grown in individual pots, others in open ground. Many, such as foxgloves and mullein, look good when they are grown mixed in with perennials in a border, while others, such as wallflowers, do well as bedding plants, perhaps mixed with bulbs, such as tulips. However, none of these rules is sacrosanct – large drifts of foxgloves look good as bedding, while wallflowers and sweet williams can be effectively mixed into the border.

Prepare the planting areas in advance, digging them over, removing weeds and adding organic material. Break down the soil to a fine tilth and plant out, setting the plants to the same depth they were in the nursery beds or in their pots. Water.

BIENNIALS

Campanula medium (Canterbury bells)
Dianthus barbatus (sweet williams)
Digitalis purpurea (foxglove)
Erysimum (*Cheiranthus*; wallflowers)
Hesperis matronalis (dame's violet)
Lunaria annua (honesty)
Matthiola incana (Brompton stock)
Oenothera biennis (evening primrose)
Papaver nudicaule (Iceland poppy)
Verbascum (mullein)

TIDYING SUMMER BEDS

Although annuals should be removed as they go over, there is always quite a bit of tidying up to do in the autumn. Remove all parts of the remaining annuals, even if they are still green. Also remove any weeds that are in the bed. Dig the soil, adding well-rotted compost or manure to it. Leave it for the winter weather to break down so that it is ready for planting next spring.

Some of the short-lived annuals, such as forget-me-not (*Myosotis*), *Collomia grandiflora* and the poached-egg flower (*Limnanthes douglasii*), have been over for many weeks. Being self-sowers, however, they will have shed their seeds and will have already produced young plants. These are likely to require thinning, or they will be starved and not make a very good display. The thinnings can be planted elsewhere or even give away. At the same time as thinning, remove any weeds they may have grown up among them.

Foxgloves, *Digitalis purpurea*, create an old-fashioned, cottage garden effect.

BULBS

Most spring-flowering bulbs should be in the ground by now, but if you are behind there is still time to get them in. Tulips, however, can still be planted over the next couple of months, and lilies can also be planted this month (p. 136). Many gardeners like to put a handful of grit at the bottom of the planting holes of lilies, partly to help with drainage and partly to discourage slugs from attacking the bulbs.

Dahlias (see below) should be lifted and stored before they are frosted.

If you have collected or managed to acquire seeds of any bulbs, now is the time to sow them. Some seeds, particularly those of the lily family, including lilies, fritillaria and tulips, benefit from being sown fresh. This usually means that it should have been sown last month if it is your own seed, but if you have been sent seeds from friends or suppliers, this month will do. The seed will germinate if it is sown next spring, but it may take longer.

STORING DAHLIAS

Dahlia tubers are not frost hardy, and they should, therefore, be lifted and stored in frost-free conditions. In some warmer areas it may be possible to leave them in the ground, but even here, the depredation of slugs is such that they may well be better off above ground.

On a dry day, cut away any foliage at 10–15cm (4–6in) above ground level. Make sure that the remaining piece of stem retains a label because one dahlia tuber looks very much like another and the different varieties can easily become muddled. Dig up the tubers and remove any soil. If there are any damaged or diseased tubers, cut off the affected areas and treat the wound with a powdered fungicide. Stand the tubers upside down for a few weeks until the remaining stem has dried out completely and then pack the tubers (right way up) in dry peat, peat substitute or composted bark. Store them in a cool, but frost-free place until they are needed for planting out for the next season.

In most areas dahlia tubers must be lifted and stored in a frost-free place. There are dozens of varieties for the dahlia enthusiast, including the small waterlily-flowered 'Gerrie Hoek'.

Autumn Bulbs

While most people think of bulbs as bringing flowers to the spring garden, they can also make quite a display in the autumn. One of the best known is the so-called autumn crocus – it is, in fact, not a crocus but a colchicum. They produce large purple or white goblets that are particularly noticeable because they do not have any leaves at this time of year (hence another of their common names, naked ladies). The leaves appear in spring and will have faded away by the time the flowers emerge. There are quite a number of different varieties of colchicum, and it is worth buying a few for their brilliant display. They can be bought dried and planted in the spring, but are better bought 'in the green' or in pots.

There are autumn species of crocus but these are not so spectacular. Even so it is worth growing several, in particular the blue *Crocus speciosus*, with its distinctive orange-red stigma. Another, much rarer, but very beautiful species, *C. banaticus*, is worth looking for. This has the most beautiful lilac-blue colouring. Unusually for a crocus it grows in moist soil and prefers a little shade. If you get interested – and it is very easy to become infatuated with this beautiful genus – there are a lot more crocus species that flower at this time of year.

Another crocus look-alike is *Sternbergia lutea*, which flowers this month and next. This has striking greeny-yellow petals. It needs a warm sunny position – against a wall, for example. Another plant for the same area is *Amaryllis belladonna*. This is not the big bulbous plant that are often seen at Christmas (although it often called amaryllis this is, in fact, *Hippeastrum*). Amaryllis have tall, naked stems topped with bright pink trumpets. Another naked plant with pink flowers is the nerine, which also likes warm conditions.

The most startling or at least unexpected of all autumn flowers is the autumn snowdrop, *Galanthus reginae-olgae*. They look very similar to ordinary snowdrops and, unless you are an expert, you may be forgiven for believing that they had simply got their timing wrong.

AUTUMN-FLOWERING BULBS

Amaryllis belladonna
Colchicum
Crocus
Cyclamen
Galanthus reginae-olgae
Nerine bowdenii

FRUIT

Fruit harvesting is tailing off now, although there are still some late varieties of apples to gather if you happen to grow them. Quinces are beginning to ripen and judgement is required as to whether to pick them before the autumn winds bruise them or blow them off, or whether to leave them on just a bit longer to ripen fully.

Finish cutting out old fruiting canes of blackberries and raspberries (p. 156) and tying in the new growth, which should be a continuing process, from the moment they first start to lengthen. If it is left too late, they will thrash around in the wind, damaging themselves and other canes.

Once the leaves have dropped it is time to take hardwood cuttings of gooseberries and currants. The simplest way of doing this is to cut 30cm (12in) of stem and stick them into the ground about 15cm (6in) apart. If your soil is on the heavy side, make a slit or narrow trench in the ground with a spade and line it with sharp sand before inserting the cutting and firming back the soil. Leave until the following autumn when the rooted plant can be lifted and transplanted.

Apple trees and cherry trees benefit from having grease bands placed around their trunks this month. Although this can be a messy process, it prevents the wingless female winter moths getting up into the trees and laying their eggs. These, in turn, hatch to produce caterpillars, which damage leaves as well as fruit and blossom buds.

Apples

Apples have always been popular in gardens, and it is mainly thanks to gardens that many of the older varieties are still being produced. Shop-bought apples give a very limited choice, whereas the gardener can choose from thousands of varieties. The flavours of some of these are domestically produced fruits are unbelievably different from commercially grown apples.

When you are choosing trees there several things to take into consideration. You should decide whether you want to grow dessert or cooking apples. You must also decide what flavours you prefer and whether you want apples that keep or those that should be eaten when ripe. On the more practical side there are different types of tree, ranging from full-sized standards to dwarf trees, and from pillar trees to those grown as cordons. Different rootstocks will give different size of tree (p. 36). Another factor to bear in mind

is that most apple trees need a different variety planted
nearby as a pollinator. This means that you must choose
and plant compatible trees. It may well be, for example,
that your neighbour has trees that will act as pollinators.
Get advice on this at the time of purchase.

The site for apples needs to be sunny, but protected
from the wind, especially cold winds. The soil should be
moisture retentive and have plenty of organic material
worked into it before planting, particularly if you are
planting dwarf trees. Plant bare-rooted trees between
autumn and mid-spring, and support them with a stake
until they are established (p. 162). Cordon, fan or espalier
trees should be supported by horizontal wires, walls or
fences (p. 10).

It may be necessary to protect buds from bullfinches
during the winter and early spring. Covering small trees
with nets is one possibility, but see also p. 53. Thicker nets
can be used on small trees to help protect them from late
frosts if particularly cold weather is forecast for late spring.
Thin the young fruit if necessary (p. 95). Water during any
dry spells, especially when the fruit is swelling, and apply a
general fertilizer once a year, in early spring, at a rate of
100g per sq m (3oz per sq yd).

Pruning Apple Trees

Pruning is perhaps the most important of the maintenance
routines. Once they are established, trees and bushes should
be pruned once a year during the winter months. Remove
all dead and dying wood, as well as any weak growth and
any branches that cross or touch other branches.

There are two types of apple trees – tip bearers, on
which fruit is mainly carried at the tips of the branches,
and spur bearers, on which the fruiting spurs are carried
along the whole shoot. For obvious reasons, if you cut
back the shoots of tip-bearing varieties, you will remove
the fruiting buds. On these varieties, therefore, cut out a
few of the older fruiting stems each year, so that new,

vigorous shoots are formed. On spur-bearing varieties cut
out the straight new growth to stimulate the formation of
more spurs on the older wood because apples are borne
on wood that is two or more years old. On older trees,
where there is a tangle of spurs, thin them out, removing
the older ones. Trained forms of trees also require summer
pruning to prevent them becoming overgrown. Cut back
the new growth to one leaf.

PEARS

Pears are grown and cared for much in the same ways as
apples. However, to give good crops they need warmer
situations than apples, and they do particularly well
against brick or stone walls. They flower earlier than
apples and the blossom can be cut back by the frost. Pears
are grown on quince rootstock (p. 36). There is a wide
variety of both dessert and culinary varieties available,
but, like apples, they must have compatible pollinators, so
always grow at least one pair of different varieties. Check
times of pollination when purchasing.

RECOMMENDED VARIETIES *of* PEAR

As with apples, it is best to taste the various varieties
available before selecting.

Early varieties
　‘Beth’: dessert
　‘Clapp’s Favourite’: dessert
　‘Jargonelle’: dessert
　‘Williams’ Bon Chrétien’: dessert

Mid-season
　‘Beurré Clairgeau’: dual purpose
　‘Beurré Hardy’: dessert
　‘Concorde’: dessert
　‘Conference’: dessert
　‘Doyenné du Comice’: dessert
　‘Improved Fertility’: dual purpose
　‘Onward’: dessert
　‘Pitmaston Duchess: dual purpose

Late season
　‘Beurré Alexandre Lucas’: dessert
　‘Black Wooster’: culinary
　‘Catillac’: culinary
　‘Glou Morceau’: dessert
　‘Joséphine de Malines’: dessert
　‘Winter Nelis’: dessert

Supporting raspberry canes

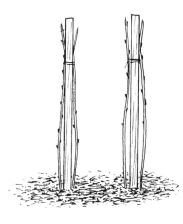

Single post driven into the ground at interval can be used to support individual plants.

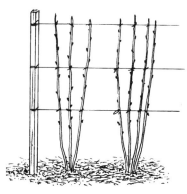

If two parallel rows of raspberries are grown, they can be held by wires running at right angles and at intervals of about 60cm (2ft) to the main horizontals.

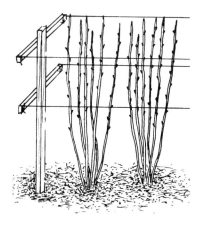

Raspberries are often tied into wires held horizontally between two posts. The wires should be about 75cm (30in), 1m (40in) and 1.5m (5ft) from the ground.

RASPBERRIES

As long as there is room, no garden should be without raspberries. Fortunately, the increase in the number of varieties means that raspberries can be available not just in early summer but for a long season, lasting right into autumn. Anyone making a new bed, rather than planting a single variety, should try to include a few canes for each season so that they have a continuous supply. Raspberries are best fresh but they can be cooked, frozen or bottled.

Raspberries prefer an open position, but it should not be too hot. In hotter areas, in fact, a little shade will be beneficial. It will be necessary to create a framework against which the canes can be tied. This is normally created from posts at each end of every row (with intermediate posts at 3m (10ft) intervals if the row is a long one) with galvanized or plastic-covered wires stretched between them. The lowest wire should be about 75cm (30in) from the ground, with two more above this, 45cm (18in) apart.

Raspberries like a rich, free-draining soil, but it must be moisture retentive. The addition of plenty of well-rotted organic material to the soil at the time of digging will help considerably. Either dig a trench in which to plant the canes or dig a wide hole for each one. Plant the canes, 45cm (18in) apart, in autumn or early winter, at the same depth as indicated by the existing soil mark on the stems. Reduce the stems to about 25cm (10in).

Tie in the canes as they grow. These will produce fruit in the following season. Pick fruit as it ripens and do not leave rotten or damaged fruit on the canes. Once they have fruited, cut the canes out completely, leaving that season's crop of new canes to fruit in a yet another year's time. The canes should be tied individually against each of the wires. In winter cut back the growing tip of each cane to about 15cm (6in) above the top wire. Regular mulching with compost will help to conserve the moisture.

Birds are one of the worst pests, but the use of a fruit cage will keep them at bay. Raspberry beetle is the other main worry. It is the larva (or maggot, as it is more commonly known) of the beetle that causes the problem, and the only way to control the problem is to spray with malathion or derris just as the fruit begin to turn pink. Apply a second spray two weeks after the first.

RECOMMENDED VARIETIES *of* RASPBERRY

Early varieties
 'Delight'
 'Glen Cova'
 'Glen Moy'
 'Lloyd George'
 'Malling Promise'

Mid-season varieties
 'Glen Lyon'
 'Glen Prosen'
 'Julia'
 'Malling Jewel'

When it is grown under glass the vine 'Black Hamburg' will produce delicious dessert fruit.

GRAPES

Grapes generally need warm, dry climates, but an increasing number of varieties suitable for cooler regions is becoming available, making it possible for vines to grown in more gardens. Most of the sweeter grapes that are used for dessert are still grown in greenhouses, but wine grapes can be grown outdoors. These are often grown properly trained on wires, but they can also be grown as decorative features over pergolas or arbours, providing pleasantly dappled shade under which meals can be taken.

Greenhouse Cultivation

Grow directly into the greenhouse bed where the soil should be free-draining and reasonably fertile. In conventional greenhouses, site the vine at the end opposite the door and train it up and along the ridge of the roof. In lean-to greenhouses, train the vines against the solid wall. It is important that the greenhouse is kept well ventilated, especially during the winter and after the fruit is set. The temperature in the greenhouse should be well regulated so that it does not fluctuate violently. There is no need to heat the greenhouse in winter because the vines need a chilling, but if you want an earlier crop, bring the vines into early growth by providing heat in late winter and early spring.

   The main problems are botrytis (which is caused by insufficient air circulation), pests getting into the house and eating fruit (net the openings) and red spider mite (keep the atmosphere humid by damping down the floor). Tight bunches of grapes will need thinning with a pair of fine-pointed scissors to allow the remaining grapes to develop fully. Once the fruit has coloured up, leave it for two to three weeks to finish ripening completely. Remove the leaves around the fruit so that sun can get at them. Top dress the soil around the roots with well-rotted compost every year in spring.

In a smaller greenhouse pruning should be for a single cordon, with wires fixed to the back and sloping roof of the house to take the branches. Each year laterals should be allowed to develop and then cut back once they have reached five or six leaves. Bunches of flowers are restricted to one on each lateral. Side shoots should be restricted to one leaf. In winter laterals are cut back to one bud. The following summer the process is repeated.

RECOMMENDED GREENHOUSE VARIETIES *of* GRAPE

   'Alicante': black, dessert
   'Black Hamburg': black, dessert
   'Buckland Sweetwater': white, dessert
   'Foster's Seedling': white, dessert
   'Gros Maroc': black, dessert
   'Reine Olga': red–black, dessert
   'Seyval Blanc': white, wine

Outdoor Cultivation

In cooler areas outdoor varieties of grapes are mainly for wine-making, although there are increasing numbers that can be used as dessert or dual-purpose varieties. The soil should be well drained and the site warm.

Grape vines are trained against wirework, which can be against a wall or fence, or in the open on posts set at 2m (6ft) intervals. Between these are tensioned wires, the bottom one being about 45cm (18in) above the ground and subsequent ones at 30cm (1ft) intervals. Plant one vine at each post.

There are several ways of pruning vines, the simplest is the one described above. Another method, producing a more prolific crop, is to allow three shoots to develop each year. Two of these shoots are tied down horizontally on either side and are allowed to develop vertical fruiting shoots. The third (central) shoot is cut back to three buds, which develop the three shoots for next year. Any side shoots that develop on fruiting shoots are cut back to one leaf. In winter all the fruiting stems are cut out and the remaining three stems treated in the same way as the previous year. Size is not important for wine grapes, so there is no need to thin.

There is no need to water once the fruit starts to develop except in extreme drought because water adversely effects the qualities of the grapes. Treat with 70g per sq m (2oz per sq yd) of a general fertilizer in spring and top dress around the plants with organic material every year.

RECOMMENDED OUTDOOR VARIETIES *of* GRAPE

'Brant': black, wine
'Chardonnay': white, wine
'Incana': black, wine
'Léon Millot': black, wine
'Madeleine Angevine': pale green, dual purpose
'Madeleine Sylvaner': white, wine
'Müller Thurgau': white, wine
'Noir Hatif de Marseille': black, wine
'Perlette': black, dual purpose
'Pirovano 14': red-black, wine
'Précoce de Malingre': white, wine
'Riesling': white wine
'Royal Muscardine': white, dessert
'Siegerrebe': golden, dual purpose
'Triomphe d'Alsace': black, wine

THE GREENHOUSE

The main thing to do at this time of year is to prepare the greenhouse for winter.

PREPARING FOR WINTER

The first task is to make certain that the greenhouse is clean both inside and out. All remaining shading should be removed, the glass washed down and all hinges and catches oiled. Any used pots that are empty should be washed out. If tomatoes are grown in beds the soil should be removed and replaced with fresh. Fresh soil will also be of benefit for other crops, but it need not be changed every year.

Any beds that are to be used for winter vegetables should be dug over, with some well-rooted organic material being added to it. Winter lettuce can be sown now.

Once the greenhouse has been cleaned, any secondary glazing can be erected. In most greenhouses this consists of sheets of bubble plastic or just plain polythene. This is attached the inside of the framework to help conserve the heat, but it is not necessary in cold greenhouse except in areas where very low temperatures are expected, and then it may be of benefit even to quite hardy plants. Cover ventilators separately so that they can still be opened.

Use a disinfectant to sterilize pots and tools – and don't forget to clean and oil anything that is kept stored in the potting shed.

GREENHOUSE HEATERS

Check that all heaters are in working order. The best form of heater is an electric fan heater, which has the advantage that it can be set to a particular temperature and will only come on when that temperature is reached, thus saving fuel during warm periods or once the greenhouse has warmed up. Another advantage of this type of heater is that the fan causes the air to move, which helps prevent the fungal diseases caused by damp stagnant air. The main disadvantage is that you are left without heat if there is a power cut. Another problem is, of course, that you need to lay on electricity to the greenhouse, which, when it is done properly, might be expensive.

Paraffin heaters are also popular. These are relatively inexpensive to run and the initial outlay is not very high. There main disadvantage is that they pump out a lot of moisture into the atmosphere, which can encourage fungal diseases such as mildew and botrytis. Another point against them is that they need regular attention – filling, trimming the wick and lighting – and you may not be at home at the right time. Once lit, they are on constantly until turned off, no matter what the temperature in the greenhouse. Overall, electricity has the edge over paraffin, but a paraffin heater is a very useful standby in case of power failures.

Gas heaters for greenhouses are available, and they can be run off the mains or on bottled gas. They have the advantage that they can be fitted with thermostats so that temperature can be controlled, but gas, bottled propane gas in particular, can produce water vapour and fumes.

Other systems are far grander and need a large greenhouse to justify it. They generate heat by means of a boiler, which circulates warm water through pipes or emits warm air through ducts. These are easy to control and produce a safe heat, but they are expensive both to set up and to run.

It may not be necessary to heat the whole greenhouse. Long greenhouses can be divided into two with one section being heated and the other left cool. On a much smaller scale many gardeners manage to use only a small area by encasing part of a bench with a temporary polythene frame and using undersoil heaters buried in sand to provide just enough heat to keep the more tender plants alive. Some use a heated propagator for the same purpose if it is not needed for propagating until the spring.

Frost alarms are a useful device. They let you know if you need to light paraffin heaters and they will also tell you if there is a power failure and the electric heater is not on.

Do not overheat your greenhouse. It is very important that fresh air is allowed in and is able to circulate. Ventilation should be left open during the day as long as and whenever the outside temperature allows. Ventilation is especially important when paraffin or gas is used, although it unfortunately reduces their efficiency.

LAWNS

Winter is not a very good time for lawns and grass paths. They are usually wet and cannot be used, and if they are used they quickly turn into mud baths, which not only ruins the grass but also breaks down the structure of the underlying soil. The best advice is to keep off the grass altogether unless it is well drained or the weather is dry. Even in dry weather, dew can be sufficient to cause problems unless the lawn is not so sheltered that the wind can dry it off.

For paths that are in constant use or if a lawn must be regularly crossed – to a garage, say – it is a good idea to lay stepping stones. This allows the area to be predominantly grass but at the same time makes it accessible in the wetter months. If you need to work from the edge of a lawn or from a grass path – while you are tending borders, for example – during the winter, work from planks or sheets of wood if possible.

There are several jobs that should be attended to before winter sets in to make sure that the grass is at its best next season. Continue to mow if the lawn is dry enough but not if it is wet. A rotary mower works better at this time of year. Check that the blades are set high because you do not want to cut the grass too short, just cut enough to keep it even and under control.

Give the lawn a thorough scarifying to remove the thatch (p. 59). This helps to let air into the soil and prevent dead grass smothering the living. This can be done either by hand with a spring-tined rake or with a special machine, which can be hired.

Another way to allow air in to the roots is to aerate the lawn. If not already been done, there is still time to do it. As well as air, the process allows water to sink into compacted lawns, which will keep them drier in the winter (p. 123).

In warmer areas it is still not too late to apply an autumn fertilizer. This is not the same as a spring fertilizer because it contains less nitrogen. However it is applied in the same manner (p. 60).

WORM CASTS

Worm casts become more apparent in autumn and winter. If they are left they form muddy patches on the lawn, smothering the grass. They can also blunt the mower if it is used. Make it a regular part of your routine to scatter the casts with a birch broom (besom) or by swishing the grass with a long cane. If you consider it a real problem, it is possible to get rid of the worms by applying a wormicide, but think carefully about this because worms do a great deal of good in the lawn, breaking down grass cuttings, taking them into the soil and aerating the soil. Do not waste worm casts. They can be mixed with peat substitute and grit and used for potting composts.

If weeds are troublesome treat the lawn with a special weedkiller (p. 79). Moss may also be in evidence at this time of year. Much of it will be removed by scarifying, but it should be treated to get rid off it by next season. You can use a specific moss-killer or use one that is incorporated with a weedkiller.

Once all the various tasks have been completed, the lawn can be top dressed with a mixture of sieved loam, sieved peat or leaf-mould and sand. Use this to fill in any holes or slight indentations and work it into the grass with a broom (besom) or lute. Larger holes or damaged turf can be repaired in the spring.

A regular task that must be carried out is to remove any leaves that fall on the lawn (p. 174). If they are left, they will cause bald patches in the grass. Brush or rake them off or use one of the special blowers/vacuum cleaners that can be bought or hired for the purpose (p. 23). Don't waste the leaves – compost them.

PERENNIALS

Signs of activity are coming to an end in the borders. A few lingering plants struggle to put on a display, and in some warmer areas a lot of late-flowering plants – such as *Vernonia* – are still in full spate, while many other – penstemons, for example – still have a lot of bloom left on them. Physical activity increases, however, as it is time to start clearing the borders, removing all the dead and dying vegetation and generally renovating the borders (p. 143).

Many perennials can be sown in pots now – in fact, a number prefer it because it allows them to have a winter's chilling before germination. If you are in doubt when to sow seed, sow half now and half in early spring. Leave pots of perennial seeds out in the open. There is no need to cover them except in very wet years or if the seeds germinate.

If you have prepared the beds and if you do not live in cold wet areas, new plantings can be made now.

GROUNDCOVER

A pet hate of many gardener is the weeding. There is, in fact, really no way round this if you want a first class garden, but there are ways to make life easier. One of these is to use groundcover plants. These tend to make a dense mass of foliage, under which weed seedlings cannot germinate. These mass planting are often of tough plants, which will grow in areas that more decorative plants

eschew, so they can be used in drifts – for example in shady areas or on banks.

There is no limit on what constitutes a groundcover plant as long as it has plenty of leaves to cover the ground – a closely planted perennial border has the same effect – but many true groundcover plants are evergreen so that they not only prevent weeds germinating during warmer periods in the winter but also form some point of interest during these barren months.

The real secret to using groundcover is to clear the ground of all weeds before you start. Many people feel that as it is groundcover it will not matter about existing weeds. Groundcover plants will suppress germinating weeds but not perennial ones, and unless these are removed they will constantly force their way up through the groundcover. Because the groundcover is likely to be in position for many years, thoroughly dig the ground, adding plenty of organic material. Once it is dug, break down any large lumps of soil and leave it for a month or two to make certain that all perennial weeds have been killed or removed. Any scraps of root that are left will soon push up new leaves and can be removed.

GROUNDCOVER PLANTS

Ajuga repans
Bergenia
Epimedium
Erica
Hedera
Hosta
Houttuynia cordata
Hypericum calycinum
Lamium maculatum
Lysimmachia nummularia
Symphytum
Tanecetum densum
Tiarella cordifolia
Vancouveria
Vinca

Once you are certain that the ground is clear plant up the area. To start with there will be gaps between the plants, until they fill out and merge with one another. Again, weeds will develop in these gaps and will have to be removed. Eventually, the gaps will cover over and the groundcover will be fully functional. Once it is in place, groundcover tends to be forgotten about, and it can become a bit of a tangled mess. Some plants like to be

Periwinkle, *Vinca minor*, makes an excellent groundcover. To keep it from becoming too straggly, trim it with shears at least once a year, preferably after flowering. This will keep it tight and compact. Although periwinkles will flower in shade, they will be more floriferous in a more open, sunny position.

sheered over regularly. Try to work in some organic material between the stems from time to time, because the cover may soon starve the ground. Another thing to watch out for, especially if the groundcover is near a drive or road, is litter. It is surprising how many cans and packets end up among the plants.

PERENNIALS IN WOODLAND CONDITIONS

Most perennial borders are made out in the open, where the plants can enjoy the sunny conditions. There are, however, many attractive plants that like woodland conditions and a small area of such plant in a garden can enhance it greatly. The best situation is a wood itself, but in smaller gardens a credible bed containing such plants can be made under one tree or perhaps using the shadow cast from a building.

The shade should not be too dense – dappled shade is the ideal – and as long as the soil is not too dry the site can have sun for part of the day provided it is not the hottest part of the day. If you have a choice, create the bed under deep-rooted trees, oak for example, rather than shallow-rooted ones, such as birch or ash, which will quickly send their roots into the bed and draw any moisture and nutrients from it.

The soil should be friable and moisture retentive. In the wild this is likely to be created by the leaf-mould on the woodland floor, and this is the type of consistency to aim for. A good loam with plenty of leaf-mould or rotten organic material is ideal. As with all borders, thorough preparation and the complete removal of all weeds is the best possible start. One advantage of woodland areas is that grass and many other weeds are not such a problem, but they can still be a nuisance.

Plant in the autumn or spring and tend them in the same way as perennials in any other part of the garden.

Woodland plants often appear in drifts rather than as isolated specimens, and if you have space, try and develop this effect. Many like to flower early, before the leaves develop on the trees and quickly retire back under ground. Tidy up the old stems of these as soon as they have finished flowering.

If the trees above get to dense it may be necessary to thin out the branches a little. Quite a lot of light can be admitted by removing lower branches, particularly if they are low-sweeping ones.

WOODLAND PLANTS

Actaea	*Helleborus*
Anemone nemorosa	*Hosta*
Arum italicum	*Iris foetidissima*
Aruncus	*Kirengshoma*
Bergenia	*Lilium martagon*
Brunnera macrophylla	*Meconopsis*
Campanula latifolia	*Paris*
Cardamine	*Polygonatum*
Cardiocrinum	*Primula*
Clintonia	*Pulmonaria*
Convallaria majalis	*Smilacina*
Dicentra	*Stylophorum*
Epimedium	*Tellima grandiflora*
Euphorbia amygdaloides	*Trillium*
var. *robbiae*	*Uvularia*
Geranium	

🍃 TREES AND SHRUBS

From this month onwards the winds can get strong and it is wise to check that all the stakes supporting trees and shrubs are sound and that the ties are all tight enough without cutting into the bark. You should also make certain that all climbers are firmly attached to their supports and check that the supports themselves are still sound.

PLANTING TREES AND SHRUBS

This is the time of year when you should be considering planting any trees and shrubs that you want. This applies as much to fruit trees and bushes as it does to ornamental ones. From now until spring, as long as the weather is not too cold or the ground too wet, both bare-rooted and container-grown plants can be planted. After the spring the weather is too hot and dry for bare-rooted plants to be able to survive, although container-grown plants, where the roots are not disturbed, can be planted throughout the year as long as they are well watered in dry periods.

If possible, prepare the ground well in advance, taking particular care to remove all perennial weeds. Dig in plenty of well-composted manure or other organic material. This will help to get the tree or shrub off to a good start. Dig a hole wider than appears necessary and put the supporting stake into the ground before you plant the tree as a precaution against driving it through the roots. Put the tree into the hole, spread out the roots and fill in with good quality soil. The planting depth of the tree or the shrub should be the same as it was in the nursery bed or container, as indicated by the ring of soil around the stem. Firm down and fill to the top. Water and then cover with a mulch.

The final thing to do is to fasten the tree or shrub to its stake. This is necessary so that the rootball is held firm and cannot rock, so breaking roots that are attempting to

Staking trees

A low stake is used to allow the tree trunk to move about a little. Drive in the stake so that 60cm (24in) or less protrudes.

An angled stake can be added after planting. Drive in the stake at an angle of 45 degrees and use an ordinary tie.

A single, high stake for a long-stemmed plant such as a standard rose requires two ties. Use padded or buckle and spacer ties to prevent the ties from chafing the tree trunk.

move out into the surrounding soil. On the other hand, the top should be free to move in the wind. The tie between the plant and the support should, therefore, be quite low down – about 45cm (18in) from the ground. If the tree is already planted it is safer to use two or three stakes, which are placed further away from the trunk, outside the range of the roots. Longer ties will obviously be needed. Alternatively, a stake can be driven in at an angle of 45° and secured with a normal tie. For tall, thin-stemmed trees and bushes, such as standard roses, a high stake will be required. This should be secured with ties both low down and higher up. A stake will not hold a mature or large tree that has been transplanted. It will be necessary to use three angled stakes connected to the tree with guy ropes.

To prevent climbers thrashing around and damaging themselves and other plants, fasten them securely to their supports with string or plant ties.

Two further measures may be required to protect a new tree. The first is to provide rabbit guards, plastic sleeving that goes round the young trunk to prevent browsing animals getting at the bark. It also protects the trunk against strimmers and lawn mowers. The second is to erect a windbreak. A new tree or shrub may transpire more quickly than it can pick up moisture, so it is important to protect it from the wind, which will remove moisture very quickly. This protection will also reduce wind pressure on the plant as well cut down the chilling effect of the wind.

Autumn Colour

Autumn is a glorious time of year for trees and shrubs. The deciduous leaves change colour before dropping off, but not all trees and shrubs produce a spectacular display. Choose carefully if you want to fill the garden with glowing, fiery colours.

Trees and shrubs that provide autumn colour are not treated any differently from any other type of tree or

Heeling in

If bare-rooted trees or shrubs are delivered at a time when it is impossible to plant them, heel them in to the ground. This means digging a hole or a trench if there is more than one, laying the tree in it at an angle to support the trunk, and firming the soil around it. This is only a temporary measure.

Planting a container-grown tree

Dig a hole that is about one and half times deeper than the plant's root ball. Remove any perennial weeds and use a fork to loosen the soil in the bottom of the hole and at the sides.

If you are going to use a stake to support the tree, position it now to avoid damaging the roots by driving it in when the tree is in the hole. Add some soil and well-rotted organic material to the bottom of the hole.

Carefully remove the tree from the container. Take care not to break up the root ball, but tease out the roots a little.

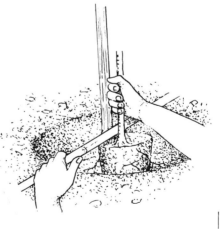

Place a cane across the centre of the hole and carefully place the tree in the hole. Use the cane to check that the tree will be planted to the same depth as it was in the container. Add or remove compost from the bottom of the hole as necessary.

Fill the hole, making sure there are no air pockets by firming it gently as you work. Tread the surface lightly and water thoroughly.

The sumac, *Rhus typhina*, has beautiful foliage all year round, but in autumn it surpasses itself in a blaze of reds and oranges. Unfortunately, it has a habit of producing a lot of suckers, which must be removed.

shrub, but you should try to make certain that they are planted where they will make maximum impact – where the evening sun will shine through the leaves, for example, or where the early morning sun will catch them. When you are choosing trees and shrubs, select those that have the most to offer – flowers in spring, good foliage and shape in summer and rich autumn colours.

TREES *for* AUTUMN COLOUR

Acer (maples)
Amelanchier
Betula (birch)
Carpinus betulus (hornbeam)
Crataegus (hawthorn)
Liquidambar
Malus (crab apples)
Nyssa sylvatica (black gum)
Parrotia persica
Prunus (ornamental plums)
Quercus (oaks)
Rhus typhina (sumac)
Sorbus (rowans)
Stuartia

SHRUBS *for* AUTUMN COLOUR

Berberis
Ceratostigma
Cornus (dogwoods)
Cotinus (smoke bushes)
Cotoneaster
Enkianthus
Euonymus (spindles)
Fothergilla
Mahonia
Nandina domestica
Stephandra
Viburnum

VEGETABLES

As one year draws to an end so another begins. The last of the vegetables are being harvested now and will go into store this month, just as the first of next year's crops are planted. It is, for example, time to plant out the spring cabbage that was sown last month (p. 130), to plant garlic (see below) and to plant broad beans (p. 16), although the last can wait until next month or even later.

The main activity in the vegetable garden is digging. Whenever the weather permits, the vegetable plot should be dug over so that it is ready for the frosts and rains to break it down.

STORING VEGETABLES

Some vegetables can be left in the ground for the winter. They are hardy enough to stand the frosts and snows, and they can be picked or dug as required. Parsnips, leeks, kale, cabbage, Brussels sprouts and swedes fall into this category, but it must be borne in mind that when the ground is frozen hard it is impossible to get at the parsnips and leeks, and so it is a good idea to harvest a few in preparation when such hard frosts are forecast.

Root crops can be lifted and stored in trays of just-moist sand. Carrots, beetroot, turnips and, in colder areas, parsnips and swedes can all be treated in this way. Clean the vegetables of loose soil, remove any foliage and place them on a layer of sand. Cover the crop with more sand and then put in more vegetables and so on until the box is full. Store somewhere that is cool but frost proof.

Potatoes should be lifted in early or mid-autumn and, when dried, placed in hessian or paper sacks and stored in a similar position. In addition, they should be stored in a dark place, because potatoes turn green if exposed to light, which makes them poisonous. They can also be stored in boxes provided that all light can be excluded.

Many of the other crops, such as peas and beans, can be stored by freezing. In some cases their quality is better maintained if they are first blanched in hot water. Although most of the varieties can be frozen, many are specially bred for freezing and, if you intend to store them in this way, you should select them for planting. Although they are fiddly and time consuming, some people still prefer to use old-fashioned, pre-freezer ways of preserving – bottling and salting.

Some crops, notably beans, can be stored by drying. Hang the whole plant upside down to dry. Once the pods are brittle, extract the beans and store in a dry place.

Planting garlic

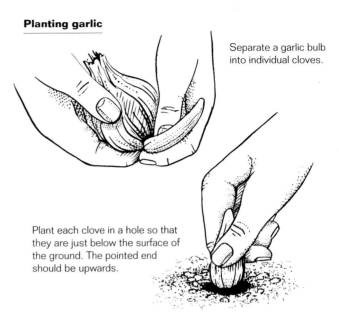

Separate a garlic bulb into individual cloves.

Plant each clove in a hole so that they are just below the surface of the ground. The pointed end should be upwards.

GARLIC

Mid- or late autumn is the time to plant garlic. This is a member of the onion family that has been greatly valued since ancient times, not only for the flavouring it imparts to cooked dishes but to its wide range of medicinal properties. It is very easy to grow, very widely used and yet it is not often seen in gardens. Perhaps it is because many gardeners do not think in terms of planting vegetables in the autumn.

Garlic consists of a bulb made up of a number of individual cloves. It likes a sunny position and a well-drained, fertile soil. Add well-rotted compost to the soil when digging. Plant the cloves individually, either in single holes or in a drill so that just the tip shows. They need very little attention except for weeding. Lift the bulbs in mid- to late summer when the foliage begins to die back. Dry in the sun, like onions, tie them into ropes or store them in net bags and keep in a cool but frost-free place.

RECOMMENDED VARIETIES *of* GARLIC

Many gardeners either use bulbs saved from the previous year or just buy plump bulbs from the greengrocer and use these. There are, however, some varieties are specially marketed for the gardener.

'Long Keeper'
'Red Bulbed'
'Rocambole'
'White Bulbed'
'White Pearl'

NOVEMBER

The leaves are falling now and the garden is beginning to take on its winter clothes. Although there is always plenty to do at this time of year, it really is a matter of getting on with things when you are able to do so because the weather is not always suitable. Never try to get onto the soil when it is wet – you will do more harm than good – but, even so, do not use this advice as an excuse for doing nothing. If you are able to work steadily throughout the next few months it will make life much easier next year.

Late autumn and winter are the most vital times in the garden. Although in many respects spring is the busiest time, the next few months will really set the agenda for coming year. If you do manage to get a lot done, your garden will be a lot better for it.

We haven't quite finished with the current year yet, though. There are still things in flower in the border and in milder areas there are still fruit to be harvested and vegetables to be dug.

CHECKLIST

General

- Continue to collect leaves for composting (p. 174)
- Plan next year's ornamental display (p. 124) and vegetable crops (p. 126)
- Order seeds (p. 120)
- Shred all prunings and old herbaceous material (p. 23)
- Cover compost bins (p. 172)
- Thoroughly clean and oil all tools before winter (p. 22)
- Drain down or lag all outside water pipes (p. 150)

Annuals and Tender Perennials

- Finish clearing up last year's displays (p. 134)
- Pot up sweetpea seedlings individually for show plants (p. 180)
- Finish planting out biennials in mild areas (p. 75)
- Prepare beds for next year's displays (p. 143)
- Clean all containers not used for winter displays (p. 152)

Bulbs

- Finish planting tulips (p. 153)
- Lift and divide autumn-flowering snowdrops (p. 21)

Fruit

- Heel in bare-rooted trees and shrubs when they arrive (p. 162)
- Plant new fruit trees and bushes when the weather and soil conditions allow (p. 162)
- Carry out formative pruning on new trees and bushes (p. 10)
- Remove any secondary growth that occurs after summer pruning of trained fruit (p. 10)
- Check stored fruit (p. 168)

Greenhouse

- If you have not all ready done so, clean and disinfect greenhouse (p. 113)
- Protect plants from frost if necessary (p. 158)
- Finish insulating the greenhouse (p. 158)
- Water carefully and only when necessary (p. 122)

Lawns

- Mow if conditions are right but not too closely (p. 140)
- Remove fallen leaves and debris (p. 23)
- Prepare ground for laying lawns in spring (p. 141)
- Turf new lawns on previously prepared ground (p. 182)
- Scatter any worm casts if they are formed (p. 159)
- Aerate if not already done so (p. 123)

Perennials

- Remove and shred dead and dying herbaceous material (p. 23)
- Clean and tidy borders (p. 173)
- Remove, clean and store re-usable plant supports (p. 80)
- Sow seeds in pots (p. 20)
- Finish planting prepared borders (p. 152)
- Prepare new beds and borders for spring planting (p. 143)
- Finish lifting and dividing clump-forming plants (p. 40)

Rock Gardens

- Sow seeds in pots (p. 41)
- Remove weeds (p. 63)
- Stop watering alpines in pots (p. 144)
- Clear away leaves and debris (p. 41)
- Top dress beds with gravel or small stones (p. 41)
- Protect plants that hate winter wet with sheets of glass (p. 189)

Trees and Shrubs

- Start planting deciduous trees and shrubs (p. 162)
- Heel in bare-rooted trees and shrubs if weather prevents planting (p. 162)
- Collect and compost leaves (p. 174)
- Take hardwood cuttings (p. 154)
- Prune roses (p. 42)

Vegetables

- Sow broad beans (p. 16)
- Plant garlic (p. 165)
- Plant rhubarb (p. 177)
- Check stored vegetables (p. 165)
- Continue autumn digging when weather allows (p. 165)
- Order seeds for next year (p. 185)
- Protect brassicas from birds (p. 177)
- Bring in chicory and seakale for forcing (p. 177)

 FRUIT

Make a habit of regularly checking fruit that is in store. Any that is rotting should be thrown out before it affects the others.

STORING FRUIT

Not much fruit can be stored through the winter in its fresh state. Apples, pears, quinces and nuts will store if the conditions are right, and other fruit can be frozen or bottled as well as being made into preserves, such as jams, cheeses and chutneys. Frozen fruit will never return to its pre-freezing state, and the soft fruits, such as strawberries and raspberries, in particular, become very soft and squashy. Some varieties do freeze better than others, however, and if you want to freeze a lot of fruit it is worth growing those cultivars.

Always choose perfect fruit for storing by any of the above methods. It should be just ripe but not over-ripe. The point of ripeness is usually when the fruit comes away easily from its stem. It should contain no blemishes and show no signs of decay or bruising. Pick, if you can, on a dry day

Grapes can be stored for up to three weeks by cutting them so that a piece of curved (hook-like) stem is attached and inserting this in a bottle of water.

Apples and pears can be stored for several weeks and even, in the case of some varieties, for months. The best method is to wrap the apples individually in paper – grease-proof paper is best – and put them in trays, which are stored in a cool but frost-free place, away from mice and other creatures that may eat them. A traditional method of storing apples is in special sheds, which had a series of special racks built from slats, between which air can easily circulate. The apples are laid, unwrapped, on these so that they are not touching. The atmosphere is dark and cool. Early apples do not store very well because they shrivel quickly, but they can be kept for a while, sealed in polythene bags with a few holes. Quinces can also be stored in a cool place, but do not wrap them and do not put them near to other fruit or they will imbue them with their distinctive smell.

QUINCES

Quinces are not widely grown, partly because they need warmth in late autumn if they are to ripen properly. In good years, however, a crop of golden quinces is worth their weight in gold for cooking and making delicious jelly and paste. A quince in the kitchen will fill it with the most beautiful aroma.

They like a sunny but sheltered site and a moisture-retentive soil. Traditionally they were often grown near ponds and they seem to do well in such situations. One of the advantages of quinces is that they need very little attention. Pruning is more or less restricted to cutting out any dead or damaged wood and it thinning out if it get overgrown. Do not pick the fruit until it is ripe, which may be late autumn.

RECOMMENDED VARIETIES *of* QUINCE

'Champion'
'Lusitanica' ('Portugal')
'Meech's Prolific'
'Vranja'

GOOSEBERRIES

Gooseberry bushes are not always appreciated in the garden because of their thorns, but they produce a good crop of fresh-tasting berries each year, which can be eaten as they are or cooked. They usually crop sufficiently well that even one bush will produce enough to make jam. They can be grown as open bushes or trained as standards, cordons or fans. The standard form is very decorative, which means that even a small garden can accommodate at least one bush because standard bushes can be used in an ornamental border. They are self-fertile, so you need no more than one bush.

Gooseberries prefer cool conditions, and this may mean that you need to provide a little shade in the hottest part of the day in hot districts. However, in the main they like a sunny position. Well-drained but moisture-retentive conditions are ideal, and on the whole they do best on heavier soils. Prepare the soil well, preferably adding plenty of well-rotted organic material.

Container-grown plants can be planted at any time, but the best time for planting these and bare-rooted specimens is during the autumn or winter as long as weather conditions permit. Plant at 1.2–1.5m (4–5ft) intervals for conventional bushes, 1.8m (6ft) for fan-trained bushes and 30–5cm (12–14in) for cordons. Cordons and fan-trained bushes will need supports: wires, a wall or a fence are all suitable.

Gooseberries are best planted in autumn or early winter, unless the ground is cold and wet, when spring will be a better time.

RECOMMENDED VARIETIES *of* GOOSEBERRY

Early season
  'Broom Girl' (yellow): dessert
  'Early Sulphur' (yellow): dessert
  'Golden Drop' (yellow): dessert
  'Keepsake' (greenish-white): culinary/dessert
  'May Duke' (red): culinary/dessert

Mid-season
  'Bedford Red' (red): dessert
  'Careless' (green/white): culinary
  'Green Gem (green): culinary/dessert
  'Invicta' (green): culinary, thornless, mildew
    resistant
  'Keepsake' (green): culinary/dessert
  'Lancashire Lad' (red): culinary, mildew resistant
  'Langley Gage' (greenish-white): dessert
  'Leveller' (yellow): culinary/dessert
  'Whinham's Industry' (red): culinary/dessert
  'Whitesmith' (green/white): culinary/dessert

Late season
  'Howard's Lancer' (greenish-white):
    culinary/dessert
  'Lancashire Red (red): culinary/dessert
  'London' (red): culinary/dessert
  'White Lion' (white): culinary/dessert

PLUMS

Plums are not as often grown as formerly, either as a garden or as an orchard fruit. However, those gardeners who do grow them are usually delighted with the fruit – luscious plums straight from the tree are a real treat. Plums are generally divided into two groups, dessert and cooking, although there are a few that can be used for both.

One of the main problems with plums is the pollination. Many trees flower early and are prone to being caught by the frost. Choose a warm, sheltered position and avoid frost pockets and windy situations. The soil should be well-drained but at the same time moisture retentive and reasonably fertile. Plant in late autumn or early winter.

There are several aspects to choosing the varieties. The chief of these is taste – choose the fruit that you like best. Experimental fruit stations and collections often have open days at which fruit can be tasted. The next

---

Formative pruning and pruning for bushes is carried out in winter (p. 154). Regular pruning for cordons and fans is carried out in both winter and summer once they have reached their full size. The procedure is very simple – just shorten all the new growth back to five leaves. These will be cut back in winter to two buds.

Bullfinches can strip the buds of the bushes in spring so they should be covered with nets. Once the fruit has developed, birds are generally not a nuisance as with other fruit. The most common disease is powdery mildew. There are some varieties, such as 'Invicta', which are more resistant to the disease. Dry conditions promote the disease, so a moisture-retentive soil, mulching and regular watering help considerably. If it does become a problem, spray with the appropriate fungicide.

consideration is pollination. Some plums are self-fertile and present no problem, but others need pollinators – that is, you need at least two varieties. This is complicated by the fact that not all plums blossom at the same time, so you must choose two that are compatible. Check this at the time of purchase. The final factor is size. Those grown on 'Pixie' rootstock will provide dwarf trees, while those grown on 'St Julien A' will be more vigorous (p. 36).

Plums can be trained as bush, half-standard, pyramid, spindlebush or fan. The bush and half-standard need little pruning once they are established other than the removal of any damaged or over-vigorous growth. The other shapes need more attention, both in winter and summer. Once the shape is established, it is mainly a matter of restricting the summer growth by cutting back new shoots to five or six leaves, reducing this to three leaves in the late autumn.

Thin fruit during prolific years so that the plums are 5–7.5cm (2–3in) apart. This will ensure that the remaining fruit fills out properly and be fully flavoured. During dry spells water thoroughly; mulching will help to retain moisture.

Damsons, which are closely related to plums, must be among the least demanding and easiest of all fruit trees to grow. The small black fruits are tart when unripe, but sweeten as they mature, and they are excellent for cooking, especially for jams and preserves. The can be treated in the same way as plums. Although some gardeners may frown on it, it is possible to follow the traditional habit of planting them in a hedgerow, where they will take up virtually no garden space and yet, even without any attention, still produce a good crop of delicious fruit. Apart from removing dead or damaged wood, no pruning is required.

RECOMMENDED VARIETIES *of* PLUM

Dessert varieties
'Ariel': red, late
'Cambridge Gage': yellow, mid-season
'Coe's Golden Drop': golden, late
'Early Laxton: red, early
'Greengage': green, late
'Jefferson': golden, mid-season
'Kirke's Blue': purple, mid-season
'Marjorie's Seedling': dark blue, late
'Merton Gem': yellow/purple, mid-season
'Oullin's Gage': golden, mid-season
'Victoria': reddish, mid-season

Culinary varieties
'Belle de Louvain': purple, mid-season
'Czar': purple, early
'Early Rivers': purple, early
'Laxton's Cropper': golden, late
'Pershore Yellow': yellow, mid-season

RECOMMENDED VARIETIES *of* DAMSON

Dessert varieties
'Bradley's King Damson': late
'Frogmore Damson': mid-season
'Prune' ('Shropshire' or 'Westmoreland'): late

Culinary varieties
'Farleigh': mid-season
'Merryweather': early

PEACHES

Peaches have always been grown in gardens but they have never been as popular as they are now. Although they will withstand a moderately cold winter, they do need warm, sunny summer conditions, but even in cooler areas they can be grown under cover. The main problem is that they blossom early and are therefore prey to spring frosts. However if wall-trained trees are grown, these can easily be protected with hessian or polythene-covered frames.

They need a well-drained but moisture-retentive neutral soil with plant of organic mater added when the bed is prepared. They are best planted against a brick or stone wall, which will not only help to keep them warm but also protect them from wind. they can also be grown as free-standing trees or bushes as long as they are in a well-sheltered position.

The most common method of cultivation is as a fan. Build up a basic fan framework (p. 121), tying in the branches to wires on the wall. Once trained, the idea is to remove the old fruited stems and allow them to be replaced by new ones each season. Pinch any unwanted side shoots in early summer, thinning them to one every 10–15cm (4–6in). Late in the summer, pinch out the tips of these side shoots, back to four or five leaves. Thin fruit if there is a heavy crop, leaving one peach every 15cm (6in). After fruiting remove the fruited shoot back to the its replacement. On established bush trees, remove any dead or dying wood and generally tidy the tree in spring. In summer reduce the length of the new growth on both main branches and side shoots.

Most peaches are grown on the dwarf 'Pixy' or more vigorous 'St Julien A' rootstock. Most are self-fertile, so only one tree is necessary to obtain fruit because no cross-pollination is required.

RECOMMENDED VARIETIES *of* PEACH

'Amsden June': early
'Bellegarde': late
'Duke of York': early
'Dymond': late
'Peregrine': mid-season
'Red Haven': mid-season
'Rochester': mid-season
'Royal George': mid-season

NECTARINES

Nectarines are grown in exactly the same way as peaches (see above), except that they need warmer conditions. The fruits have smoother skins than peaches and are slightly smaller, and the trees produce lighter crops.

RECOMMENDED VARIETIES *of* NECTARINE

'Independence': mid-season
'John Rivers': early
'Lord Napier': mid-season'
'Pineapple': late

THE GREENHOUSE

Soon it will be time to start propagating in earnest as the new season starts. Make certain that you have the right equipment for your needs and that everything is in working order.

PROPAGATORS

One of the most useful pieces of equipment for the greenhouse is a propagator. Its main use is as an enclosed space in which both temperature and humidity can be controlled. The purpose of this is to aid the germination of seeds and the rooting of cuttings. Some seeds will germinate only when the soil and ambient temperature reach a certain level, while the germination of other seeds is speeded up by warmer conditions. Cuttings generally root better when they are provided with some bottom heat, and an enclosed atmosphere means that they do not wilt in the same way as they would if they were standing on the open bench.

There are two basic types of propagator – those that are heated and those that are not. The unheated type is, obviously, not as useful as its heated counterpart, but it nevertheless has its uses. The unheated type of propagator normally consists of a seed tray on which sits a transparent plastic lid. Seeds can be sown, or cuttings placed, directly into the tray or pots can be stood in it. The lid ensures that a close atmosphere is maintained, although most have ventilators in the lid so that you can start to harden off the plants by letting in fresh air. Heat is provided by placing them within a warm environment, such as in a heated greenhouse, or somewhere indoors. A good, light windowsill is suitable, but the propagator should not be placed in direct sunlight, nor should a curtain be drawn across it at night, leaving it in a potential frost pocket because it is likely to be insulated from the warmth of the room.

More sophisticated and, inevitably, more expensive are the heated propagators. These are generally larger – sometimes so large that they are almost mini-greenhouses – and the bottom half incorporates a heating cable, which is covered with damp sand. In some that is all there is, and this cable provides enough bottom heat to warm up the compost in the pots as well as keeping the air slightly warm. A more complicated version has air-heating wires around the inside of the case, and these warm the air above and around the plants. Both sets of heaters are controlled by thermostats and can be set at the required temperature. The main drawback is that the propagator can be set at only one temperature at once so that all seeds, irrespective of their individual require-ments, are given the same treatment. In practice this is not usually too much of a problem because most will tolerate quite a degree of variation and so a compromise can generally be found.

HOMEMADE UNITS

Propagators can be expensive, but it is possible to make your own at a fraction of the cost, and a homemade propagator will have the advantage that it is tailor-made to fit both your own greenhouse and your own requirements.

The simplest unit can be made from four pieces of wood nailed together to form a bottomless box and covered with a loose sheet of glass. This can be made safer by enclosing the glass in a frame, and further by attaching the frame with hinges to the box. The sides can be about 15cm (6in) deep, with the width and length varying according to your requirements or the size of the materials you have available. This propagator can stand on the sand-covered bench and be used very successfully for large quantities of cuttings.

A slightly more sophisticated version can be made with the two side pieces angled – water will run off the now-sloping lid. In both these versions it is easy enough to put soil-warming cables into the sand below the unit as well as cables around the inside of the box if you wish. Such cables are readily available from garden centres. They are supplied ready-assembled and come with full instructions, so they are safe and you do not require a qualified electrician to install them.

ORGANIC MATERIAL

One of the most important ingredients at the disposal of a gardener is well-rotted organic material. This covers a wide range of materials, from farmyard manure and garden compost to spent hop waste and old mushroom compost. Whatever material you have, it should be capable of breaking down into a rich, fibrous substance that will not only help feed the plants but also improve the structure of the soil. Most organic materials are rich in nitrogen and usually in other nutrients as well. The fibrous material helps to break up the soil as well as holding a certain amount of moisture. It frequently also has the effect of darkening the soil, which, in turn, helps to warm up the ground more quickly in spring.

One source of organic matter that is available to all gardeners is garden compost. This consists of the remains of all vegetation that is not required. Grass cuttings and the remains of plants are the main source. Weeds can also be used as long as they are not in seed and are not perennial varieties that will continue growing. In theory, the compost heap should get hot enough to kill both the weed seeds and the perennial weeds, but in practice a lot always escape and become a nuisance in the ground on which the compost is used. Non-cooked, vegetative kitchen waste, such as peelings and discarded leaves, are another good source of compost.

Tougher stems and hedge-cutting should be avoided unless you have a shredder. This machine is invaluable if you have a lot of such material because it will chop it up into fine pieces and it can them be composted and returned to the garden as a mulch or soil conditioner. It can be either kept in its own bin or mixed with other compost.

Cottage gardeners used to throw everything in heap for a year, but although this works, it is not the most efficient way. A properly constructed compost bin, either purchased or homemade, is ideal. This keeps the compost together, allows air in at the sides and keeps the heat in. Make or buy at least three bins – the first is the one to which you are currently adding material, the second is rotting down, and the third is the one from which you are taking compost to use on the garden.

Material is added to the compost bin as it becomes available, but try not to put too much of one type of material into a thick layer, especially grass cuttings. The process can be speeded up by the addition of a chemical activator, which can be purchased at a garden centre. Alternatively and preferably, you can add a layer of farmyard manure. Add water to the heap if it is dry, but cover it with a sheet of polythene so that the pile does not get too wet. Some bins have lids to help keep the heat in. As the compost breaks down it is likely to get very

MIST UNITS

Mist units have been used by professional nurseries for years, but in recent times a cheaper version of the equipment they use has become available to amateur gardeners. It is used for rooting cuttings. The idea behind the unit is that if cuttings are kept in a moist atmosphere they will root much more quickly. The unit therefore has one or more nozzles that produce a fine mist, which is sprayed over the cuttings. The spray is not continuous but is switched on when the cuttings begin to dry out and is switched off as soon as they are covered with the fine mist. An artificial 'leaf' acts as a sensor and turns the water on and off. To make the treatment even more effective, under-soil heating cables are placed in sand under the pots or trays.

The units can be set up on a greenhouse bench. Very little superstructure is needed, although some growers drape polythene round the sides and even over the top of the unit to prevent the spray going all over the greenhouse. The nozzles, piping and control units can be purchased from larger garden centres or from specialist suppliers.

warm – this is a natural part of the composting process and is, in fact, to be encouraged.

There are a number of other sources of organic material if they can be found. Farmyard manure is one of the best, but it must be well-rotted, because if it is left to decompose in the ground it will extract nitrogen from the soil to aid its progress and thus deplete rather than supplement the nutrients. Bear in mind that some farmyard manure will contain a lot of weed seeds from the hay that was given to the animals.

Waste from various processes is also useful, but some kinds will have involved chemicals, which will still be

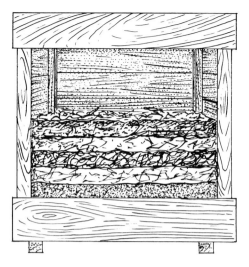

A homemade compost bin. When you are adding material, try to avoid having too much of one kind together. The aim is to have layers of different kinds – manure, kitchen waste and so on – to encourage the circulation of air.

present in the waste. Hop waste, which is available from breweries, is excellent, as is spent mushroom compost. However, you should be aware that the mushroom compost incorporates horse manure, and to counter the acidity, mushroom growers add chalk, so do not use this near lime-hating plants. Waste from the forestry industry is becoming widely available in the form of chipped and composted bark. Chipped bark has not broken down far enough to be used in the soil but it makes a good top dressing. Composted leaves are an invaluable material in the garden, but make your own (p. 160) and do not raid the woods.

PERENNIALS

The main activity in the borders at this time of year is to tidy them up and prepare them for the next season.

HERBS IN WINTER
Most herbs die back in winter
but is possible to dig up some, such as chives and mint, pot them up and bring them into a greenhouse or even an inside windowsill. Throw away the plants at the end of the winter. Some – parsley, for example – will continue to grow in the open garden as long as they are covered with a cloche.

One of the advantages of growing herbs in containers is that in winter they can easily be brought inside.

TIDYING BORDERS

The real art of ornamental gardening is to prepare in advance. Too many gardeners leave the borders to their own devices until the warm weather comes in early summer and then try to turn them into something attractive. This rarely works. The key is to do the preparation in the period between mid-autumn and late spring, so that by the time the plants come into growth there is no more work to be done. If you leave it until the weather gets warm, the weeds will already be growing away and it will be difficult to catch up.

Start in the autumn and work your way through the borders whenever the soil is dry enough for you to get on it. If you are lucky you will be able to renovate the borders in plenty of time to go through them again quickly just before growth starts, removing any new weeds that have appeared. If you do this, your life will be considerably easier next spring, the borders will look better, and you will have time to relax and enjoy the garden.

The first job is to cut back all the old vegetation. Some gardeners are reluctant to do this in the autumn. They prefer to wait until spring, partly because the dead stems contain seeds and insects on which wild creatures, particularly birds and small mammals, can feed and in which they can find some protection, and partly because the stems afford some protection to the crown of the plant beneath. The first argument is a good reason for leaving the border, but, depending on the size of your borders, it may take some time before they are all cut back and there may well be other sources of food nearby. The second reason is debatable. Often, the dead foliage does not allow air to circulate around the plant and fungal diseases develop. In addition, only a few plants need protection and these can always be cut back later. Moreover, if the plants come into growth and there is a wet spring, it may not be possible to cut down the old stems before the new ones are so high that they are damaged in the process. The advantages of getting on top of all the chores before spring seem to outweigh the disadvantages.

Cut back the old stems right to the base and do not leave snags sticking up. Remove any weeds growing in or around the crown. Any woody material removed from the borders should be shredded and put on the compost heap or composted separately and put back on the borders.

Once the border has been cut back and weeded, check to see if any plants need moving or dividing. Evidence of congestion is the vigorous new growth around the edge of a clump and a dead area of starved growth in the centre. If you find this, it is time to dig up the plant, rejuvenate the soil and then replant the young, outside growths. Discard the rest. Consult notes made in summer when everything was in full growth to see if any of the plants need moving or whether you want to introduce new ones.

Once you have finished making any alterations, lightly dig over the border, digging in any organic material left from the spring. Cover the soil with a new layer of rotted compost, 7.5–10cm (3–4in) deep if possible. This will be broken down and worked into the soil by the worms during the winter and may well need topping up again in spring.

TREES AND SHRUBS

One of the worst aspects of autumn in the eyes of many gardeners is the fall of leaves – they all need clearing up.

CLEARING UP LEAVES

If possible, clear up leaves as soon as they fall, because the longer they lie on the ground the more difficult they are to clear up. It is essential to remove them all because they not only smother plants, but they create conditions in which fungal diseases thrive and make perfect homes for slugs. There is another beneficial side to clearing up leaves and that is that it allows you to make leaf-mould, one of the most valuable commodities in the garden.

Leaves should be swept or raked up and put into a bin for composting. If you have a large garden and lots of trees it may pay to buy a blower/vacuum cleaner (p. 23). These machines can be used either to blow the leaves up into a heap or to suck them up into a bag. Although it is convenient to have the leaves in a bag, it is surprising how much time is taken up in emptying the bag, which fills very quickly. Where the vacuums are useful is in removing leaves from between plants in a border. Some models have shredder attachments incorporated in them, and these shred the leaves, meaning that more can be accommodated in the bag and that when they are composted they rot down more quickly. Another type of machine that is useful for wide open spaces is a gadget rather like a push mower except the blades are replaced by a rotating brush. This flicks the leaves up into a large hopper, which is suspended between the handles.

Never throw away leaves or burn them. They should always be composted, and the best way to do this is to make one or more leaf pens. All that is required is to knock four posts into the ground in a square and to

If you cannot immediately plant out a bare-rooted plant, heel it in until it can be planted in its final position. Dig a trench into which the plant can be placed at an angle, with its trunk supported. Cover the roots and lower part of the trunk with soil and keep it moist.

stretch wire netting stretched around them. An extra piece of netting to go on the top to prevent leaves from blowing away is useful but not essential.

The bin will fill up remarkably quickly, but, equally remarkably, by the time they have rotted down, the leaves will take up only a fraction of the space. What remains is perfect for all kinds of use in the garden. It can be added to soil to make it moisture retentive; it makes the perfect mulch; it can be used in making potting composts; and it can be mixed with soil for rock gardens and raised beds.

When you are collecting leaves, do not forget to clear them out of the bottom of hedges. Some gardeners with large gardens erect low fences of wire netting in front of hedges and in other strategic positions to catch the leaves as they blow about. Drifts of leaves collect against these and can easily be picked up.

PLANTING HEDGES

Late autumn and winter is a good time for planting trees and shrubs (p. 162). It is also a good time to plant a hedge.

Decide what type of hedging you want and order the plants well in advance. The cheapest way of acquiring them is as bare-rooted specimens, which are grown in rows at the nursery and are dug up to meet your order. In some ways pot-grown plants are more convenient, but they are more expensive, and you will also have the problem of transporting all the plants in their pots. If bare-rooted plants are delivered when you are unable to plant them heel them in. This means digging a trench and laying the bunches of plants in the trench at an angle of 45 degrees. Firm the soil back on top of them.

Also well in advance, prepare the line of the hedge. Hedges usually remain in position for many years, so it is worth spending some time at this stage. Make certain that the site is well drained – yew trees in particular dislike waterlogged soil. Double dig the soil in a strip that is at least as wide as the eventual width of the hedge times a half. This means that a 60cm (2ft) wide hedge should have strip of prepared soil 90cm (3ft) wide. Dig in plenty of well-rotted organic material to help feed the plants and keep the roots moist.

Using a garden line to make sure that the hedge is straight, plant the shrubs at the appropriate planting distance. A wide hedge or one that you wish to be particularly thick and impenetrable can be planted in two rows, with the plants staggered. This method is frequently used with beech hedges.

Once they are planted, water them in and mulch. Keep the plants watered in dry periods until the hedge is firmly established. An annual mulch of compost of manure will

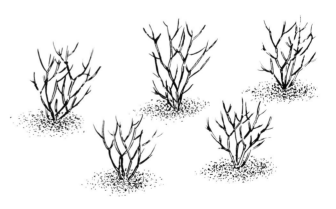

Double plant for a dense or especially impenetrable hedge, alternating the plants. This is especially useful if you are planting beech.

CAMOMILE LAWNS

If you want to try something different, a traditional camomile lawn might be worth considering. This does not make a neat sward in the same way that grass does, but it makes an acceptable alternative for an area that is not heavily used. One advantage is the smell. As soon as it is trodden on, it gives off the wonderfully distinctive aroma of camomile.

Although any kind of camomile (*Chamaemelum nobile*) can be used, the best is a variety called 'Treneague'. This is low growing and does not flower, thus making a dense carpet that requires little maintenance. Obtain several plants and then increase these by taking cuttings until you have enough to cover the area required. The ground should be prepared in the same way as for a conventional lawn (p. 141). Planting can take place in late autumn or in spring. Set the rooted cuttings about 23cm (9in) apart, planting so that they are not in rows because these may still show up once the lawn has developed. A random, but even covering is best.

Water regularly and remove any weeds until the lawn has fully developed. Once it is established, still keep an eye out for weeds. Cut regularly with hand shears or with a strimmer; do not use a lawn mower, which may tear it out at the roots and will, in any case, cut it too tight.

help to keep it healthy. For the first couple of years it may need to be protected by plastic netting if it is in a windy area.

Cut back the shrubs by about one-third on planting and again by the same amount the following year. This will make them branch out and become thick and bushy. Cut back by smaller amounts each year until it has reached its eventual height and width. When you trim it, shape the hedge so that it slopes in towards the top.

HEDGING SHRUBS

Buxus sempervirens (box): evergreen, 30cm (12in) apart

Carpinus betulus (hornbeam): deciduous, 45cm (18in) apart

Chamaecyparis lawsoniana (Lawson cypress): evergreen, 60cm (24in)

Crataegus monogyna (hawthorn): deciduous, 35cm (14in) apart

× *Cupressocyparis leylandii* (Leyland cypress): evergreen, 75cm (30in) apart

Fagus sylvatica (beech): deciduous, 45cm (18in) apart

Ilex aquifolium (holly): evergreen, 45cm (18in) apart

Ligustrum ovalifolium (privet): semi–evergreen, 30cm (12in) apart

Lonicera nitida (poor man's box): evergreen, 30cm (12in) apart

Taxus baccata (yew): evergreen, 60cm (24in) apart

Thuja plicata (thuja): evergreen, 60cm (24in) apart

Box, *Buxus sempervirens*, is the best choice for small, decorative hedges. It is slow growing and therefore needs trimming only once a year.

VEGETABLES

This is a good time to sow overwintering broad beans (p. 16), and in areas that suffer from bad weather they can be given the protection of cloches. There is still time, too, to plant garlic before winter really sets in. This is also a good month for planting rhubarb (see below).

Any addition to winter crops is welcome, so if you grow them, bring in some chicory and seakale for forcing (p. 147).

As winter deepens so birds become more hungry and search for food in the garden, not only food that has been put out for them but plants growing in the vegetable garden. Pigeons can be an especial nuisance and can quickly strip all the Brussels sprouts and cabbages. Put up netting to protect them now before the worst attacks start.

Whenever the weather allows, continue with the winter digging (see below), including preparing a trench for next year's runner beans (p. 86).

WINTER DIGGING

If possible dig most of the vegetable garden during the autumn and winter. Get as much done as you can in the autumn while the soil is still relatively dry, and if it gets very wet in the winter, leave it until spring. You will do more harm than good by getting onto the ground when it is wet. Digging the ground and allowing it to rest before planting gives time for any compost you have

incorporated into the soil to finish rotting and for the soil to be weathered to a fine tilth and to improve its structure. Digging also breaks up the surface, allowing rain and water to sink into the ground rather than lie on the surface or run off.

Unless you are intending to do a major rejuvenation job, there is no need to double dig (p. 25), a single spit will be sufficient. As you dig, clear any weeds that have appeared and mix in well-rotted organic material.

RHUBARB

Rhubarb always seems to fall between two stools: it is grown as a vegetable and used as a fruit. It is well worth growing however you classify it. Rhubarb is a permanent crop – that is, once planted, it remains in the same place for a number of years before it is dug up. It likes a sunny position and a well-drained soil. The soil should be deeply dug, with plenty of well-rotted organic matter mixed in.

Rhubarb can be grown from crowns or seed. Crowns are more reliable in terms of quality (seed-raised plants can vary), and they will crop a year earlier, but many gardeners find that seed is easier to acquire.

Plant out the rhubarb crowns at any time between late autumn and the end of winter. Seed-raised plants, sown in spring, can be planted out at the same time of year. Mulch around the plants and water them during dry summer weather. Cut out any flowering stems as they develop, because these use a lot of energy and weaken the plants.

Harvest during the spring and early summer, by gripping the base of the stems and pulling. Earlier stems may be had by forcing, which can be achieved in the garden, by covering the crown with something such as a large bucket to keep the light out. Alternatively, crowns may be lifted and kept inside in the dark, in a cellar or shed perhaps. Do not eat raw rhubarb and only cook the stems, not the leaves.

Rhubarb can left in the same place for at least five years and, in the right conditions, up to twenty years. When the plants begin to look tired, lift them, split off some of the outside segments with a spade and replant these in new or rejuvenated soil.

RECOMMENDED VARIETIES *of* RHUBARB

'Champagne Early'	'Redstick'
'Holstein Blood Red'	'Timperley Early'
'Glaskin's Perpetual'	'Victoria'

DECEMBER

The garden has now taken on a definite winter look. At a time when we feel the wind at its keenest and the frost at its sharpest, it is, perhaps, the moment to look at how best we can protect the garden from the excesses of the weather. It is possible to alleviate the wind and to protect plants from the frosts.

Even at this time of year, it is surprising how many different plants are in flower. In some cases the plants are those that are early visitors from next year – primroses, for example – while others are still blooming from the previous year – penstemons being a good example.

When the weather and soil conditions permit, keep on top of the various chores that need doing at this time of year.

General

- Shred all prunings and old herbaceous material (p. 23)
- Drain down or lag all outside water pipes (p. 150)
- Continue to collect leaves for composting (p. 174)
- Continue digging when soil conditions allow (p. 25)
- Plan next year's ornamental display (p. 124) and vegetable crops (p. 26)
- Order seeds and plants (p. 120)
- Thoroughly clean and oil any tools used during winter (p. 22)
- Clean and sterilize pots and trays (p. 152)
- Avoid walking on wet or sticky soil (p. 25)
- Create ice-free zones in ponds (p. 187)

Annuals and Tender Perennials

- Sow sweetpeas (p. 180)
- Check overwintering annuals have not suffered wind-rock or frost upheaval (p. 50)
- Deadhead winter-flowering containers (p. 134)
- Plan next year's displays (p. 124)
- Order seeds (p. 120)

Bulbs

- Lift and divide autumn-flowering snowdrops (p. 21)

Fruit

- Heel in bare-rooted trees and shrubs when they arrive (p. 162)
- Plant new fruit trees and bushes when the weather and soil conditions allow (p. 162)
- Carry out formative pruning on new trees and bushes (p. 10)
- Winter prune fruit trees and bushes (p. 10)
- Prune greenhouse grape vines (p. 157)
- Replace netting to prevent buds being stripped by birds (p. 53)
- Knock snow from netting to prevent it breaking (p. 35)
- Check stored fruit (p. 168)

Greenhouse

- Protect plants from frost if necessary (p. 158)
- Regularly check heating arrangements (p. 158)
- Prune grape vines (p. 157)
- Water plants only when in growth (p. 122)
- Ventilate except in cold weather (p. 77)

Lawns

- Lightly mow if conditions are right (p. 140)
- Remove fallen leaves and debris (p. 23)
- Prepare ground for laying lawns in spring (p. 141)
- Turf new lawns on previously prepared ground (p. 182)
- Scatter worm casts if they are formed (p. 159)

Perennials

- Finish preparing new beds and borders for planting in spring (p.152)
- Continue maintaining beds when conditions allow (p. 23)
- Shred and compost discarded material (p. 23)
- Take root cuttings (p. 142)

Rock Gardens

- Prepare new beds (p. 63)
- Continue sowing seeds (p. 41)
- Order seeds from catalogues (p. 101)
- Order plants from nurseries (p. 101)
- Protect plants that dislike winter wet with panes of glass (p. 189)
- Take root cuttings (p. 142)

Trees and Shrubs

- Plant trees and shrubs when conditions allow (p. 162)
- Heel in bare-rooted trees and shrubs if weather prevents planting (p. 162)
- Protect marginally hardy shrubs and climbers with hessian during cold spells (p. 186)
- Check stakes and ties (p. 41)
- Prune trees (p. 27)
- Take hardwood cuttings (p. 154)
- Remove snow before it breaks or disfigures trees and shrubs (p. 187)

Vegetables

- Check stored vegetables (p. 165)
- Order seeds for next year (p. 185)
- Protect brassicas from birds (p. 177)
- Take chicory, rhubarb and seakale inside for forcing (p. 177)

🍂 ANNUALS

SWEETPEAS

Early winter seems an odd time to be thinking about annuals, and it is certainly far too early to consider sowing any of the half-hardy varieties. This is, however, a good time to be thinking about sweetpeas, which are surely one of the best loved of all annuals. Their delicate flowers and wonderful scent make them welcome both in the garden and as a cut flower for the house. Sweetpeas are also excellent exhibition flowers, and many gardeners spend hours producing the best possible blooms.

The season starts early, because most exhibition growers and many ordinary gardeners like to sow their seeds in mid-autumn. These are either sown directly into the soil in warmer areas or, more usually, in pots. The resulting plants may be planted out in the late autumn or early winter or overwintered under glass and set out in the early or mid-spring. Other gardeners like to wait until the early spring and sow then, planting out the seedlings a few weeks later. Autumn sowing produces an earlier crop and often a better crop, which is less prone to disease.

Most gardeners prefer to sow the seeds in pots or trays. The seed of sweetpeas has a hard coat, which makes germination slow and irregular. To speed things up the seeds should be 'chitted'. This consists of making a nick with a knife or file in the coat of the seed on the side opposite the 'eye'. This is fiddly but effective. Although some gardeners do not like it, because a few seeds may rot, a much easier method is to soak the seeds in warm water overnight before sowing. Unless it is vital that every seed survives to germinate, soaking produces good results for most gardeners. There is no need for heat if you are not in a hurry, but they will germinate more readily if kept at about 15°C (59°F). If they are staying under glass for any length of time – throughout winter, for example – prick them out into individual pots.

Harden off the seedlings and plant them out in spring. The soil should be prepared in the previous autumn, when plenty of humus should be added. Erect a framework up which the peas will grow. This can be a row of canes or a framework with strings or netting. It can also be a traditional row of peasticks. Wigwams of canes or peasticks are a good way of growing sweetpeas in a limited space, and they are decorative features in a flower border. Set the plants about 25cm (10in) apart along the row or round the wigwam. Keep them watered during dry spells

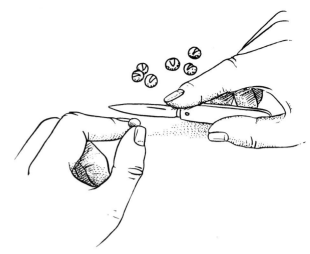

Chitting seed – knicking the hard coat with a sharp knife – will speed up germination. It is a technique that is often used with sweetpeas and with other hard-coated seeds such as legumes.

and deadhead regularly to get the best out of the plants. For a longer season, sow a few seeds two to three weeks later than the rest.

Most sweetpeas grow to 1.2–1.5m (4–5ft), but there are also dwarf varieties that form bushes. These are more useful as decorative plants in a border or for planting in containers. Although they are not supposed to need support, they often benefit from a little help from some twigs or canes. Their colours are usually mixed.

RECOMMENDED VARIETIES *of* SWEETPEA

'Anniversary': white and pink, fragrant
'Black Prince': dark maroon
'Blue Mantle': deep blue, fragrant
'Cambridge Blue': pale blue, scented
'Charles Unwin': creamy pink, fragrant
'Cream Southbourne': cream, fragrant
'Cupid': dwarf, fragrant
'Daphne': mauve, fragrant
'Diamond Wedding': white, fragrant
'Her Majesty': red, fragrant
'Memories': pink, slightly fragrant
'Mrs Bernard Jones': pink, fragrant
'North Shore': blue
'Old Times': cream, fragrant
'Queen Mother': salmon
'Red Arrow': red, slightly scented
'Royal Wedding': white, fragrant
'Snoopea': dwarf, fragrant
'Southbourne': pink fragrant
'White Supreme': white, fragrant
'Wiltshire Ripple': red striped, fragrant

 # FRUIT

NUT TREES

Several types of tree that produce edible nuts can be grown, although the most popular are cobnuts (hazel), filbert nuts and walnuts. Sweet chestnuts can also be grown but they take up a lot of space, and in warm areas, almonds can be grown.

COBNUTS AND FILBERTS

Although cobnuts and filberts are very similar, they are, in fact, different species, *Corylus avellana* and *C. maxima*, respectively. The filbert has a much longer husk than the cobnut, and it often encases the nut completely. Some have frilly husks.

Both of these trees prefer a cool situation, preferably where they are partially shaded. The soil should be free-draining and reasonably moisture retentive, but it should not be too rich. Plant new trees in autumn or winter (p. 162). They should be set at 4.5m (15ft) intervals. The trees are trained as open goblets – that is, open centred – with their height restricted to about 2.1m (7ft). Pruning should be carried out in late winter (p. 27). Remove all suckers (p. 102).

Cobnuts and filberts ripen in the autumn and should be picked and stored in a cool dry place away from mice and squirrels. Squirrels will also reduce the crop on the trees.

RECOMMENDED VARIETIES *of* COBNUT

'Cosford'
'Fuscorubra'
'Pearson's Prolific' ('Nottingham Prolific')
'Web's Prize Cob'

RECOMMENDED VARIETIES *of* FILBERT

'Butler'
'Frizzled Filbert'
'Gunslehert'
'Kentish Cob'
'Red Filbert'
'White Filbert'

Although walnut trees (*Juglans*) take several years to produce a reasonable number of nuts, you should find that you have a small crop within a few years.

WALNUTS

Walnut trees (*Juglans*) can eventually grow very large, and they need a reasonable amount of space. They are ornamental and create a pleasant, dappled shade, however, so they can be used as specimen trees on a lawn. If space is limited. choose a self-fertile variety, otherwise you may have to plant a pollinator. Most trees take many years before they bare fruit, although some will produce the odd nut after five years or so.

Choose a warm site, away from frost hollows. The soil should be well-drained and yet moisture retentive with plenty of organic matter added to it before planting. The tree may well seem to take a while getting established, but it will suddenly begin to grow more speedily. Apart from the removal of dead or damaged wood, no pruning is required.

The time to harvest the nuts is in autumn when you see the outer cases beginning to crack. If you want to pickle the walnuts, they must be gathered in the summer before they start to harden. Store in a cool, but slightly humid place.

RECOMMENDED VARIETIES *of* WALNUT

'Broadview'
'Buccaneer'
'Corne de Périgord'
'Franquette'
'Granjean'
'Lara'
'Marbot'
'Parisienne'

SWEET CHESTNUTS

There is not much point in growing sweet chestnuts (or Spanish chestnuts) unless you have plenty of space as the tree are likely to grow up to 30m (100ft) high and half of that across. If you have the space and like chestnuts, there are several varieties to try. They are not difficult to grow and require no pruning. They prefer a moist, woodland-type soil but will grow in any fertile, moisture-retentive ground.

RECOMMENDED VARIETIES *of* SWEET CHESTNUT

'Bournette'
'Marron de Lyon'
'Paragon'

LAWNS

LAYING TURF

Although preparing a new lawn from seed is much cheaper, laying from existing turves is quicker and it will not be disturbed by birds or pets before it is established. New turf lawns look green and established as soon as they are laid, and they can be in use as soon as their roots reach down into the soil, which is usually after a few months.

Turves can be purchased in a number of different grades. Some turves are specially seeded from grass seed of varying types, while others are the result of lifting existing meadow grass. Meadow turves may simply be straight meadow grass, which may well contain all manner of weeds, ȯr it may be treated meadow grass, taken from a field that has been treated to get rid of the worst weeds. Needless to say, the specially sown grass is the most expensive type and the untreated meadow grass the cheapest. Order well in advance and, if you have the opportunity, have a look at the grass to check what you are getting. It is useful to have someone waiting to meet the lorry when the turf arrives so that you inspect it and make certain that it is stacked where you need it.

Turf lawns can be laid at any time between autumn and spring as long as the weather conditions allow you to get onto the ground without breaking down its structure. The ground should be prepared at least a month, preferably more, in advance, so that it can settle and any perennial weeds that have been missed can be removed.

Before laying the turves, loosen the surface with a rake and fill in any depressions that have occurred since the bed was prepared. Lay the first row of turves against a straight edge. Put a plank on the laid turves and stand or kneel on this to lay the second row. The second row should be

STORING TURVES

If the turves are delivered and you cannot use them on the same day, it is important that they are not allowed to dry out. Water the exposed earth and roots in the stack. Do not leave them rolled up for longer than 24 hours or the grass will turn yellow and even die. Unroll the turves and lay them, grass upwards, on a sheet of polythene or large paved area such as a patio or drive. Water and do not allow to dry out. Lay the turves as soon as possible.

Laying turves

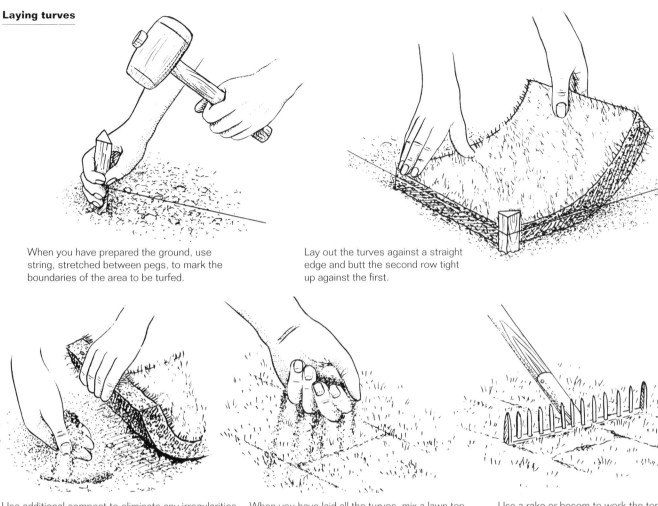

When you have prepared the ground, use string, stretched between pegs, to mark the boundaries of the area to be turfed.

Lay out the turves against a straight edge and butt the second row tight up against the first.

Use additional compost to eliminate any irregularities in the turves or to fill any depressions you missed when you prepared the soil.

When you have laid all the turves, mix a lawn top dressing and sprinkle it over the surface.

Use a rake or besom to work the top dressing into the joins between the turves.

Lifting turf for re-laying

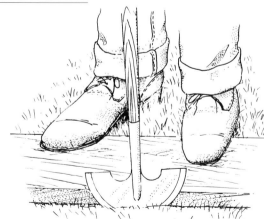

If existing turf is to be re-laid, use a plank as a straight edge along which to cut the strip.

Divide each strip into pieces about 45cm (18in) long and lift them, making sure that each piece is at least 2.5cm (1in) deep. Do not allow the grass to dry out before it is re-laid.

butted up tight against the first and the joints should overlap, much in the manner of brickwork. Continue to lay the turves until the whole area is covered. Cut turf that butts against a hard surface, but allow it to overlap onto borders. Do not place a short piece at the end of a row. Use a longer piece and put the shorter piece further into the lawn. Once all the turves have been laid, use the plank as a guide to cut a straight edge or use a flexible hosepipe as a guide to cut curved edges.

Go over the new lawn with a light roller or tamp down the turves with the back of a rake. Fill in any gaps between the turves with a lawn top dressing (p. 38). Do not allow the turves to dry out because the new roots are liable to shrivel and the turves will shrink, leaving gaps. Once the turves have rooted through to the soil, they will take light traffic and can be mown, at first with a high cut (p. 38).

TREES AND SHRUBS

EVERGREENS

Evergreen trees and shrubs are a vital ingredient in the design of any garden, providing continuity of form and colour throughout the year. Long after the flowers and fruit of the other trees and shrubs have faded, the evergreen leaves are still there providing interest. Some evergreens are not particularly beautiful in their own right, but they form a solid backbone to the garden. They make good hedges, keeping out winds and prying eyes throughout the whole year, and their colour usually makes a good foil against which herbaceous borders and other plants can be appreciated. Many evergreens, however, have very attractive foliage – colourful and variegated or with an interesting texture. Many evergreens have shiny foliage, while many conifers and the hollies have interestingly shaped leaves.

It is in winter, of course, that many evergreens come into their own – when other plants have died down or lost their leaves, the evergreens still put on a show. Holly is the king of the winter, but other more colourful shrubs are most welcome. The silver or golden variegated forms of *Elaeagnus* always makes a splash and provide valuable cutting material for flower arrangers even in the depths of winter.

There is no real difference in the treatment of deciduous and evergreen trees and shrubs, although a few minor variations are worth noting. Bare-rooted evergreens are usually planted in autumn or in the spring, unlike deciduous plants, which may be planted throughout the winter. Container-grown specimens can be planted in summer as long as they are well watered.

Most evergreen shrubs, especially the conifers, do not need a great deal of pruning. Many suffer die back during the winter and all affected stems and branches should be removed in mid-spring. The flowering stems of short-lived shrubs, such as lavender and santolina, which are frequently used along with perennials should be trimmed back after flowering and then cut back to almost the old wood in spring, just as growth is beginning.

Snow can create problems for evergreens if the branches get bowed down, leaving the shrub or tree misshapen and frequently broken. Knock off any heavy snow from the branches.

CONIFERS

Conifers come in an astonishing range of shapes and sizes. Tall, thin ones, conical ones and round ones, even some prostrate forms. There is also a good variation in colour, from shades of green to blues and golden-yellows. Always check what you are buying, although you may not live to see it – some species are capable of growing to 30m (100ft) or even more.

Small conifers, such as this *Chamaecyparis lawsoniana* 'Minima Aurea', add structure and all-year-round colour to a garden.

HEATHERS

Heathers (*Erica*, *Calluna* and *Daboecia*) are an extremely useful group of evergreen shrubs. The tree heathers are large and decorative, but it is the smaller ones that most gardeners know best, although they do not always realize that they are shrubs. They make very good groundcover and provide colour all the year round, both with their foliage and with their flowers. There are some cultivars that flower in midwinter, and the foliage can provide large splashes of gold at the same time of year. There are hundreds of different cultivars, all with subtle differences. Heathers are not difficult to grow. The vast majority will grow only on acid soils, although a few will grow on alkaline ground. Pruning usually consists of shearing the plants over in spring (autumn in warmer areas) to keep them compact.

Heather is a useful winter-flowering plant. Here *Erica carnea* 'Springwood Pink' is undaunted by the covering of frost.

Unless they are used as hedges, conifers need very little attention, and they generally do not like being pruned or cut back.

DWARF CONIFERS

Abies balsamea; *F. hudsonia*
Chamaecyparis lawsoniana 'Minima Aurea'; *C. obtusa* 'Nana Aurea'
Cryptomeria japonica 'Nana'
Juniperus chinensis 'Echniformis'; *J. communis* 'Compressa'
Picea abies 'Pigmea'; *P. glauca* 'Alberta Globe'; *P. pungens* 'Montgomery'
Pinus leucodermis 'Schmidtii'; *P. strobus* 'Radiata'; *P. sylvestris* 'Beuvronensis'
Thuja orientalis 'Aurea Nana'

PROSTRATE CONIFERS

Juniperus conferta; *J. davurica* 'Expansa'; *J. sabina* 'Blue Danube'; *J. communis* 'Depressa Aurea'; *J. virginiana* 'Grey Owl'
Picea pungens 'Procumbens'
Podocarpus nivalis

VEGETABLES

Once in a while check stored vegetables to make sure that they are still in good condition. Throw out any rotting ones and take suitable action if you discover that they are being eaten by rodents.

Early winter is a good time to sit down and browse through the seed merchants' catalogues. It is worth keeping notes of what you buy and, more to the point, what you like, because there is such a bewildering number of varieties to choose from that it is easy to forget which ones you want to choose again. Put in the order as soon as you can to avoid disappointment through stocks being sold out. It may be an idea to go through the catalogue with a friend and make up a joint order. Many of the packets will contain far more seeds than you will require, and sharing the seeds or the resulting plants will save money.

Now is the time to move chicory and rhubarb indoors for forcing (p. 177).

SHALLOTS

Shallots, which, like onions, need a fertile, well-drained soil, are planted out in late winter or early spring. Push them into the soil or into a shallow hole made by a dibber so that just the tip shows. They should be 15cm (6in) apart in rows 25–30cm (10–12in) apart. Birds are keen on digging them up, so either cover them with netting until they are established or check regularly and replant any that have been disturbed.

Lift once the foliage begins to shrivel. Remove any soil and dry off the clusters of bulbs in a dry sunny place. Once they are dry, separate the individual bulbs and tie them into a rope or put in a net bag and store in a cool, but frost-free place.

RECOMMENDED VARIETIES *of* SHALLOT

'Delicato': red skinned

'Dutch Red': red skinned

'Dutch Yellow': yellow skinned

'Giant Red': red skinned

'Giant Yellow': yellow skinned

'Golden Gourmet': yellow skinned

'Hâtive de Niort: brown skinned

'Success': red-brown skinned

'Topper': yellow skinned

WINTER WEATHER

The weather, obviously, has a great effect on the way we garden, and the winter weather is probably the greatest single influence on what we grow and how we grow it. The main problems arise from frost, wind, snow and rain.

FROST

In many ways frost is good for the garden – it helps to break down the soil, for example – but also causes quit a few problems. Severe frost during the winter can kill or severely damage plants, although it is, of course, possible to take precautions to protect plants, especially if we live in areas that are regularly affected by hard winters. What causes most problems, however, are unexpected frosts early and late in the year.

If you have any choice in the matter, do not choose a garden that is in a frost hollow – that is, an area of ground where cold air collects. On the whole these are in valleys and dips in the ground, but they can also occur where cold air, rolling down a slope, is blocked. A hedge or wall can cause this, so where this is practicable, leave gaps so that

ORNAMENTAL KALE

Kale is not only for eating. There are some very ornamental varieties, which are good for adding colour to the garden during winter months. They can be used as bedding plants or planted in containers. Most seed merchants list them in their catalogues so you can grow your own from seed, but they are also available as young or even grown plants from garden centres and nurseries.

the cold air can filter through. Another solution is to put a hedge on the uphill side of a garden that is arrow-shaped or that slopes to one side so that the cold air is deflected around the garden.

Whatever your position and however carefully you try to make sure that there are no frost pockets in the garden, you are still going to get frosts, and it will be necessary to protect plants. Tender plants should be overwintered indoors where a temperature that will not fall below freezing point can be maintained. These plants should not be planted outside again until the threat of frost has finally passed. This applies equally to tender perennials and annuals that are raised from seeds each year.

The cold greenhouse or coldframe should also be protected against the frost (see pp. 37 and 158). If you have a coldframe, cover it with an old carpet or, in extreme conditions, use bales of straw.

Some plants – shrubs, for example – are too large to be moved and need protection where they stand. One of the first lines of defence is to think ahead at planting time and to position them in the warmest part of the garden. This is usually against a wall facing the direction of the sun. The next step is to wrap up a plant that may be affected by severe winter cold. Some plants should be wrapped up in autumn and left until growth restarts in spring. However, in general it is better for the plant's overall health if it is in the open air and, if possible, use the wrapping only in for brief periods in really cold weather. One of the best forms of protection is to wrap the plant in straw, which can, in turn, be covered with polythene to keep it dry. Some shrubs that are only slightly tender can be wrapped in hessian or plastic netting.

Tender herbaceous plants that retire back below ground are still vulnerable when the temperature drops sufficiently to freeze the ground. These can be covered with an extra layer of bark or straw, held in place with a piece of wire netting. An easy removable method is to fill a shallow tomato tray with straw and to invert this over the plant.

Plants are always especially vulnerable in spring, when they are coming into growth. Stems that can take a frost when they are mature are too soft in spring and can be burnt off. If frost threatens, a covering of loose newspapers is usually sufficient to protect the new stems. Always use at least two sheets so that air is trapped between them. Fleece is also a very good insulator.

Very often, the damage is done not by the freezing itself but by the rapid thaw that follows. This is true of many buds – camellias are a well-known example – and one way around this is to position the plants where they do not get the morning sun, which allows them to thaw out more slowly. Another method is to spray cold water on the affected plant so that it thaws out slowly. It is a laborious chore, but one that could well save a precious plant.

When the ground is frozen it may be impossible to lift vegetables such as parsnips and leeks, so if such weather is forecast, lift a few and store them. Nothing can be more desperate than spending a cold winter's morning with a pick axe, trying to excavate vegetables for lunch.

Most ponds will tolerate being frozen, although the stresses on a concrete pond can be considerable. To alleviate these, place a rubber ball or a piece of polystyrene in the water. The theory is that the ball or the polystyrene will squash, taking up sufficient of the expansion to reduce potentially damaging pressure on the pond walls. Fish will not suffer from the cold as long as the water in the pond does not freeze solid, and this should not happen if the pond is deep enough for fish in the first place. Prolonged freezing will deplete the oxygen in the water, however, and may cause a build up of harmful gases below the ice. To prevent either of these, keep at least a small area free of ice. Never break the ice by trying to crack it with a hammer, because the shock waves may harm the fish. Instead, make a hole by standing a container of hot water on the ice. A better alternative is to instal a small water heater especially designed for the job; these can be obtained from garden centre or specialist water plant suppliers.

WIND

Wind is the scourge of many gardens. It not only batters the plants, even knocking them over, but also scorches them, especially when it is a hot or cold wind. A certain amount of air circulation is necessary in a garden, but too much can be decidedly harmful.

Fortunately, there are ways of protecting a garden simply by setting up some sort of barrier. The best protection is a hedge. Unlike a solid barrier, such as a wall or solid fence, a hedge allows the wind to filter through it, reducing its speed considerably. A wind hitting a wall causes turbulence as it passes over it, often becoming more of a nuisance than the wind itself. In addition to the main windbreak, dividing a garden up with a series of internal hedges helps considerably. The effect of a windbreak is to reduce the effects of the wind for up to approximately ten times its height.

As a temporary solution, plastic netting, sold especially for creating a windbreak, can be used. This is usually not particularly attractive and should, if possible therefore, be used only until a hedge is established. The hedge itself will grow faster if it is protected by such netting. Netting can also be used within the garden to give localized protection, perhaps to a transplanted shrub.

Individual plants or clumps of plants should be given extra support by the use of stakes or some other form of support (see p. 80 for staking perennials and p. 162 for staking trees).

Gardens that are near to the sea have special problems. In the first place they are rarely without a wind and, second, the winds are often laden with salt. Again the use of hedges and other windbreaks is of paramount importance. The other key to success is to use plants, both in the garden and as hedges, that will tolerate these special conditions.

SNOW

Snow can be both good and bad news for the gardener. The good news is that when the ground and plants are wrapped in snow, they are protected from the worst excess of winter winds and frosts – the snow acts as kind of winter blanket.

The main disadvantage is that the weight of the snow can break branches and cause bushes and hedges to become misshapen. Whenever possible, knock the snow off as soon as possible. Hedges should be cut so that they slope towards the top as this makes it less likely that snow will lie on top of the hedge. Flat-topped hedges tend to split open with the accumulated weight of snow. If the snow does remain on a hedge for several days so that it is left spread out, with gaping holes in the top, pull it back into position and tie it into shape with strong string or rope.

Another disadvantage that might arise if the snow cover lasts too long is that plants that are in leaf will be unable to

Opposite: Winter can be a beautiful time in the garden. Many people are 'summer gardeners' and miss the wonders that are available to them at this time of year.

Right: Not only do cabbages supply welcome vegetables for the kitchen in midwinter, they also provide colour in the garden. These are ornamental kales that can be bought as seed or young plants.

photosynthesize because no light can reach them. When the snow eventually goes the plants may be quite yellow. In areas where it is normal to have prolonged periods of snow most natural vegetation, except trees, is herbaceous or deciduous and the problem does not occur.

RAIN

Rain is one of the life-forces of the garden, but in winter excessive rain can be a nuisance because dormant plants do not like to lie in waterlogged soil. Obviously, it is impossible to stop the rain, but it is possible to improve the drainage. If your garden is constantly wet, think seriously of putting in a proper drainage system. If it is wet only because the soil is heavy, you should try to improve the general condition of the soil. Adding plenty of humus and grit to the soil will work wonders.

Many alpine plants can stand considerable degrees of cold but they cannot do so if the cold is combined with wet conditions. One way to overcome this is to give them individual protection with panes of glass or to make wooden frames covered with polythene that can cover several plants at one. Make sure that you do not enclose the plants completely because it is vital that air is allowed to circulate freely around them. The problem for some plants, such as *Ramonda*, can be solved by planting them on their side in vertical crevices in or between rocks (p. 41).

Rain supplies essential moisture, however, and if you are able, catch as much as you can in barrels, tanks, ponds or underground cisterns so that you can use it in dry weather in summer.

INDEX

PICTURE CREDITS